To my good friend
Bill Diez

Orlando

One old soldier to another

Perilous PURSUIT

Perilous PURSUIT

THE U.S. CAVALRY
AND THE NORTHERN CHEYENNES

STAN HOIG

University Press of Colorado

© 2002 by the University Press of Colorado

Published by the University Press of Colorado
5589 Arapahoe Avenue, Suite 206C
Boulder, Colorado 80303

The University Press of Colorado is a cooperative publishing enterprise supported, in part, by Adams State College, Colorado State University, Fort Lewis College, Mesa State College, Metropolitan State College of Denver, University of Colorado, University of Northern Colorado, University of Southern Colorado, and Western State College of Colorado.

The paper used in this publication meets the minimum requirements of the American National Standard for Information Sciences—Permanence of Paper for Printed Library Materials. ANSI Z39.48-1992

Library of Congress Cataloging-in-Publication Data

Hoig, Stan.
  Perilous pursuit : the U.S. Cavalry and the northern Cheyennes / Stan Hoig.
    p. cm.
Includes bibliographical references and index.
  ISBN 0-87081-660-8 (hardcover : alk. paper)
    1. Cheyenne Indians—Wars. 2. Cheyenne Indians—Relocation. 3. Cheyenne Indians—Government relations. 4. United States. Army. Cavalry, 4th. 5. Mackenzie, Ranald Slidell, 1840–1889. I. Title.
  E99.C53 H66 2002
  978.004'973—dc21
                                                          2001007763

Design by Daniel Pratt

11 10 09 08 07 06 05 04 03 02   10 9 8 7 6 5 4 3 2 1

CONTENTS

PREFACE

THIS BOOK TAKES EXCEPTION TO CERTAIN ASPECTS of the Cheyenne trek north as presented by other authors. In doing so, it challenges their overreliance on the delayed memory of some who were involved in the ordeal. Two prime examples are Little Wolf, whom George B. Grinnell interviewed in 1897 and 1898, and scout George W. Brown. Both men contributed much valid information regarding their experiences in the ordeal, but both occasionally erred in their distant recall. This is true of other participants as well.

The Northern Cheyennes were and are a very honest people, and there is no intent here to question their veracity. The long-after-an-event memory of most humankind, however, is subject to fault. It is simply asking too much of most people—white, Native American, or other—to relate many years later the precise details in a series of dramatic, fast-moving events. Some people can do so, and some cannot. In many aspects of the retreat, the Cheyenne participants offer valuable insight and perspective that could not be obtained elsewhere. On a number of provable matters, however, their memory was badly in error, as was that of some non-Indians who were involved. Many of these inaccuracies have been routinely repeated by writers and have become widely accepted as fact.

The basis for this challenge lies in two important bodies of information: (1) reports of the various Fourth Cavalry officers supplied independently on order of Gen. Edward Hatch, and (2) the testimonies of Fourth Cavalry officers, enlisted men, and others presented in the Hemphill, Gunther, and Rendlebrock court-martial cases. These two sets of documents, especially the latter, provide extensive details concerning the Cheyenne retreat that are available nowhere else.

Further, some studies of the Cheyenne retreat either slight seriously or totally fail to use the very pertinent Cheyenne/Arapaho Agency papers in delineating the intercourse of agency and military officials with the Northern Cheyennes during the difficult period of 1877 and 1878. Official records must be weighed against hearsay evidence offered long after. Either may be valid, and either may be tainted; but neither should be ignored. To question some aspects of the Northern Cheyenne retreat as previously told by no means denies the wrongs done the Northern Cheyennes. This study, as the reader will see, joins others in giving testimony to their maltreatment and justness of purpose in returning to their homelands.

For a writer of history, it is imperative to examine existing records and recollections as thoroughly as possible. Another valuable perspective comes from visiting the sites of historical events. Such visits often provide much insight that records, personal reports, and maps simply do not offer. Early in this study, I knew I wanted to travel the Northern Cheyenne route from Oklahoma, where I reside, to their northern homeland. I particularly wished to visit the sites of their conflicts with the U.S. troops.

There was nothing about the comfortable auto trip my wife and I made in May 1999 that would in any sense approach the heroics of the beleaguered Cheyennes or the physical punishment of the Fourth Cavalry's ride in pursuit. Still, our journey was extremely illuminating in terms of the terrain and logistics. Further, we were benefited enormously by the generous assistance of residents and museum archivists along the way. I am indebted to a number of people who contributed to an understanding of events in their particular areas.

Wanda Shipley and Mary Erskine of Alva, Oklahoma; DeWayne and Lillian Hodgson of Freedom, Oklahoma; Bob Klemme and Glen Payne of Enid, Oklahoma; Bud and Sue Martin, Woods County, Oklahoma; Bob Rea of Fort Supply, Oklahoma; and Dr. Bill Lees all participated in the ongoing search for the Turkey Springs battle site. Two participant maps— one by Captain Rendlebrock and another provided at the court-martial hearings—are contradictory in part and have failed to disclose the precise battle location.

Floreta Rogers of the Pioneer Krier Museum in Ashland, Kansas, offered information regarding the Cheyenne flight across Clark County and local landmarks. At Scott City, Kansas, Tom and Patsi Graham added greatly to the lore of Punished Woman's Fork; and their son, geologist Rodney Graham, provided a cook's tour of the battle site.

Tom Buecker, curator at the Fort Robinson Museum, graciously contributed both the valuable resources of his office and his personal knowledge in addition to an instructive tour of Fort Robinson and the old Red Cloud Agency site. B. J. Dunn of Chadron, Nebraska, and Dr. Don Green of Chadron State College provided an informative auto excursion of the region involved in the Fort Robinson outbreak, including the Antelope Creek death pit located very close to B. J.'s boyhood home.

We had no intention while there of probing for artifacts in the pit once consecrated by brave Cheyenne blood. But almost eerily, from a sandy mound of a freshly dug animal hole at the side of the pit, a circular metallic shape— the butt end of a .45-caliber slug—gleamed forth. The round, undoubtedly fired by a Third Cavalry trooper during the final assault of January 21, 1879, is now deposited with the Nebraska Historical Society.

This study benefited greatly from research material furnished by Bob Rea, Fort Supply Historic Site supervisor, and from the positive criticism and advice of the anonymous manuscript readers for the University Press of Colorado. And, as always, I must acknowledge the very generous and helpful assistance of my wife, Patricia Corbell Hoig, in the construction of this book.

Good words do not last long unless they amount to something. I am tired of talk that comes to nothing. It makes my heart sick when I remember all the good words and all the broken promises. If I cannot get to my own home, let me have a home in some country where my people will not die so fast. Let me be a free man—free to travel, free to stop, free to work, free to trade where I choose, free to choose my own teachers, free to follow the religion of my fathers, free to think and talk and act for myself—and I will obey every law or submit to the penalty.

—CHIEF JOSEPH, NEZ PERCÉ, *North American Review*, April 1879, regarding the removal of his tribe to Indian Territory

1

Contested
HOMELAND

B RIG. GEN. HENRY B. CARRINGTON GAZED OUT FROM HIS TENT on the grassy bank of Big Piney Creek in northern Wyoming where his troops were busily erecting a log palisade military post. The army had decided to call it Fort Phil Kearny.[1] Off to the west towered the rocky buttresses of Cloud Peak and the Bighorn Mountains. Snow-streaked slopes and valleys stood decked with pine, hemlock, ash, balsam, box elders, fir, willow, spruce, and cottonwood. Here in season could be found wild plums, cherries, currants, strawberries, gooseberries, raspberries, grapes, sweet peas, wild onions, and Indian potatoes. The region was also replete with a wide assortment of game: buffalo, bear, deer, antelope, rabbits, and sage hens.[2]

Carrington was exuberant. He felt that nothing on the Platte River to the south could rival this rich, beautiful country fed by the snows of the Bighorns. To him, the land presented a glorious prize for the United States in its post–Civil War expansion westward. No matter that it had long been a favorite haunt of the Sioux, Cheyennes, Arapahos, Snakes, and Crows. No matter that these choice hunting grounds featured much that was vital to the survival of these native tribes. Now the native inhabitants of this veritable Eden of the American Northwest would have to submit to the dictates of U.S. concerns.

Carrington had been sent forth to enforce those concerns. The discovery of gold in Montana prompted the U.S. government to open a road along the Bozeman Trail that ran through the Sioux and Northern Cheyenne country of north-central Wyoming. Despite the two tribes' bitter opposition to further white intrusion, Carrington was ordered to construct two new forts along the Bozeman. He arrived at Fort Laramie in June 1866 with 700 construction troops of the Eighteenth Infantry. From there Carrington marched north to Crazy Woman Fork, where he upgraded previously established Camp Connor and renamed it Fort Reno. This chore completed, he continued on up the eastern slopes of the Bighorn Mountains. Soon after Carrington arrived at the site of the new fort, a message came from Northern Cheyenne chief Black Horse. The Cheyenne asked: Had he come for peace or war? Carrington responded by inviting the chief to come and talk with him.

"I shall be happy to have you come and tell me what you wish," he wrote. "The Great Father at Washington wishes to be your friend, and so do I and all my soldiers."[3]

Two days later, on July 16, the Cheyennes arrived in grand style. Carrington had planned a formal reception. He and his officers had unpacked their dress uniforms from trunks, polished the epaulets, and neatly brushed their dress hats. The U.S. flag was hoisted above the camp. As the Cheyenne chiefs rode in, the infantry band played a gala air. Every effort was made to present an aura of state dignity to the proceedings. Carrington provided tobacco and other gifts to the guests as they gathered in a great council circle for talks.[4]

The Cheyennes, who said they represented 176 lodges, were unyielding at first. They told Carrington that if he pushed no further into the Powder River country and built no more forts, he and his men would not be molested. They wanted the white traffic moving westward to Oregon, however, to continue its route along the Platte River and not to turn north through their hunting grounds.

"What are you doing in this country anyhow?" the Cheyennes asked. "You come here and kill our game; you cut our grass and chop down our trees; you break our rocks [conduct mining], and you kill our people. This country belongs to us, and we want you to get out of it."[5]

The Cheyennes remained friendly with the whites through summer and fall of 1866 even though the Sioux attacked citizen trains and killed and scalped several whites, including a soldier, near Fort Phil Kearny. Despite the peaceful inclinations of the Cheyenne chiefs, the Sioux war medicine exerted a powerful influence on the Cheyenne warriors who attended a huge gathering of Northern tribes on the Powder River. The assemblage vowed to destroy forts encroaching on the Indians' hunting grounds. The Northern Cheyennes and Arapahos joined with them. When Carrington went ahead with building Fort Phil Kearny and began constructing still another post, Fort C. F. Smith, to the north on the Bighorn, the tribes began harassing the Fort Phil Kearny troops and transportation.

During mid-October an estimated 100 warriors attacked a wood detail 5 miles from Fort Phil Kearny, killing 2 men and wounding 1. Carrington rode out with 30 men and a howitzer and chased the attackers away. A second altercation occurred on December 6 when a party of 300 Sioux and Cheyennes fell on a wood train near the post. Again Carrington led a force from the fort, this time losing an officer and a sergeant who were cut off by the Indians and killed.[6]

The attackers appeared in strength again on December 19. A sentry stationed on Pilot Hill, half a mile from the post, signaled with a mirror that a large force of Indians had a wagon train corralled. Capt. James Powell led a detachment in relief, driving the Indians back to Lodge Trail Ridge, which he had orders not to cross. He returned to the post to say he was certain that had he crossed the ridge where the warriors were concentrated in force, he and his men would never have survived.[7]

Two days later, still another assault on a wood train was signaled to the fort. This time Carrington ordered out a command of seventy-six troops and four civilians under Capt. William J. Fetterman, issuing strict orders not to follow the Indians beyond Lodge Trail Ridge. The zealous Fetterman, however, failed to heed the order and, by pursuing the raiders, led his men into a deadly trap.[8]

Fetterman suddenly found himself surrounded by a mass of 1,500 Sioux warriors under Red Cloud, Arapahos under Eagle Head and Black Coal, and Cheyennes under Dull Knife, Little Wolf, and Strong Wolf.[9] The troops turned and attempted to escape, but their retreat was cut off. Their only option was to stand and fight. With every man needed for combat, the troops' unattended horses broke away and escaped. The odds were hopeless, and the Fort Phil Kearny command of seventy-six men, three officers, and two civilians was completely wiped out in the worst defeat suffered by the frontier army of the United States to that date. The Cheyennes lost two men, the Arapahos one, and the Sioux eleven.[10]

There were other clashes, all pointing to the weakness of U.S. frontier forces and the need for an arrangement with the Northern Cheyennes and Arapahos. On May 10, 1868, a peace commission led by Gen. William T. Sherman met with the tribes at Fort Laramie, Wyoming. Both Dull Knife and Little Wolf were present when a pact was eventually agreed on. The

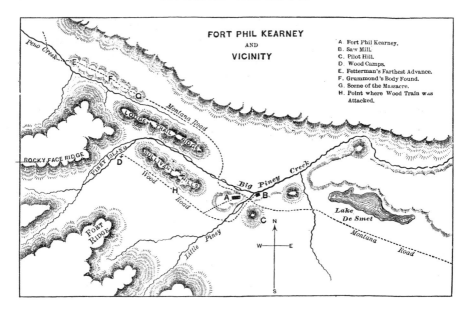

treaty stipulated that within one year the Northern Cheyennes would go and live either with the Crows on the Yellowstone in Montana; with the Sioux on the Missouri River near Fort Randall, South Dakota; or with the Southern Cheyennes and Southern Arapahos in Indian Territory. Of critical importance to them, the two tribes would retain the right "to roam and hunt while game shall be found in sufficient quantity to justify the chase" beyond their accepted reservation.[11]

With the election of President Ulysses S. Grant and the institution of his plan for Quaker management of Indian operations, a U.S. Indian Commission toured various Indian agencies of the West. Members met with the Northern Cheyennes at Fort Laramie during September and October 1870.[12] With no one available to interpret the Cheyenne tongue, the commission depended on a Sioux interpreter to communicate largely through sign talk. After a brief statement by Medicine Man, Dull Knife spoke for the Northern Cheyennes. He first asked that traders be sent to his people in the upper country. He said he did not want to use the same trading post as the Sioux. The two tribes did not always get along, and the Cheyennes wanted their own traders.

The commissioners said they did not wish to talk about "little things" like traders and the white man's road through the tribal hunting grounds. They wanted to know how the Cheyennes felt in their hearts and if they were willing to be peaceful. The chiefs answered that they could not live in a house on a reservation and had no wish to go south. They insisted further that the north country belonged to them and that "the white man that came to make treaties told untruths."[13]

More was said that the Sioux interpreter could not translate, and the council ended. In ensuing talks, however, the Cheyennes promised they would do no wrong to whites. They said they wished to stay in the Sioux country, as Red Cloud was agreeable to. The commissioners told them they could either do that or go to the reservation of the Southern Cheyenne, but they had to choose one or the other and not go back and forth.[14]

In autumn of 1871 runners arrived at Fort Fetterman to announce that a Northern Cheyenne band under Chief Little Wolf was on its way. Little Wolf and his people were returning after a lucrative hunting season in the Powder River country with pelts and robes and dried buffalo tongues to trade for goods of the white man at Fort Fetterman. The larger body of the Northern Cheyennes under Dull Knife and Turkey Leg were only a day behind.

The following afternoon a vedette alerted the Fetterman garrison to a dark mass moving up the valley of the Platte River.[15] Upon reaching the post, the Cheyennes selected a spot near the river, and the women began industriously preparing camp. Ponies were unloaded before being led off and picketed by young boys. In a short time, the tepees were erected; then bundles of trade robes, bags of pemmican, strings of jerked meat, and cooking pots were carried in and stowed.[16]

Col. George A. Woodward, commanding the post, listed three men as the head chiefs of the Northern Cheyennes: Little Wolf, Dull Knife, and Turkey Leg. He knew Dull Knife and Little Wolf and possibly Turkey Leg had taken part in the Fetterman massacre. Little Wolf (Oh-cum-ga-che) and Dull Knife (Tah-me-la-pash-me, or Morning Star) had signed the treaty of 1868. Woodward particularly admired Dull Knife, whom he considered the superior of the three men.

"Tall and lithe in form, he had the face of a statesman or church dignitary of the grave and ascetic type. His manner of speech was earnest and dignified, and his whole bearing was that of a leader weighted with the cares of state."[17]

Although Little Wolf appeared less officious, he impressed Woodward with his soldierly bearing. The officer held a lesser opinion of Turkey Leg.

During 1872, 1,342 Northern Cheyennes were attached to the Red Cloud Agency, which had been relocated that year from the Platte to the White River in far northwestern Nebraska. Their tribal number was provided by their own estimates. The chiefs refused to be counted for fear an enrollment would result in rations being issued directly to families instead of through leaders of the bands. Such a policy would severely reduce their control over the tribe.[18]

The government still sought a resolution to the matter of relocating the Northern Cheyennes and Arapahos. Accordingly, in 1873 it was arranged for a delegation of those tribes to visit Washington, D.C., and talk directly with President Grant. The Northern Cheyenne group consisted of Dull Knife, Little Wolf, Black Hawk, Strong Wolf, Spotted Wolf, Lame White Man, Crow, Old Wolf, Bear Who Pushes Back His Hair, and White Powder. The Northern Arapahos were Old Eagle, Iron, Eagle Dress, Plenty Bear, and Friday. Col. John E. Smith was in charge of the Northern delegation, and Jules Ecoffee, William Rowland, Joseph Bissonnette, and Thomas Reed were their interpreters.[19]

A delegation of Southern Cheyennes and Arapahos from Indian Territory arrived in the capital at the same time. Chiefs Stone Calf, Little Robe, Whirlwind, White Shield, Pawnee, and White Horse represented the group.[20] This constituted the first formal meeting of Northern and Southern Cheyenne leaders in many years.

Commissioner E. P. Smith and the two delegations held a preliminary meeting on November 13, 1873. Dull Knife spoke for the Northern Cheyennes and Plenty Bear for the Northern Arapahos. They told Smith they wanted to go to their old reservation in Nebraska. When the commissioner replied that by treaty they had given up those lands, the chiefs denied they had done so. Further, they said, they had come a long way to talk with the Great Father and did not propose to deal with subordinates. Smith insisted that because neither the Crows nor the Sioux would accept them, the Cheyennes would be forced to go south in line with the 1868 treaty.[21]

The meeting with the president took place at the White House the following morning with the visitors sitting in a large circle on the floor of the president's office. Grant opened the talks by stating his full approval of what the commissioner had said. The government was doing all it could to benefit them, he declared, and the tribes would be better off in the south where they could be better provided for. Plenty Bear, spokesman for the Northern Arapaho, replied that he had understood he was to remain in the north for thirty-six years before going south.

"By that time," Grant responded, "the whites would have crowded you in, and the Arapahos might well be gone. If you go south, you can be protected by the government. The southern agency has more game, the climate is milder, the winters are shorter, and you would be much better provided for if you go there."[22]

Chiefs Little Wolf (*left*) and Dull Knife during their visit to Washington in 1873. Courtesy, National Museum of American History.

Dull Knife rose and stepped forward. When he signed the treaty, he said, he had not known he would be required to go south. The president replied that it must have been the interpreter's fault, for he knew General Sherman would not intentionally harm the Cheyennes. During this meeting in Washington, Whirlwind invited the Northern Cheyennes to come among them.

"We are the biggest part of the tribe," he said, "you are the smallest part; we have plenty of buffalo and other game to hunt; we would very much like to have you come down here with us."[23]

The Northerners knew, however, that some of the Southerners such as Chief Little Robe were not pleased with the idea. But it did not matter; the Northern Cheyennes had no intention of leaving their beloved homeland. Yet when they returned to Red Cloud Agency, they found their trip to Washington had done them little good. The government now turned to hunger as a weapon. By its appropriation act of June 22, 1874, the U.S. Congress prohibited the Northern Cheyennes and Arapahos from receiving annuities until they relocated with the remainder of their tribes in Indian Territory.[24]

That fall at Red Cloud Agency, following several seasons of unproductive hunting, the Northern Cheyennes and Northern Arapahos met with agent J. J. Saville and asked to be allowed to settle and remain there. The lack of game had left them destitute of food and clothing. A group from the two tribes was persuaded to sign a paper agreeing to go to the southern reservation whenever the president directed if they could continue to remain at Red Cloud and receive rations until then. Little Wolf, Limber, Big Wolf, and Standing Elk represented the Cheyennes. But although the older Cheyennes were in favor of signing the treaty, the young soldiers of the tribe under Medicine Wolf rebelled and threatened to kill anyone who supported it.[25]

The move had still not taken place during spring of 1876, however, when the government sent commissioners Felix R. Brunot and Robert Campbell to exert further pressure on the tribes. The Chicago *Inter Ocean* reported that although the Indians were threatened with being deprived of their annuities unless they agreed to go south, "they remained deaf to all threats or persuasion."[26]

Invasion of the Black Hills by a gold-seeking expedition under Lt. Col. George Armstrong Custer and the ensuing flood of whites into the region antagonized both the Sioux and Northern Cheyennes, whose war parties struck against white intrusions into their homeland. The conflict came to a head during spring of 1876 when Gen. Phil Sheridan launched a three-pronged invasion of their mountain retreats in southern Montana. In an effort to force the tribes to their reservations, Col. John Gibbon pushed east from Fort Ellis, Montana; Gen. Alfred Terry drove west from Fort Abraham Lincoln, Dakota Territory; and Brig. Gen. George Crook struck north from Fort Fetterman, Wyoming.[27]

In early March Col. Joseph J. Reynolds, with 900 men of Crook's command, attacked a village on the Powder River, believing it to be an Oglala camp. Only after driving the villagers into the frozen countryside and burning their tepees was it discovered that they were predominantly peaceful Cheyennes under Chief Old Bear. Reynolds's victory was lessened considerably when the determined Cheyennes returned and recovered their pony herd.[28]

When Crook renewed his advance northward into the Indian stronghold, he was met on the Rosebud River by a combined force of Northern Cheyennes and Sioux who inflicted enough damage to cause him to withdraw temporarily. Eight days later, on June 25, Custer and his Seventh Cavalry launched an attack on a large Sioux and Northern Cheyenne encampment on the Little Bighorn River. Custer and 215 men under his command were annihilated in the famous conflict. Eventually, the Northern Cheyennes involved in the Custer defeat split from the Sioux to form their own village in the Bighorn Mountains. They were joined there by other Northern Cheyennes from the Red Cloud Agency. On July 12 one of those bands was intercepted on War Bonnet Creek in far northwestern Nebraska by a Fifth Cavalry force under Col. Wesley Merritt and turned back. Dull Knife and Little Wolf, however, were able to evade the troops and make their way west.[29]

Although neither had been involved in the great Indian victory, both knew they might be held responsible. For this reason, they took their camps deep into the Laramie Mountains of Wyoming where they hoped the white soldiers would be unable to find them.

2

Attack at
RED FORK

THE COLD MIST OF A WINTER DAWN SHROUDED THE FROST-CRUSTED VALLEY of the Red Fork of the Powder River in northern Wyoming as Col. Ranald Mackenzie rested his forces and waited for enough light to attack. From the Cheyenne encampment on the river less than a mile ahead came the throb of a drum and the chanting of warriors who had danced their war medicine through the night. Mackenzie ordered his troops to remount.

The friendly Indian scouts were to take the front and lead the charge. Without hesitation they made ready for battle, casting off their extra clothing and unneeded articles, then anxiously jostled their mounts into line as if vying for a racing position. Behind them the cavalry troops tightened their saddle girths and checked their carbines and pistols. The bitter cold caused most of the soldiers to keep their overcoats on even for battle. A Pawnee Indian blew on his pipe, producing a shrill humming tune that cut through the air with a unique wildness. That sound was obliterated when the order was given to make the charge. Around 1,500 horses surged forward simultaneously, the roar of their hooves echoing against the canyon walls and rolling down the valley like an approaching thunderstorm.[1]

Mackenzie's attack on the Northern Cheyenne village under Chiefs Dull Knife and Little Wolf took place on November 25, 1876, just five months after the Sioux and Northern Cheyenne annihilation of Custer and a large portion of his Seventh Cavalry on the Little Bighorn River. Mackenzie's command consisted of ten troops of Third, Fourth, and Fifth Cavalry supported by 400 Arapaho, Bannock, Lakota, Shoshone, and even some Northern Cheyenne scouts. The force had been sent forward from a Crook expedition that also included fifteen infantry companies and one of artillery under Lt. Col. Richard I. Dodge and accompanied by a supply train of 168 wagons and 400 pack mules.[2]

The Fourth U.S. Cavalry, the largest segment of Mackenzie's military force, had been seasoned by several years of Indian fighting in Texas. During March 1872 Mackenzie led the Fourth out of Fort Concho to make a surprise raid on a Comanche village in the Texas Panhandle, capturing a large number of Indians and 3,000 ponies. Then in May 1872, on orders from Gen. Phil Sheridan, Mackenzie followed Kickapoo and Lipan Apache raiders 160 miles south of the Rio Grande into Mexico. The unit killed 19 warriors and captured 40 women and children along with a number of ponies before burning three villages and the property in them. During the outbreak of 1874 and 1875, the Fourth had helped to defeat the Southern Plains tribes and drive them back to their Indian Territory reservations.[3]

On the basis of this success, Mackenzie and seven companies of the Fourth Regiment were ordered to Camp Robinson, Nebraska, in August 1876. There Mackenzie took charge of the military's District of the Black Hills, which included both the Red Cloud and Spotted Tail Indian Agencies. When Oglala Lakota chief Red Cloud refused to come in to the Red Cloud Agency, Mackenzie led the Fourth Cavalry on a 40-mile overnight march to the Sioux camps. After capturing 400 of their horses, he surrounded the camps and forced the Sioux to surrender their arms and horses and return with him to the agency.[4]

In early November Mackenzie marched to Fort Laramie and then on to Fort Fetterman, Wyoming, where he joined the overall command of Brig. Gen. George Crook for an expedition against the Sioux under Crazy Horse in southern Montana. While Crook's army waited out a snowstorm in Wyoming at old Fort Reno, however, scouts reported the presence of Dull Knife's Cheyenne camp on the Red Fork of the Powder River a short distance to the west. Crook ordered Mackenzie to find the Cheyennes and attack them.[5]

The Northern Cheyenne village lay nestled comfortably in a mountain-rimmed valley four miles long through which the mountain stream ran west to east. A narrow gap protected the eastern entrance to the canyon, but beyond there the valley opened into an elongated bowl defined by flat-topped bluffs and mountain slopes on the south and on the north by perpendicular, strata-lined cliffs that rose nearly a thousand feet above the canyon floor. Footing the north bluffs was a broad plateau that stood twenty feet above the river. This relatively level area was dotted by a scattering of conical buttes and cut by several dry gullies and arroyos that sliced snakelike down to the river. The most prominent of these was a deep, steep-sided ravine at the center. Around 200 Cheyenne lodges straddled the river amid the cottonwood and willow that lined its course, their cross-pole tops and skyward drifts of smoke visible above the thick underbrush.[6]

The Northern Cheyenne camp had been forewarned. Their scouts had discovered Mackenzie's army camped on Crazy Woman's Fork. A council was held, and many thought they should move and rejoin the Oglalas. But Last Bull, leader of the Kid Fox soldier society, arrogantly insisted that all would stay to fight the white man's army. Meanwhile, they would hold a dance to celebrate a recent victory over a Shoshone hunting party.[7]

The fete continued well into the morning before many finally retired. The majority of the camp was asleep when Mackenzie launched his attack. When the boom of Mackenzie's charge struck the village, the tribesmen who were still awake sounded the alarm. They yelled out warning cries, fired their guns, and began beating a large drum that had been presented to Chief Dull Knife during his visit to Washington in 1873. Pvt. William E. Smith, Troop E, Fourth Cavalry, observed a Cheyenne sentinel atop a big rock at the valley entrance. The lookout fired a warning shot before mounting his pony and galloping for the village.[8]

Aroused from their sleep, the panicked villagers poured out of their lodges into the subzero weather and snow-blanketed terrain. Women, children, and those too old to fight scrambled for safety among the surrounding bluffs even as half-clad warriors grabbed their guns and belts of ammunition and rushed into battle. The encampment, by estimate, held 400 to 500 Northern Cheyennes highly reputed for their fighting ability and to-the-death determination.

"They are the very best soldiers on this continent," Lieutenant Colonel Dodge once opined of the Northern Cheyennes, "indeed, I think, the best in the world."[9]

Although taken by surprise, the Cheyenne warriors had no intention of giving up without a fight. The noncombatants of the village were herded up the rock-strewn hillsides as a rear-guard action was being engaged. Many Cheyenne men swarmed to the high points above the village and began pouring rifle fire down on the troops. Others took up positions in the ravines where they met the troops closer on, setting up a stinging counterfire that blunted the charge of the scouts and Mackenzie's troops. Their coolness under fire and the warriors' willingness to take any risk in battle led Mackenzie's men to agree that "they had no cowards to encounter in the Cheyennes."[10]

The Indian scouts had been arranged with the Shoshones and Bannocks to the right; the Sioux, Cheyennes, and Arapahos at the center; and the Pawnees to the left. During the charge the Shoshones and Bannocks under Lt. Walter Schuyler broke off to occupy the heights above the plateau on the south. The Pawnees, commanded by Maj. Frank North, were ordered to charge the Cheyenne village. They did so, veering off to the left across the Red Fork, their drive slowed by having to ford the stream. Once inside the streetless arrangement of the Cheyenne lodges, it was every man on his own to fire at the fleeing forms before him. When the scouts emerged from the village, the unit was badly disorganized. North quickly regrouped the Pawnees on the north bank and drove to the west end of the canyon, where they captured the main Cheyenne horse herd.[11]

Private Smith, riding as an orderly to Mackenzie, gave his account of the action by the troops:

> We started now on the charge but jest as we goot near the camp, the Indians [friendly scouts] turned up the side of the mounten and this left us right to the front. Well this did not stop the Genroll [Mackenzie] and we dashed on. Now there was about 10 of us a way a hed of the collom. When the Indians [Northern Cheyennes] saw the Indians on the hill they all turned out and commenced a heavy fire on them. They had not seen us yet. When we were wright in to the camp, the Genral looked around and says We were all a lone. He goot a little excited and says go back and tell them companys to charge in hear.[12]

The two battalions of cavalry galloped side by side in sets of four across the north bank. One battalion consisted of two troops of Third Cavalry, two of the Fifth, and one of the Fourth. This last, Troop M of the Fourth, was led by 1st Lt. John A. McKinney, serving on detached duty from Fort Reno, Indian Territory. A second battalion consisted entirely of Fourth Cavalry Troops B, D, E, F, and I under the overall command of Capt. Clarence B. Mauck, a native Hoosier who had won Civil War brevets during the battle of Stone River, Tennessee, and the Atlanta campaign.[13]

The momentum of the cavalry charge was stymied somewhat, first by the troops having to cross the Red Fork at the east end of the valley and soon after by a swale that lay in their path. This gave the Cheyennes the instance they needed to find firing positions along the rocky hillsides and in the ravines. Maj. George Gordon's battalion charged the ravines on the

Facsimile of Big Back's drawing of Mackenzie's attack. No. 7 indicates Lieutenant McKinney; No. 5, Bull Hump; No. 6, High Bull. Dodge, *Our Wild Indians*, Plate 4. Courtesy, Western History Collection, University of Oklahoma.

right, driving the Cheyennes back until defensive rifle fire from the hillsides forced them to take shelter behind a bluff.

Early in the action, a group of Cheyennes was seen moving to rescue a pony herd on the western half of the plateau. Mackenzie sent word by regimental quartermaster Henry W. Lawton, Fourth Cavalry, to McKinney and his Company M to make a charge and cut off the Cheyennes. This forced McKinney and his men to cross the deep center ravine. McKinney, brandishing his cavalry sword, was in the lead of his column of fours upon reaching the chasm. Suddenly, a party of Cheyennes rose up from almost underneath him and fired at point-blank range. McKinney was hit six times and knocked from his horse. Even as he fell, he called to his men: "Get back out of this place; you are ambushed!"[14] Despite this, his first sergeant and five of his men were wounded. McKinney lived twenty minutes, long enough to mumble a few words about his mother as the life went out of him.[15]

The Cheyennes' barrage threw Company M into confusion. Following McKinney's warning, several of the sets of four troopers immediately behind him wheeled about to retreat. Their horses crashed into those still driving forward, creating chaos down the line. In their rear Capt. Henry W. Wessells responded by yelling to his Company H, Third Cavalry, to "dismount and fight on foot!" Moving forward as skirmishers, Company H drove the Indians up the ravine toward the mountains. In this action Sgt. James S. McClellan outdueled and killed a Cheyenne. He then took the warrior's gun and gun belt, discovering that the belt carried a silver plate with the name "Little Wolf" inscribed on it. He later learned it was not the Cheyenne war chief whom he had bested, although the belt had been given to Little Wolf while he was in Washington.[16]

Capt. Alfred B. Taylor, Fifth Cavalry, of Gordon's battalion was ordered to lead a charge through the village on the north bank. In this skirmish the Cheyennes killed and scalped Pvt. John Sullivan of Company B, Fourth Cavalry. Four horses were lost.

Mauck's battalion, its charge also halted by the Cheyennes' fire, had dismounted and rushed forward to take shelter behind some bluffs on the west end of the now-vacated village.[17] The battalion became a target for Cheyenne riflemen in the bluffs. Fourth Cavalry Company I under Capt. William C. Hemphill moved forward on the left, but Cheyenne sniper fire quickly forced the troopers to abandon the ground they had gained.

Capt. Wirt Davis and Troop F, Fourth Cavalry, had taken a position behind a bluff when several Cheyenne warriors suddenly emerged from some rocks and charged them. The troopers ran back to a gully that provided cover and from there were able to kill several Cheyennes. Others were forced to retreat to the shelter of a cave. Supported from above by the fire of the Shoshones and Bannocks and on the ground by the sabre-wielding Capt. John Hamilton, Troop H, Fifth Cavalry, Davis's men engaged the Cheyennes in fierce hand-to-hand combat.

The main fighting lasted a little over an hour. After that it settled down into a rifle contest, and the entrenched Cheyennes held the upper hand, their infantry rifles outdistancing the cavalry carbines. Mackenzie realized the futility and high cost of attempting to drive them from their rocky fortresses.

"The talk of the Cheyennes was still fierce enough and their courage was unabated," John Bourke surmised; "had we foolishly attempted to force them out of their improvised rifle-pits in the crevices and behind the rocks on the hill sides, the loss of life would have been fearful."[18]

Mackenzie was content to take the captured horses and burn every vestige of the Cheyenne village. Before the torch was applied, the men and scouts were given the privilege of gathering the spoils of their victory. Among the items found was clear evidence that warriors in the village had been involved in the Custer defeat. There was a silk Seventh Cavalry guidon; a memo book listing the three top marksmen in one of Custer's massacred companies; a letter written by a Seventh Cavalry soldier to a young lady, stamped and ready to post; a Seventh Cavalry guard roster; plus saddles, canteens, nose bags, currycombs, brushes, axes, photographs, a gold pencil case, watches, officers' coats, and other paraphernalia of the lost command. One coat was thought to have been that of Tom Custer, who was killed in the fight.

Around 500 Indian ponies had been captured, and they were later given to the Indian scouts. This in itself constituted an enormous loss to the Cheyennes, but additionally their entire winter supply of dried meat and a large quantity of ammunition had been left behind during the assault. The Indian scouts were permitted to load more than fifty packhorses with buffalo robes and other goods from the deserted lodges.[19]

"Those of us who were in the fight with Mackenzie," Bourke observed, "knew the severity of the blow he had dealt the Cheyennes in the total destruction of their fine village."[20]

Before leaving the battlefield, Mackenzie sent interpreter Bill Rowland, who was married to a Cheyenne woman, to talk with the Cheyennes about surrendering. Rowland and some of the scouts crawled up close enough to parley with Dull Knife. The chief said (according to Col. Homer Wheeler in *Buffalo Days*) that three of his sons had been killed in the fight and that although he was willing to surrender, he could not persuade other chiefs to do so. Other Cheyennes called out to the Indian scouts, saying, "Go home! You have no business here! We can whip the white soldiers alone but can't fight you, too."[21]

The Cheyennes' misfortunes by no means ended in the village. With many of their people wounded, they had been driven into the mountains without shelter, clothing, food, or horses in the throes of winter. Uncounted numbers died in the frozen hills. Those who had somehow survived managed to reach the Oglala camps under Crazy Horse on the Powder River. The Cheyennes later said they lost forty of their tribe on the Red Fork.[22]

Among Mackenzie's troops, the Fourth paid the greatest price, comprising the majority of his casualties. Five of the seven men killed in the battle were Fourth Cavalry troopers, with McKinney the only officer slain. The dead Fourth Cavalry men included Cpl. Patrick F. Ryan and Pvt. James H. Baird of D company, Pvt. Alexander Keller of E Company, and Sullivan. Further, of the twenty-six men wounded in the battle, eighteen were from the Fourth Cavalry.[23]

"I then hird someone say Leut. McKiney was shot," Pvt. William Earl Smith wrote in his diary. "But not a word of lots of privits that I could se laying a round ded."[24]

The Fourth Cavalry learned a significant lesson about battling the Northern Cheyennes, one that would have important bearing in another historic conflict with them two years later. As Bourke put it, once they got into the rocks and fortified themselves, "One Indian is equal to 10 Cavalry men."[25] This fact and the fighting spirit of the Northern Cheyennes would be well remembered by the Fourth Cavalry units under Mauck and Hemphill as well as by Wessells and his Third Cavalry troops. In time, fate would bring these commands and the Northern Cheyennes into deadly conflict once again.

3

Farewell THE MOUNTAINS

A FTER THE FIGHT AT RED FORK, MACKENZIE REJOINED CROOK at Canton-
ment Reno and continued on north up the Belle Fourche to the
head of the Little Missouri. Hampered by subzero weather, bliz-
zards, poor water, a scarcity of forage for its animals, and lack of success, the
expedition was ordered back to Fort Fetterman. Mackenzie and the Fourth
Cavalry returned to Camp Robinson, where the unit took on the much less
rigorous garrison duties for a time. There, during spring of 1877, they witnessed the surrender of Dull Knife and Little Wolf.

The bands of those two chiefs, along with those under Two Moon, White
Bull, and Little Chief, had wintered with the Lakotas along the Tongue
River valley below Hanging Woman tributary. During early January 1877
Gen. Nelson A. Miles marched south from the Yellowstone and attacked
the joint camp. Afterward, several of the Northern Cheyenne surrendered
to Miles on the Yellowstone, but Dull Knife, Little Wolf, and Standing Elk
went to Red Cloud where their people had been before.[1]

Red Cloud Agency sat comfortably established on a grassy plateau in
the White River valley of far northwestern Nebraska. To its north towered
the sheer bluff of the Pine Ridge escarpment that stretches from South Dakota westward to the Rocky Mountains of Wyoming. Constructed fortlike
in the form of a 200-by-400-foot corral surrounded by a 10-foot-high board

Issue day at Red Cloud Agency near Camp Robinson during spring of 1876. *Harper's Weekly,* March 13, 1876. Photocopy, Western History Collection, University of Oklahoma.

enclosure with bastions at two corners, it featured a two-story agent's house, offices, hospital, large storehouse, council room, mess house, schoolhouse, blacksmith and carpenter shops, an inside well, and a barn. For a time, the agency operated a steam sawmill.[2]

Little Wolf surrendered first at the agency on April 4 at the lead of 1,400 tribesmen, most of whom were Cheyennes. He explained that because his part of the band had the best ponies and was not encumbered with wounded, they had been able to come in well ahead of the others. Even so, some of his people were nearly dead from the effects of hunger and privation. Lieutenant Bourke, who was present at the surrender, was much impressed with Little Wolf, whose resolute face was framed by hair that hung loose over a red shirt and black pantaloons.[3]

Another portion of the Cheyennes under Turkey Leg surrendered at the Dakota Territory Spotted Tail Agency. He had been wounded in the Mackenzie fight, and his Cheyennes had lost everything. Although his people were destitute to the extreme and he was partially paralyzed, the chief expressed the intense pride they held as warriors.

"These are the Cheyennes," he told Crook. "You who have fought us know what we are. We claim for our people that they are the best fighters on the plains."[4]

Little Wolf and his warriors willingly joined the company of scouts headed by Lt. William P. Clark. The Cheyennes, who knew him as "White Hat," thought highly of Clark.[5] The 200 or so scouts, divided into four companies, were composed of Lakotas, Cheyennes, and Arapahos from both the Spotted Tail and Red Cloud Agencies. Mustered in and paid like regular army soldiers, the scouts were provided with arms and ammunition. They furnished their own ponies, but because it was generally believed they knew more about cavalry tactics than the cavalry officers, they were not drilled.[6]

The Northern Cheyenne bands under Dull Knife and Standing Elk arrived at Red Cloud Agency on April 21. A newspaper correspondent described the event:

> Yesterday morning, the hostile Cheyennes came into this agency and surrendered. They approached the agency from the north, and, as they came over the hills into the valley, began singing and firing their guns. The warriors were formed in companies, and maneuvered with as much apparent ease as companies of cavalry. The leading company carried a white flag, in front of which rode Standing Elk, Dull Knife, and other chiefs, these being preceded by Lieut. Clark and Interpreter Rowland.
>
> A place was cleared for their camp in the valley of White Earth River, just behind the agency, and then the warriors rode up to the stockade where were assembled Gen. Crook, Gen. Mackenzie, Gen. [James W.] Forsyth of Gen. Sheridan's staff, and a number of other officers. Standing Elk and the other chiefs dismounted, and the first named addressed Gen. Crook, saying that he had come in to shake hands and be friends. He desired to surrender his gun to Gen. Crook in person, as did the other chiefs, and said all his warriors would surrender their arms at once, and hereafter live in peace with the whites.[7]

Despite this picturesque pageantry, the eighty lodges of Cheyennes presented a scene of abject despair. Completely impoverished of all the necessities of life, their shelters consisted of makeshift tents of old canvas, skins, and gunnysacks. They had very few blankets or robes and no cooking utensils. A number of the tribe were still suffering from limbs frozen following Mackenzie's attack on their village. The group contained 550 Cheyennes, 85 of whom were fighting men who turned over 600 ponies, 60 rifles, and 30 pistols to the military. There were a large number of widows among the Cheyennes. Some of the band were nearly dead from the effects of hunger and privation. It was reported that one tribesman was so famished that when he was fed he ate so much that he died.[8]

One widow was the daughter of Dull Knife. Her husband had been killed in Mackenzie's attack, and in mourning she had slashed her arms severely in three or four places. Bourke estimated the chief's other two daughters as sixteen and eleven years of age, "both bright and pretty, the youngest especially so."[9]

Before holding a formal council with the Cheyennes, Crook gave them a chance to rest, eat, and have their sick and wounded treated. At noon the following day, the Cheyenne principal men met with Crook and Mackenzie. The Cheyennes seated themselves in a circle on the floor, passing the peace pipe from one to the other. The officers and chiefs shook hands all around.

"I am glad you have come in, and I hope you will listen to reason hereafter," Crook told them through interpreter Rowland. He asserted that he did not talk one way and act another. At the same time he asserted blandly, "This country is large enough for all of us."[10]

Standing Elk agreed, saying "I think it is as you say. There is room enough for all of us in this country."[11]

Bourke found Standing Elk to be "a fine-looking Indian with hair divided in the center with a vermillion stripe and hanging down over his shoulders. Vest trimmed with brass-headed tacks, necklace and breast-plate of porcelain pipe-stems."[12]

Mackenzie spoke to the chiefs as well. "Those who remained in, you can see, were well treated," he told them, "and had you all remained, it would have been better for you. Behave well, and you will have nothing to fear hereafter. All we want is good faith and good actions. Sitting Bear and Crow, who remained here with me, are my friends, and there must be no bad talk about them. From this time throw away all foolish talk."[13]

Holding his green blanket about him, Dull Knife spoke for his people. "When your messengers came to us," he said, "we listened to their words and came right in. I am glad to meet you all here to-day. Anything you say to us we will believe hereafter. We hope there will be an everlasting peace."[14]

The Northern Cheyennes would soon learn, however, that the government was still fully determined to remove them south to Indian Territory. Despite General Crook's talk about there being room enough for both whites and Indians in the North, the issue of removing the northern tribes to Indian Territory had not gone away. Writing from Red Cloud Agency on April 19, 1877, a news correspondent revealed that the subject was still under discussion by officials there: "The Indians here all oppose removal to the Indian Territory, or even to the Missouri River, and until they are all disarmed, dismounted, and thoroughly accustomed to the new order of things, it would hardly seem to be a good policy to remove them."[15]

Both the Cheyennes and Arapahos would bitterly oppose being sent to join their southern cousins, the agent at Red Cloud observed. They would not go unless forced to do so.[16]

Mackenzie, however, reported the opposite to Sheridan:

> Col. McKenzie telegraphs me that the Northern Cheyennes, numbering in all not over 1,400, desire to go to the southern agency at Fort Reno, on the Canadian River, Indian Territory, and that one officer and 12 men can move them. I have consulted Gen. [John] Pope, who says he has no objections, and that he can perfectly control them, and that no bad results will happen to the Indians there.[17]

Although most Cheyennes were much against going south, a faction among them was agreeable to removal. Standing Elk, who did most of the speaking for the Cheyennes, and others of his band had relatives among the southern bands. They had been thinking of moving to Indian Territory for some time. So Standing Elk stood up and declared that the Cheyennes were willing to go south.[18] Wooden Leg, a Northern Cheyenne who was among those at Camp Robinson, later stated that his people did not like the soldier talk about joining as one tribe with the Southern Cheyennes. They wanted to remain in the north country near the Black Hills. Standing Elk, however, insisted that the northern people would be better off if they went there. As a result, Wooden Leg claimed, the soldier chiefs gave Standing Elk extra presents and would talk only with him, ignoring the other forty-three chiefs: "I think there were not as many as ten Cheyennes in our whole tribe who agreed with him. There was a feeling that he was talking this way only to make himself a big Indian among the white people. . . . One day he went around telling everybody: All get ready to move. The soldiers are going to take us from here tomorrow."[19]

So, reluctantly, the Northern Cheyennes accepted their fate and agreed to go south to Indian Territory. But it was clear in their minds that they were doing so only to see if they would like it there. Otherwise, they would return.

On May 28, 1877, the Northern Cheyennes under Dull Knife and Little Wolf began their journey south from the Red Cloud Agency to Indian Territory. It was not a particularly unusual sight for that day, the long cavalcade of almost a thousand tribespeople stretching for nearly two miles.[20] But it was an interesting one. All was order: the Fourth Cavalry troops leading the way, Cheyenne scouts riding the flanks with rifles across their pommels, packhorses pulling their twin-pole travois laden with infants and goods, blanketed pedestrians, supply wagons bumping along with camp dogs trailing behind, and at the rear of the march a pony herd and the beef cattle that would feed the entourage on the trail.

There was no hurry. The Northern Cheyennes were far from pleased to be leaving their native homeland and going south to Indian Territory. Still, they were nomadic people. They were somewhat pleased to be on the move once more and escaping the restrictive oversight of the Camp Robinson soldiers. Few Northern Cheyennes knew anything of Indian Territory where they were headed. Some of their older men who had visited there said it was hot and not nearly as nice as the high country. Yet on this peaceful spring day, with the pine-decked cliffs to the north towering against a clear blue sky, no one could have foreseen that in less than two years many would be returning north under far different circumstances.

After the first day on the trail, the main body of Fourth Cavalry returned to Camp Robinson. This left the hard-drinking, Civil War Medal of Honor holder 1st. Lt. Henry Lawton with only fifteen Fourth Cavalry troopers and thirty Northern Cheyenne scouts who had been enlisted into army service as escort for the entourage of almost a thousand tribespeople. The scouts received the same pay as the soldiers, plus forty cents a day for the use of their horses. One of the scouts had participated in the Custer massacre the year before and proudly wore a blue army coat captured in the fight. The migration was also accompanied by Bill Rowland, his half-blooded wife, their grown son, and other younger children.[21]

The procession of Northern Cheyennes under Lawton moved leisurely toward Sidney Barracks, Nebraska, their first replenishing point on the way to Indian Territory. The length of a day's march varied from ten to fifteen miles a day depending on the water and camping situations encountered. The enlisted scouts not only rode ahead and searched out locations for making camp, but they also served as hunters and provided fresh meat for the travelers to supplement the beef supplied by the cattle driven along behind.[22] Although the situation would soon change drastically, buffalo, antelope, and other game were still in abundance on the Western plains.

Wooden Leg, who made the journey as a young man of nineteen, recalled his hunting experiences during the trip. He was friends with the soldiers, some of whom loaned him their guns to hunt with. In return he brought in the best parts of his kill and gave the gun lender his choice. The soldiers also hunted, he said, and were good shots.[23]

Some of the very old tribespeople and those who were sick were permitted to ride in military wagons, which also carried the lodge covers and provisions such as bread, sugar, coffee, and other foodstuff. These last were issued to the caravan daily along with portions of the beef cattle butchered each day. Having few lodges of their own, at night many tribespeople slept in soldier tents made of canvas.[24]

Henry W. Lawton. *Harper's Weekly,* October 2, 1886. Photocopy, Western History Collection, University of Oklahoma.

The march from Sidney Barracks led to Fort Wallace on the Smoky Hill River in far western Kansas. The Cheyennes went into camp fifteen miles east of the fort, which many of them visited. Lt. George H. Palmer of the Sixteenth Infantry, which had just arrived at Wallace from New Orleans, issued rations to the entire party.[25]

From Wallace, the migrating troupe moved south to the Arkansas River and Fort Dodge. During the journey to Fort Dodge, the hunters killed an average of 75 antelope each day and a total of 200 buffalo to feed the migrants. Also, the army had arranged for rations to be issued to the Cheyennes at the military posts along the way.

On July 11 the Cheyennes went into camp nine miles west of Dodge City, Kansas. A large number of Dodge City residents rode out to view them. Lloyd Shinn, editor of the *Dodge City Times*, described the Northern Cheyenne encampment for his readers. He told of the Cheyennes' hundred or so tents pitched in a circle around an open area of several acres on the flat bank of the Arkansas River. Grazing near the camp were 1,200 fine-looking ponies.[26]

It was nearly six P.M. when he arrived at the camp, and the newsman found the women busy cooking over outside campfires. Fifty chiefs and warriors were holding council in a large tepee. The men sat cross-legged in a circle on the ground, smoking and discussing a matter they wished to present to the six-foot-six Lawton, whom they called "Tall White Man."[27]

When the council was finished, the Cheyennes took their concern to the officer. They found him relaxing in a camp chair in front of his Sibley tent. The chiefs formed a large semicircle before him, passing a long-stemmed pipe around for each to puff before beginning their talk. Turkey Leg and Wild Hog did the talking. They requested permission to send a small detail of warriors ahead of the main party. Lawton listened, but he refused the request on the grounds that it would lead to others doing likewise and cause the band to become separated.

Evidently relying on interpreter Rowland as his source of information, Shinn identified Standing Elk as the principal chief of the Cheyennes. The elderly Dull Knife, he noted, had held that position but had lost it, possibly because of his advanced age. One military office referred to him as an "incurable invalid."[28] Still, this "remarkable chief" was often chosen to speak for the Cheyennes in meetings with U.S. authorities. Big Head, a Cheyenne closely associated with Dull Knife, also spoke on the matter. Although formerly a chief, he said, Dull Knife had not been considered so for a long time except by the whites. Other chiefs of the band included Little Wolf, Wild Hog, Crow, Living Bear, White Contrary, and Big Wolf.[29]

Cheyenne chief Turkey Leg. Courtesy, Oklahoma Collection, University of Central Oklahoma.

The following morning the Cheyennes moved past Dodge City and went into camp on the banks of the Arkansas River opposite Fort Dodge. During the day, the tribespeople flooded into town and mixed amiably with the townspeople. In recognition as the leading chief, Standing Elk accompanied Lawton and Rowland to visit Col. William H. Lewis, commander of Fort Dodge. Both men were oblivious to the irony that fourteen months later Lewis, a man sympathetic to the plight of the Northern Cheyennes, would perish in battle with these same tribesmen. That afternoon a dozen of their young men, gorgeously painted, held a dance in the town's main street. One dancer wore a colorful feathered headdress; another's head was bedecked with horns.

Before renewing their march, the Cheyennes were issued rations at Fort Dodge consisting of sugar, coffee, tea, rice, beans, bacon, beef, and tobacco. En route to Camp Supply, they were provided with beef by rancher Red Clarke, who had been contracted by the government at his Cimarron River ranch fifty-five miles below Fort Dodge on the Kansas–Indian Territory border.[30]

Another halt was made at Buffalo Springs near present Buffalo, Oklahoma, where a highly successful buffalo hunt was conducted. The Northern Cheyennes were pleased to find so much game. Even though the hot, heavy air was disagreeable and the barren scenery much to their distaste, it had begun to appear that living in Indian Territory would perhaps not be as bad as they had thought.[31]

The Northerners were met at the Persimmon Creek tributary of the North Canadian by Ben Clark, interpreter and scout from Fort Reno, which lay just across the river to the south of the Darlington Agency. He led the cavalcade the rest of the way down the river to a camping place near the agency and the post. The Northern Cheyennes reached the end of their journey on August 5 after seventy days on the trail.[32] Only then did many of them look back to the West and realize sadly that they could no longer see the green pines rimming the horizon.

4
What Are You Sioux DOING HERE?

THE NORTHERN CHEYENNES WENT INTO CAMP on the brushy but treeless
bank of the meandering North Canadian River just west of the Southern Cheyenne and Arapaho Agency. Nothing about the place was
like their homeland in the north. At this time of year the air was stiflingly
hot and humid. The woods were infested with ticks, and ravenous horseflies
attacked the horses. Even the trickling channel of the river failed in comparison to the cold, rippling streams the people had left behind. Lodge covers were left rolled up day and night to catch any breeze that might come
along, and mosquitoes swarmed in. Other than sand plums, there was little
edible plant life. Further, the region had been hunted out; the buffalo and
deer were gone. This not only left the northerners constantly hungry for the
red meat they had always known, but it left the men with nothing to do but
sit around the camp in the shade all day.

When elderly Quaker agent Brinton Darlington selected the site for an
agency in 1869, he had done so largely on the basis of its agricultural potential,
not for its hunting or gathering qualities. The agency sat at the far eastern edge
of the Cheyenne and Arapaho Reservation that extended up the Canadian
and Washita watershed to the Texas Panhandle. It was a good distance
from the agency to the buffalo grounds of western Indian Territory, and the
tribesmen were restricted from going there without military escort.

Cheyenne camp on North Canadian just west of Darlington Agency. Courtesy, Archives and Manuscript Division, Oklahoma Historical Society.

Two miles south from the agency, across the North Canadian, Fort Reno stood neatly arranged on a long, sloping, and largely barren hillside. Like the Fort Reno of Wyoming, it had been named for the Civil War general Jesse L. Reno, who had been accidently killed by friendly fire at South Mountain, Maryland, in 1862.[1] Both Maj. Clarence Mauck and Capt. Wirt Davis of the Fourth Cavalry had once commanded here. Although not a stockade-enclosed fort, it appeared to be a typical military post with a central parade ground and flagpole surrounded by administration buildings, officers' quarters, and barracks for enlisted men. Beyond these were the barns, stables, and corrals. There was no bridge over the river connecting Fort Reno and the agency until Lt. Col. E. V. Sumner (the younger) constructed one in 1885. Although a makeshift ferry was put into operation, when the North Canadian flooded, the two locations were essentially cut off from one another.

The garrison at Fort Reno in fall of 1877 consisted of Companies G and H, Fourth Cavalry, and Companies E and I, Sixteenth Infantry—a total complement of 220–230 men. Maj. John K. Mizner, an 1852 West Point graduate from Michigan, commanded the post. He had risen to the rank of brevet brigadier general of volunteers during the Civil War for action at Corinth and Panola, Mississippi. Capt. Joseph Rendlebrock, who had overall command of the two companies of Fourth Cavalry, was a Prussian who had enlisted in the U.S. Mounted Rifles in 1851. He had won three Civil

War promotions to reach the rank of brevet major. Capt. Sebastian Gunther, a native German who had served on the Western frontier before the war and fought with Sumner against the Cheyennes in 1857, commanded Company H of the Fourth. He, too, had been twice breveted in fighting for the Union.[2]

Following the war, the Fourth Cavalry was assigned to garrison duty in Texas with headquarters at San Antonio. Rendlebrock and his Company G saw duty principally at Fort Concho and Fort Clark, whereas Gunther and Company H were stationed at Fort Griffin, Fort McCavett, and Fort Richardson. Gunther had ridden with Mackenzie when he struck the joint Comanche-Cheyenne-Kiowa camp at Palo Duro Canyon on September 28, 1874.[3] Both men and their units moved to Fort Sill, Indian Territory, with Mackenzie in spring of 1875. They were left to oversee the still unsettled southern tribes, however, when the other Fourth Cavalry units were sent to Camp Robinson. After a short stint at Fort Elliott in the Texas Panhandle, Rendlebrock's Company G took up garrison duty at Fort Reno, Indian Territory, in February 1876. At the time of Mackenzie's attack on Dull Knife's village, Rendlebrock and his troopers were escorting a party of Southern Cheyennes and Arapahos on a buffalo hunting expedition up the North Canadian River.[4] Gunther and Company H transferred from Fort Sill to Fort Reno during September following arrival of the Northern Cheyennes.[5]

These two Fort Reno cavalry units, their rosters filled with raw recruits, inherited the immediate control of the former Red Cloud Indians. They were given support in oversight of the Cheyenne/Arapaho Reservation and the Northern Cheyennes by the Fourth Cavalry troops, now returning from Camp Robinson. In May 1877 the six companies marched to Sidney and from there reached Indian Territory by rail. Three of the companies were stationed at Fort Sill to monitor the Kiowa and Comanche tribes. Troops B and F under Mauck were sent to Fort Elliott, and Troop I under Captain Hemphill was dispatched to Camp Supply.[6]

Almost immediately after the Northern Cheyennes arrived at Fort Reno, a dispute arose when Lawton issued orders for the scouts to turn in the rifles they had used for hunting during the march. The Cheyennes were angry and insisted that they would still need the weapons for hunting, as well as for their own protection. The chiefs held a council with Lawton, and finally the officer gave in, permitting them to keep the guns.[7]

The day after they arrived, the northerners were visited by Colonel Mizner. With him was Mackenzie, who had arrived back in Indian Territory ahead of Lawton's entourage to take command at Fort Sill.[8] An enrollment was immediately made of the northerners. It showed 190 families with

John K. Mizner. Courtesy, Special Collections and Archives, U.S. Military Academy Library.

a total of 933 Cheyennes that included 235 men, 312 women, and 386 children. There were also 3 Arapaho men and 1 Arapaho woman.

The rolls listed their chiefs as Dull Knife, with a family that included three women and one child; Standing Elk, with two women and eight children; Living Bear, with three women and seven children; and Turkey Leg, with one woman and three children. Little Wolf, who was not cited as a chief on the rolls, had four women and nine children.[9]

Once the enrollment was made, Mackenzie ordered the Northern Cheyennes to give up most of their finest ponies. They would be allowed to keep only one to a lodge. The confiscated horses were driven off to Wichita, Kansas, where they were sold at auction. Mackenzie used the proceeds to purchase breeding stock with which the Cheyennes were to start their own cattle herds and turn to raising and tending their own livestock. The Cheyennes were upset, seeing this action as a direct betrayal of promises made to them in the North.

By the treaty of 1868, they had been promised "one good American cow and one well-broken pair of American oxen" per lodge in addition to "one pound of meat and one pound of flour per day" for each person over age four.[10] They were also promised that the president would detail an army officer to be present and attest to the delivery of such. Nothing had been said in the treaty or otherwise about giving up their horses, and the Cheyennes were particularly incensed at that loss.

"Before we came into Red Cloud," Wild Hog claimed, "we had a good many horses; after getting there we were dismounted, and our horses taken away from us; but a part of them were given back to pack our things on. After reaching the south, a part of the horses were taken away and never given back again, contrary to the promises made that those ponies never should be taken away from us."[11]

From the proceeds of the horse sale, Mackenzie purchased fifty-one cows for the Northern Cheyennes. These cows, however, were quickly devoured by the starved tribespeople. "We would not kill them if we had anything else to eat," Wild Hog's wife noted.[12] Old Crow further suggested a vital need Mackenzie had overlooked. To produce a herd, he wryly observed, it would be good to have a bull available for the cows once in a while.[13]

The Southern Cheyenne and Arapaho bands had only recently conducted a successful fall hunt on the Washita River. They returned with over a thousand hides for making lodges and moccasins, along with a large quantity of brains to be used for tanning the hides. The southerners were in a festive mood and welcomed the newcomers with a period of gala feasting and dancing that celebrated the unification of the two tribal divisions.[14]

On August 7 Mizner relinquished control of the Northern Cheyennes to agent John D. Miles and the Darlington Agency. At that time Miles issued them rations along with six beeves.[15] The procedure by which rations were distributed quickly created a problem that was very disruptive. It was the same matter that had been resolved to their liking at Red Cloud. There, the goods had been stacked in one great pile from which the chiefs and warriors would distribute them to the tribespeople.

Miles felt that with this method the lion's share was often gone by the time the women got their pick of the goods. By Miles's system the Southern Cheyenne and Arapaho women brought ration tickets that had been issued them and presented the tickets to the clerk at the commissary building to collect their annuity items.

The problem came to a head at the August 8 issue. That morning Miles had gone to the beef corral two miles northwest of the agency to oversee the operation there.[16] Upon returning to the agency he found his clerk had given in to the demands of the northern chiefs and warriors and stacked all of the annuity goods in the yard in front of the commissary. Some warriors, the agent learned, had collected all of their family's ration tickets. They had brought them to the commissary and demanded that the annuities be issued in bulk.

Miles was determined not to change his system of distributing the annuities, feeling his way was the fairest to the tribespeople. The chiefs and head soldiers objected strenuously. They had reason to be concerned. When the chiefs lost control of distributing goods to their people, they lost a great deal of tribal influence and power.

"If it is done your way," they argued to Miles, "what is there for us to do? What is the use of being chief?"[17]

The northern chiefs held councils about the matter among themselves and with the Southern Cheyennes. The latter, having already made their adjustment to Miles's mandate, eventually convinced the northerners that they, too, would have to submit to the Indian Department. Still, the matter remained a sore point with the northerners and provided another strong reason why they did not like it in the south.

A serious health problem quickly developed among the northern people who were unacclimated to the scorching hot days of August and September and the heavy air of Indian Territory. Dr. Lawrence A.E. Hodge soon reported an "unprecedented epidemic of malaria fever."[18] He informed Miles that his supplies of medicines—sulphate of quina or sulphate of Cinchonidia—were almost exhausted and that if more was not received soon, much sickness and death would result.

John D. Miles (*second from left*) with son Whit, Ben Clark, and Chief Little Robe (*standing*). Courtesy, Archives and Manuscripts Division, Oklahoma Historical Society.

Reports of Northern Cheyenne discontent, particularly with the sparsity of their rations, reached Superintendent of Indian Affairs William Nicholson in Lawrence, Kansas. He wrote to the Commissioner of Indian Affairs in Washington, saying that "the Northern Cheyennes are very turbulent. If not fed, they may fight."[19]

Despite the failure of his program to make herders of the Northern Cheyennes, Mackenzie spoke forcefully in their behalf. In a letter to Gen. John Pope he wrote:

> This is the only band at the Red Cloud or Spotted Tail agencies who have up to this time complied fully with the treaty; and I may be pardoned for saying that my position is a very distressing one, in this—that I am expected to see that these Indians behave properly, whom the Government is starving, and not only that but starving in flagrant violation of the agreement.[20]

On September 20 Lieutenant Lawton returned to Darlington from Fort Sill on orders from Mackenzie to thoroughly inspect the Northern Cheyennes' condition at Darlington. Miles was away at the time. With interpreters Ben Clark and William Rowland, Lawton visited the Cheyenne village. He interviewed Wild Hog, who had been delegated to speak for the camp.[21]

Wild Hog said his people had been drawing no corn, hard bread, hominy, rice, beans, or salt. They received yeast powder and soap only occasionally, and the weekly ration of sugar and coffee lasted only about three days. The all-important beef issue was about the same, and the animals often looked starved. Some were very lame, Wild Hog said, and appeared about ready to die on their own.

"Very soon after our arrival there," Wild Hog said later, "the children began to get sick and to die in a way they never had been known to do at the north. The climate was much hotter than at the north, and the woods were full of mosquitos and bugs, that troubled us very much."[22]

Many Bears, Crow, and Turkey Leg confirmed that what Wild Hog said was true. Turkey Leg urged Lawton to intercede with Mackenzie to allow the Cheyennes to make a buffalo hunt. He said ten of their people had died since they arrived, and many more were sick. The chief argued that they had received first-class rations at Red Cloud and all the way down, but at Darlington they had received only meager amounts of poor-quality food. When Lawton witnessed a beef issue, Clark and Rowland told him the amount distributed was much larger when he was there to observe.

The northerners also complained that they were never visited by the agency doctor and that they had to ride a long distance to Darlington to get medicine. Then they would get only one dose and have to go back again for more. Lawton talked with Dr. Hodge. The physician said he did not make it to the camp very often because he was occupied at his office most of every day. He showed the officer his report for September that indicated he had treated well over a thousand reservation Indians.

Still other factors were working against the northern people. Despite the happy reception they had received when they arrived, their relations with the southerners had quickly become strained. The southerners contemptuously called them "Sioux Cheyenne" because of their close association and intermarriage with that tribe.[23]

James Rowland, who had helped escort the northerners to Indian Territory, testified later that they had gone without knowing the country, which was how the government could get them to go. "A Northern Indian," Rowland said, "cannot live down there. Even we white people who had lived in the north got the chills as soon as we got there. At first they had enough to eat because General McKenzie seemed to look out for them. After General McKenzie went away they got less."[24]

Wild Hog charged that southern chief Little Robe had pointed a finger at him and asked, "What are you *Sioux* doing here?"[25] Constant quarreling took place between the two Cheyenne divisions. As a result, some northerners moved about 12 miles up the North Canadian toward Raven's Springs where there was better water, open country, and a good supply of wood. This remoteness made it far more difficult for Hodge to attend them—had he attempted to do so.

When Miles learned of Lawton's negative report charging him with inadequately tending the Northern Cheyennes, he was very perturbed. He tried to arrange a conference with the officer to counter some of the charges. In truth, he said, he had complained to beef contractors about the poor quality of the beef but had little choice but to take what they drove to the agency. He, like other agents, was further restricted by departmental regulations and by budget as to how much beef he could issue per person. Also, he had indeed tried to procure better medical help for the tribe.

During October 1878 a *New York Herald* reporter who arrived at Darlington to investigate charges of corruption was given free access to agency records. He concluded his report: "I have no hesitation in pronouncing him [Miles] both an honest and able man, who discharges the duties of his position with great zeal."[26] Still, Miles was annoyed by the added responsibility of the nonconforming Northern Cheyennes. His lack of concern was revealed in a comment to a Senate investigating committee. "I have been able to find but very few Indians," he observed unsympathetically, "who would not say that they could eat more beef."[27]

5

Starvation HUNT

I F ANY SINGLE EVENT CONVINCED MANY NORTHERN CHEYENNES that they did not want to remain in Indian Territory, it was the joint buffalo hunt held during December 1877 and January 1878. They had ridden out to find the abundant buffalo herds they had been told were there. Instead, they found themselves camped west of Camp Supply far from their agency in midwinter with no buffalo to kill and so totally without food that they were eating their horses and dogs.

In making treaties with the tribes of the Plains, U.S. commissioners had always offered only enough annuity foodstuff to the tribes to supplement their buffalo hunts. Essentially, the tribes remained sorely dependent on the buffalo, not only for meat but for pelts and robes that could be bartered for other staples from the agency trading post. At the same time, the federal government did nothing to prevent or impede the wholesale slaughter of buffalo by white hunters. In truth, some within government and without argued that the demise of the buffalo was the most efficient way to solve the Indian problem in the West.

Ben Clark later testified to a Senate committee:

> From my observation, [after] the arrival of the Northern Cheyenne and ever since the Agency was built here the rations would not have been sufficient if the Indians had not supported themselves on the buffalo at

least one third of the year. Heretofore during the summer months when
not on the hunt a large proportion of their robes and skins have been
traded for flour, bacon, sugar, and coffee to make up for the deficient
supplies.[1]

During their summer hunt on the Washita south of the Antelope Hills,
conducted just prior to the arrival of the northerners, the Southern Cheyenne and Arapaho hunters often had to go up to fifteen miles from their
prairie camps to find game. The length of time required to bring the prey in
made it difficult for the women to prepare the meat before it spoiled. Still,
enough small herds were found to kill 150 to 200 animals a day. The women
worked industriously, slicing the buffalo meat into strips, drying it on scaf-
folds, and curing the hides. They managed to save most of the kill.[2]

The success of that hunt offered hope for the destitute Northern
Cheyennes, who arrived in severe need of lodges and additional subsistence
beyond the rations issued at Darlington. Miles strongly favored a joint
hunting expedition, seeing it as an opportunity to conserve his supplies. He
requested permission from superiors to authorize such a venture by the tribes,
arguing that it was necessary "that we may be able to save sugar, coffee,
flour, &c., for the Indians of this Agency next spring and summer when they
must remain at the Agency and that they may have the opportunity to
secure Robes and thus supply a large deficiency in their subsistence."[3]

"They were a people brought up to live on meat," southern chief
Whirlwind noted of the northerners, "and [were used to] having meat
for their main subsistence; and when they came down here they could
not get as much meat as they had been accustomed to having; they did
not get enough to keep them from getting sick; their stomachs troubled
them."[4]

Miles further requested that hunters be accompanied by troops and be
given permission to go beyond the reservation if necessary into the Texas
Panhandle. It was late November before the hunting expedition could be
arranged. Under escort of Troop A, Fourth Cavalry, commanded by Gunther,
the hunters headed up the North Canadian toward Camp Supply. The Southern Cheyennes and Arapahos followed along the north bank. The Northern
Cheyennes, who traveled slower than the others because their few horses
were in such poor condition, followed the south bank.

The tribes soon found that the large herds Miles had been told were
east of Camp Supply were not there.[5] Adding to their misery, a severe cold
wave plunged temperatures down to five degrees below zero.[6] On December
4 Gunther dispatched a courier to Fort Reno to report the dire situation of
the hunting expedition. He wrote:

The tribes are now out of rations. They are very much dissatisfied and are in a starving condition. I have to state that there are no buffalo in this part of the country and from information received at this Post the buffalo have all moved south and southeast of Fort Elliott, Texas, and it is reported that there are about 3,000 Buffalo hunters on the line of the Territory and in Texas.[7]

Buffalo hunter John R. Cook observed that the great buffalo decimation began in earnest in 1876. Up to that time only the natural increase, not the original herds, were killed. In that one year an estimated 155,000 hides went downriver on steamboats from Montana, 170,000 were entrained east over the Santa Fe Railroad, and 200,000 more were shipped from Fort Worth, Texas. The last great buffalo slaughter, Cook said, took place during December 1877 and January 1878, the very time the Cheyenne/Arapaho starvation hunt was under way.[8]

Still another factor was complicating matters for the Darlington hunters. It had been learned that 800 Pawnees from the Loup River of Nebraska, escorted by 10 Fourth Cavalry soldiers and 30 Indian scouts, had come south to hunt the buffalo. The Cheyennes were angry that their old archenemies had been permitted to come onto their hunting grounds. Although he had no interpreter, Gunther saw signs that made him suspect that a collision between these two longtime enemies of the Plains would take place when the Cheyennes reached Camp Supply.

The German-born Gunther was no newcomer to the West. After enlisting as a private in the First Regiment of U.S. Cavalry in 1855, he had fought against the Cheyennes on the Plains. During the Civil War he rose to commissioned status and won brevet laurels for his role in the pursuit of Hood's Confederate army at Nashville and in the capture of Selma, Alabama.[9]

One evening in camp, Gunther overheard an elderly Northern Cheyenne telling of a fight he had once been involved in with U.S. troops. The former warrior began scratching a map in the sand. In the lines he drew, Gunther easily recognized the Platte, South Platte, Republican, Solomon, Smoky Hill, and Arkansas Rivers. The old man poked holes in the sand to indicate the "soldier towns," or forts. He then indicated the line of march followed in 1857 by the dragoons under Col. E. V. Sumner, driving west along the Platte, and Maj. John Sedgwick, who marched to the Rockies by way of the Arkansas River. When Gunther told the Cheyennes he had also taken part in that battle, the tribesmen were excited and pleased. As fate would have it, within a year Gunther and the same Cheyennes he was now escorting would be doing battle once more.

Sebastian Gunther. Courtesy, Kansas State Historical Society.

The Cheyennes blamed the Pawnees for driving off the herds, but in truth the Pawnees were having just as difficult a time. They, too, were desperately hungry. They had applied to Maj. Henry A. Hambright, newly assigned commander of Camp Supply, for rations and were rejected. As a result, the Pawnees began trading off practically all of the wearing apparel issued to them before leaving their reservation. Choosing to cope with the freezing weather rather than with the gnawing hunger in their bellies, they sold their clothing to soldiers at Camp Supply at bargain prices to purchase food items from the post traders. Blankets, ulster overcoats, woolen dress coats, hickory shirts, hats, boots, shoes, and other items were swapped for food.[10]

In an effort to avoid a clash between the two tribes, both of whom were well armed with breech-loading rifles as well as bows and arrows, Hambright and his interpreter Amos Chapman worked out a compromise. By agreement, the Pawnees would hunt the country to the west of Camp Supply; the Cheyennes would go south, and the Arapahos would push northwest up the Beaver.[11]

Mizner, in the meantime, had dispatched Ben Clark to Camp Supply to serve as an interpreter and guide for Gunther. Clark led the entourage of Cheyenne tribespeople southwestward up Wolf Creek, going into camp at the mouth of Little Wolf Creek twenty-five miles above Camp Supply. With the erratic Plains weather having turned unexpectedly warm, many Northern Cheyenne men shed their leggings and the long buckskin tunics that reached almost to their knees, and the women rolled up the sides of their bleached buffalo hides for air. This was one of their favorite camping spots, the Southern Cheyennes said. Plenty of buffalo were always found here.[12]

Clark—a short, bowlegged, dependable man—knew the Cheyennes, the country, and the Wolf Creek site well. Ten years earlier, in 1868, he had ridden this way as a scout with Lt. Col. George Custer and his Seventh Cavalry on their march from Camp Supply to attack Black Kettle's Southern Cheyenne village on the Washita. Afterward he had taken a Cheyenne girl, Toch-e-me-ah, as his wife. Clark came along Wolf Creek again during the 1874 uprising, this time scouting for Gen. Nelson Miles and his expedition against the Plains tribes in the Texas Panhandle.

From Wolf Creek the various Cheyenne bands began fanning out in search of the elusive buffalo herds. The Southern Cheyennes scoured the country south beyond the main Canadian and Washita Rivers. Chiefs Little Robe, Whirlwind, and White Horse left their lodges on the Canadian and searched for game even to the head of the Red River near the Palo Duro Canyon. The Northern Cheyennes and Gunther followed Wolf Creek westward to its headwaters in the Texas Panhandle. All met with little success, and some bands suffered further at the hands of roaming white horse thieves who depredated their herds.[13]

In the meantime, Miles had become concerned over the situation of his Darlington charges. Also, he had received a complaint from Gen. Edward

Hatch at Fort Elliott asking that Miles keep his charges out of the Texas Panhandle lest their presence there lead to bloodshed with white settlers—in other words, leave the buffalo to white hunters.[14] On December 13 Miles sent word directing the Camp Supply trading firm of Lee and Reynolds to make a temporary issue of beef to all those at the post who were destitute of meat.[15]

The traders refused to do so without certification from Gunther. That officer, however, was with the Northern Cheyennes under Standing Elk forty-five miles up Wolf Creek and unable to move because of the poor condition of the ponies. Eventually, the various hunting bands straggled back in to Camp Supply. On December 21 Hambright reported that 300 tribesmen under Dull Knife, Crow, Arapaho chief Little Raven, and half-blood George Bent had returned to the post. Chapman told Hambright the Indians were eating the flesh of horses that had died.[16]

Crow made a similar statement, saying, "We went out on one buffalo hunt the first winter after coming here, and that was enough; we went out, and could hardly get back; we could not find enough buffalo to keep us from starving and had to live on turkeys."[17] Some camps, he said, got one, two, or three, some possibly as high as half a dozen buffalo, but others got none. They had to scatter out to get buffalo because they were so scarce.

Wild Hog said: "We were told that, in addition to the rations issued, there would be plenty of buffalo for us to hunt; but we did not find buffalo plenty there at all. They were all gone the first winter that we went out to hunt. . . . While on the hunt we had to kill a good many of our ponies to eat to save ourselves from starving."[18]

Even white hunters coming back north past Camp Supply from as far south as the Double Mountains in north Texas reported the country void of buffalo. At the same time, Gunther sent word from his Wolf Creek camp to Miles that Standing Elk and his party had found the herds gone. They were subsisting on small game, but with that food source very scarce they were "rapidly verging on starvation."[19]

A week of constant rain set in during late December, flooding the grounds at Camp Supply and driving both Wolf Creek and the Beaver out of their banks. The bands encamped along the river bottoms were forced to move to higher ground. Then in January another blast of winter struck the area, bringing snow and freezing temperatures. The streams were frozen over several inches thick—enough that the Camp Supply soldiers were able to cut and stow 50 tons of ice.[20]

In early January 1878 Miles directed agency farmer J. K. Covington to go to Camp Supply to gather in the hunting parties and secure a beef issue to the tribes. Runners were sent out, and gradually the bands straggled in and were fed. Although he reported at the time that he found no starvation among the bands at Camp Supply, Covington later acknowledged that "when I arrived at Camp Supply they were living mostly on dogs, ponies and poisoned wolves."[21]

After receiving the rations the Cheyennes balked at returning to Darlington.[22] Chapman explained that they could not remain at Camp Supply. To receive further rations they would have to return to Darlington. Reluctantly, the chiefs accepted their fate and moved back down the North Canadian. Crow and his group, however, continued to linger at Camp Supply. One day Crow's wife brought her share of the issue to Chapman and showed how small it was in comparison to army rations. It would not last more than three days, she said. White officials suspected that Crow had intentions of breaking away and returning north.[23]

At Darlington the situation only worsened for the Cheyennes. The annuity issue included beef and cornmeal but no flour, sugar, or coffee.[24] By now it was clear to the Northern Cheyennes: the glowing promises President Grant had made at Washington on behalf of the people of the United States as well as those of the generals at Camp Robinson were all lies.

6

Summer
OF DESPAIR

URING SUMMER OF 1877 A STORM OF DISCONTENT GATHERED over the Cheyenne and Arapaho Reservation, and neither Miles nor Mizner seemed fully aware of its potential consequences. With white hunters flooding the prairie and killing the buffalo and other game promiscuously, it became increasingly difficult for the tribes to find enough fresh meat to sustain them. But when Miles issued permits for certain traders to sell ammunition to the tribes, Gen. John Pope, who commanded the Department of the Missouri, objected. The Cheyennes and Arapahos were forced to secure their guns and ammunition by trade.

"The arms we had when we left to go north again," Crow testified, "were arms we bought from the other Indians around here [Darlington], who came here trading. The Pawnees, Sacs, and Indians of other neighboring tribes used to come here to trade, and we used to buy arms from them."[1]

Even successful buffalo hunts provided subsistence for only a short time before the Cheyenne and Arapaho bands were again dependent on annuity issues of beef and other foodstuffs.[2] With government allowances falling far short of his needs, Miles turned to unauthorized confiscation from Texas cattle herds illegally grazing on the Cheyenne/Arapaho Reservation. He also borrowed bacon, coffee, and sugar from the Fort Reno commissary to help stave off hunger among his agency's bands.[3]

Fort Reno stood as one in a pentagon of forts in western Indian Territory, western Kansas, and the Texas Panhandle arranged to control the southern Plains tribes and quash any potential outbreak. Other posts included Fort Sill to the southwest in the Wichita Mountains; Fort Elliott, just west of the 100th meridian that separated Indian Territory and Texas; Camp Supply to the northwest; and Fort Dodge in western Kansas. In 1878 these locations were not yet interconnected by telegraph and depended on mounted couriers for communication.

By far the most difficult problem Miles faced following the 1874 outbreak was feeding the severely famished and suffering southern bands the U.S. Army under Miles and Mackenzie had driven in from the prairie. With the bands subdued, the army had moved north to engage the tribes in rebellion there. The resulting removal of Northern Cheyennes to the south, tragically, coincided with a sudden diminution of the great buffalo herds.

Other factors at Darlington worked against them as well. In coming south, the northern Indians contracted diseases of the white man that were new to them, principally malaria, measles, and congestive fever. Miles's requisition for more medical supplies took several months to fulfill. With no medicine available, Dr. Lawrence A.E. Hodge closed the doors of his dispensary. As Miles would later point out to a congressional investigating committee, Hodge was the only physician at the agency. One doctor was far short of what was needed to attend the hundreds of sick people—employees as well as tribal members—at the agency. Further, there was a severe lack of available medicine other than quinine at the agency, and even that was completely depleted at times.[4] Wild Hog said:

> There was a doctor at the agency; sometimes when called upon he would go and see the one that was sick; at other times, very often, he would pay no attention; he would not go nor do anything. He would doctor some of the southern Indians; but when the Northern Cheyennes would call on him, he would not go near them nor pay any attention to them.
>
> The children died of diseases we never knew anything about before; they broke out in blotches and dots all over, their noses would bleed and their heads split open. Then there was ague among the older people.[5]

In a report to the commissioner of Indian Affairs, Miles revealed that in little over a year a sizable number of Northern Cheyennes—sixteen men, twenty-six women, and forty-four children—had died from dysentery, chills, and fevers.[6]

"There was much sickness among the Northern Cheyennes," Wooden Leg confirmed. "To us it was a new kind of sickness. Chills and fever and aching of the bones dragged down most of us to thin and weak bodies. Our people died, died, died."[7]

Wild Hog's wife said, "Three or four children died every day for a while and that frightened us."[8] Wild Hog estimated that fifty children perished during their stay at Darlington.[9]

The Northern Cheyennes' situation remained bleak during summer of 1878. The scourges of hunger and disease continued to haunt the camps. An epidemic of smallpox that swept through Wichita and Kansas border towns during May had caused Mizner and Miles to restrict travel through the country. All Indian camps were removed from the line of travel, and tribespeople were warned to avoid strangers. Freighters were ordered not to enter houses and to stay away from the camps. Eventually, vaccine arrived at the agency, and Hodge soon reported that 600 Indians and all agency employees had been vaccinated. Several hundred other tribal members remained untreated.[10]

In early July a delegation of Northern Cheyenne chiefs went to Miles and pleaded for permission to go on another buffalo hunt as the Kiowas and Comanches had been permitted to do. They said their ration of three pounds of beef per week lasted only three or four days. They needed buffalo for food and lodge skins. They declared further that if they were not given permission, they would go anyway. Miles urged them not to take any action until he had heard from Commissioner of Indian Affairs E. A. Hayt in Washington on the matter. They agreed to wait until after rations were issued on July 15 and 16.[11] On July 17 Miles wrote to Hayt:

> I would respectfully inform [you] that a portion (fully one half) of the Northern Cheyennes who joined our Agency about one year ago have affiliated with the Southern Cheyennes and are willing and ready to conform to regulations while another portion, represented by "Dull Knife," "Little Wolf," "Wild Hog," and "Crow," are rather disposed to fault finding, and sometimes resort to real insolence, but taking into consideration the recent status of these Indians up north and their extreme ignorance of their own best interests, I would recommend a firm *but as liberal* [emphasis in the original] a policy as can be granted them. If we cannot at present silence them by persuasion or compulsory to work, I am satisfied that we can control them by granting them a full ration—This seems to be the extent of their present demand and in my judgment should be granted—Later in the season a more rigid policy can be adopted with safety.[12]

To this admission that a less than full ration had been issued, Miles further recommended the immediate shipment of the sugar and coffee being held in a Wichita warehouse.

The portended buffalo hunt did not take place. Reports from the field indicated that few buffalo could be found. Miles, fearing a repeat of the earlier near tragedy, concluded it was inadvisable to let the tribes go out. Instead, two small parties, one of six hunters and one of five, were dispatched. They returned to report that a thorough search discovered only one small herd of buffalo. Miles decided it would be necessary to hold off until the regular winter hunting season.[13]

There was no assurance that the supply of buffalo would be any better then, and some factions of the Northern Cheyennes were growing more and more determined to escape their dire conditions. Their people were sick— partly from disease, partly from the hot, humid climate, and partly from persistent hunger, which was only increased by the annuity-issue corn mush that disrupted their bowels.

"They gave us cornmeal ground with the cob," Wild Hog would claim, "much as a man feeds his mule, some salt, and one beef for forty-six persons to last seven days."[14]

Adding to this desperation was their intense dislike of the new country and a homesickness that gnawed at their spirits. Many of their children and old ones were dying. Too many times the Northern Cheyennes had wrapped the thin, stiff corpses of family members in blankets and interred them on a scaffold in some distant tree. The wailing for lost loved ones in their camps never seemed to cease.

Dull Knife's people asked why they ever had to leave the north. There had been plenty of game in the high country along the Cheyenne, Belle Fourche, and Powder Rivers and in the Bighorn Mountains. Buffalo, antelope, deer, bear, and other animals could always be found, and there was plenty to eat. The people yearned for the light, cool air of the north and the fresh, sweet-tasting water that came down icy cold out of the mountains. It was especially rankling that although they had been sent south, the Northern Arapahos, with whom they had been confederated for so long, had been permitted to remain in the north. Many still had family members in the north, as Crow explained.

> I love the country in the north where I was born; besides everything there is better; the water is colder, purer, and better to drink; the climate is pleasanter and healthier; it is a better hunting country than this. Almost all my relatives and friends are up there; I have a mother up there yet, and I have a daughter up there who is married to a white man; and I must live separate from them all the rest of my life.... I have laid in my lodge the most of the time, with nothing to think about but that.[15]

Both Mizner and Miles appeared almost not to have heard the Northern Cheyennes when they spoke of their determination to return to the north. Neither did much to attend the desperation building increasingly among the famished camps of the Northern Cheyennes. Miles refused Little Wolf's request to be allowed to return to the pines and mountains of the north: "If you cannot give us permission to go back there, why [not] let some of us go to Washington or do you write to Washington to get permission."[16]

During August and early September 1878, certain members of the Northern Cheyennes began making secret preparations to leave Darlington and go north. It was vital to their interests that the military at Fort Reno did not learn of this, and they made every effort to conceal their plans. Still, signs emerged that were easily readable. One was a request that they be issued their annuities to cover a two-week period instead of the usual one-week allotment. Another strong indication was revealed on September 5 when a group of Southern Cheyennes and Arapahos came to Miles with a complaint. The Northern Cheyennes were stealing their horses, the southerners claimed, and some of their young men had already gone north.

"How do you know the thieves are Northern Cheyennes?" Miles inquired. White horse thievery had accelerated to the point that Mizner had issued ten guns to the Indian police for use in pursuing the thieves.[17] "What makes you think they are not white men?"

"These thieves are particular," the southerners replied. "They take only a few good horses from a herd, always picking out the best. White men would just round up the whole bunch and run them off."[18]

Later the southern tribesmen paid Miles another visit. They said they had positive information that young men from the northerners' camps had established a camp on the Cimarron River where they were collecting a good herd of stolen horses in preparation for starting north.

Miles said he would look into the matter. He alerted the agency Indian police to go to the northerners' camps and see if any of their young men had left or were getting ready to leave. At the same time, he sent his clerk to Fort Reno to notify Mizner that some Northern Cheyennes had departed. The message became badly mangled in transmission. Mizner asked the clerk if many of the northerners had left. The man was unsure. Mizner then asked, "Was there a majority of them?" Faced with a choice of either yes or no, the courier replied, "Yes."

Mizner ordered the two troops of Fourth Cavalry then at Fort Reno into their saddles to pursue the Northern Cheyennes. Simultaneously, he sent a courier galloping off to Camp Supply with a call for assistance from Hemphill's Company I, Fourth Cavalry, from that post. He instructed, "The company of cavalry at your Post should reach the Arkansas River a little west of Fort Dodge as quickly as possible so as to intercept the Indians when they reach the Arkansas River."[19]

The Fort Reno unit was commanded by Rendlebrock. A dark-complex-ioned man, Rendlebrock still spoke with a strong German accent despite his twenty-seven years in the U.S. service. His officers included Captain Gunther; Lt. Wilber E. Wilder, a Michigan West Pointer; and 2nd Lt. David M. McDonald, an 1873 West Point graduate from Tennessee.[20] The two troops of cavalry were composed of eighty-two men. In addition to the Arapaho scouts, Thomas Donald, a man who had been among the tribes for twelve years, served as guide.[21]

Night had fallen before the troops were equipped and mounted, so they rode only a short distance on September 5. The next morning they continued on to the Cheyenne camp and found that Mizner's information was incorrect. The Northern Cheyennes were still established on the north bank of the North Canadian twelve miles from Fort Reno. Rendlebrock went into camp on the river four miles below the Cheyennes. A guide who was sent into the village reported that the Cheyennes were all there, and a courier carried that information to Mizner the next morning. Mizner sent back orders directing Rendlebrock and his troops to go into camp somewhere near the village on the North Canadian and keep a close watch over the Cheyennes. Rendlebrock moved his command upstream, camping at the nine-mile crossing of the river just northeast of present Calumet, Oklahoma, but still two miles from the Cheyenne camp.[22] The presence of the troops alarmed the Cheyennes and prompted them to move their camp into nearby sandhills and begin digging rifle pits and building fortifications.[23]

Mizner also dispatched another courier to Camp Supply rescinding his request for troops.[24] Hambright had already rushed Hemphill into the field with Amos Chapman as guide for the cavalry troop mounted entirely on gray horses. Hambright immediately sent a scout galloping to recall. Accordingly, Hemphill and Company I returned to Camp Supply on September 10—the same day it would be discovered that Northern Cheyennes had departed, this time for certain.[25]

During the four days in this camp, Rendlebrock maintained surveillance of the village through binoculars or with scouts who approached more closely or entered the village. At the same time, Northern Cheyenne warriors freely visited the soldiers' camp, in part to show the troops defiantly that they were well armed with rifles and revolvers. Some wore two belts of ammunition.[26]

Miles sent word to the northern chiefs that he wished to talk with them at the agency. When they arrived at his office on September 6, a Thursday, he demanded to know if any of their young men had gone north or were about to. According to Miles, the chiefs shook their heads and said no, none had left or were going to. It was, they said, all a Southern Cheyenne and Arapaho lie. Miles told them that to see who was telling the truth, he wanted them to bring in some of their young men so he could check against their enrollment.[27]

The chiefs replied that some of their warriors were sick and could not come in. Miles agreed that he would not ask the men to leave camp if they were too ill, but he would send the doctor out to see them and do all he could to make them well. J. A. Covington, Miles's son-in-law and head farmer at the agency, would go along and count ill persons excused by the doctor.[28]

On Friday Covington, who was well acquainted with the Northern Cheyennes, rode west up the North Canadian alone to visit their camp. He discovered that the Cheyennes were not where he expected them to be. An old tribesman directed him to the north through a stand of blackjack timber. Emerging from it, he was surprised to see a long cavalcade of Indians with their lodges, goods, horses, dogs, and camp accouterments moving toward him across a broad valley. They proved to be the Northern Cheyennes. Covington concluded that the band had started north but turned back when it failed to find water. Riding down to them, he found Dull Knife and asked the chief why the Cheyennes were out on the prairie.[29]

Dull Knife answered that the women, remembering past assaults on their villages by U.S. forces, were moving because they had been frightened by the Fort Reno troops camped so near to them. The two men were joined by Chiefs Little Wolf, Wild Hog, and Crow and the other principal men of the village. Covington noted that they were all exceedingly well armed. The men talked for an hour, with Covington reassuring them that they need not fear the soldiers. The chiefs complained strongly that their rations were insufficient and expressed their desire to return north, saying they had never intended to live in the south permanently. Still, they promised Covington that the next morning they would take their young men in to the agency. Fully convinced that the Cheyennes were not intending to leave, Covington conveyed as much to Miles and Mizner:

> He [Covington] told us—Agent Miles and myself—that he had visited every lodge in their camp; had talked with a majority of their leading men for some time, seated in a circle; they were in a very destitute condition; that he did not think they had a day's food in their camp; that he did not believe they intended to fight; that he did not think there was any fight in them.[30]

Even as this discussion was taking place, Ben Clark arrived at Fort Reno to report that he had been told the Cheyenne women were digging rifle pits. Covington insisted that while he was in their camp he had witnessed nothing of that nature. When Rendlebrock heard a similar story of the Cheyennes entrenching themselves in the sand dunes where they were camped, however, he became alarmed. Thinking he might have to drive them from the hills, he dispatched Lieutenant Wilder to Fort Reno with a request that Mizner send out the fort's two 12-pound Napoleon artillery pieces. Mizner, believing from Covington's report that the Cheyennes were quietly settled in and that the cannons might panic them into fleeing, rejected the request. He also sent orders for Rendlebrock not to interfere with the tribes or do anything to provoke hostilities.[31]

Rendlebrock was annoyed at Mizner's refusal, but he did not realize that the order may have been fortunate for him and his men. The rifle pits, thirteen miles west of Fort Reno on the north bank of the North Canadian, were later inspected by Capt. John A. Wilcox, Fourth Cavalry. The officer was highly impressed with the Cheyennes' engineering ability. Having twice been struck by U.S. troops without warning or provocation, Little Wolf and his men had constructed a nearly perfect trap for the Fort Reno troops. The Cheyennes' camp, Wilcox found, was situated close to a series of sandhills or dunes that formed a horseshoe in a sharp bend of the river. Rifle pits two to five feet deep had been dug in tiers along the sides of the dunes. From them, Cheyenne sharpshooters would have commanded every available point against the troops had they followed the fleeing villagers into the trap. "When once within this horseshoe," Wilcox opined, "the troops would have been at the mercy of the Indians, [and] a massacre would have been the result."[32]

All through Saturday, September 8, agency personnel waited for the Cheyennes to come in to be counted as promised. That evening Crow finally appeared, but he was the only Northern Cheyenne to show. Miles learned later that the chiefs had indeed tried to get the young men to come in, even to the point of taking down some of their lodges. But the hostile soldier elements of the bands, who adamantly refused to go, had stopped them.[33]

At Miles's request Covington returned to the Cheyenne camp on Sunday—this time in a buggy accompanied by Dr. Hodge—to learn why the chiefs had not come in. While Hodge went through the camp examining the sick and issuing quinine, Covington held a council with Dull Knife and the other principal men of the camp. Covington sat in his buggy, and the Cheyennes sat on the ground.

The interview did not go well. The chiefs refused to give him any firm assurance that they would go in to the agency. Covington warned them that if they took their women and children and went north, the troops would stop them. The chiefs remained noncommittal. When Hodge had finished

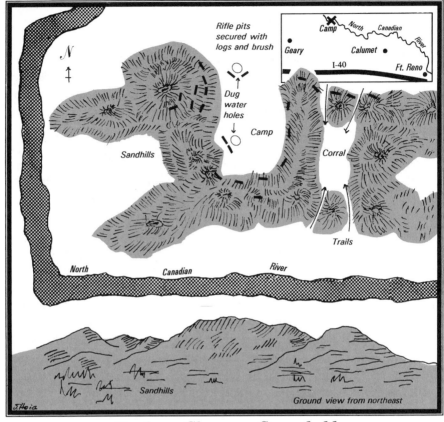

Northern Cheyenne Stronghold
West of Darlington Agency
Rendering of sketches made by
Capt. John A. Wilcox, 4th Cavalry,
showing breastworks and rifle pits

his rounds, the two men climbed back into the buggy and returned to Darlington.

Upon receiving their report, Mizner sent more detailed orders to Rendlebrock. He was to watch the village carefully and see that no one left except to go to the agency. "Have the camps visited from time to time by the Indian Police or by Patrols," Mizner ordered, "and keep yourself fully informed."[34]

The gathering of the bands on ration day, September 9, offered Miles another chance to meet with Little Wolf, Crow, and Wild Hog in his office. Mizner rode over from Fort Reno and was present when Miles told them through interpreter Edmund Guerrier that the troops camped near them meant no harm. They would be withdrawn, he said, once a count of their young men was made. If ten or fifteen of them were not present, it would not matter.[35]

Mizner supported what Miles had said, adding that until they came in to be counted, the soldiers would continue to guard their village and no further supplies would be sent to them. He also issued a threat: "If you don't come up and be counted, I will see that you do." The Cheyennes made no answer and departed.[36]

Little Wolf later claimed that Miles demanded ten of his young men as hostages against the return of three others who had left. The chief refused, arguing that three men traveling across the country could hide so they would not be found and that Miles would therefore never set his ten men free. It was then that Little Wolf reportedly made his famous speech: "I am going to leave. I am going north. I do not want to make bloody this ground about this agency. If you are going to send your soldiers after me, I wish you would let me get away from this agency a little way. Then if you want to I will fight you and we will make the ground bloody there."[37]

Mizner and Miles, however, both believed the talks had convinced the chiefs to be compliant. They were badly mistaken. Neither man really comprehended the full desperation of the Northern Cheyennes.

Shortly before three o'clock the next morning, September 10, Miles was awakened by a rapping at his door. When he opened it, the flickering light of his lamp revealed Northern Cheyenne chief American Horse and a captain in the Indian police standing there. They had startling news. The Northern Cheyennes had fled north, leaving their tepees standing and lodge fires burning to mislead Rendlebrock's spies.[38]

Miles quickly roused agency employee William Darlington, son of the former agent, and had him hurry across the North Canadian to alert Mizner at Fort Reno. At the same time, Miles sent a courier galloping off to Fort Sill with a message of the Cheyennes' escape to be wired to the commissioner of Indians Affairs. Another telegram was directed to Robert M. Wright, a trader at Dodge City, Kansas, advising him "to put the cattle men and citizens on the border, on their guard, as the Indians would undoubtedly strike some of their herds and likely show resistance, if checked in their march."[39]

Miles's militant actions would not please his church superiors. Their views were expressed in the Quaker publication, *The Friend*: "The military measures taken by the agent to restrain them [the Cheyennes] were certainly inconsistent with Friends' principles, as were those used by him on a former occasion, when the Associated Indian Committee publicly expressed their disapprobation of his conduct, and requested his resignation."[40]

7
Flight TO FREEDOM

ILENTLY BUT SWIFTLY, THE NORTHERN CHEYENNES MOVED ABOUT in the darkness, packing what camp goods and belongings they could get into their buffalo robe parfleches. Everyone would be required to travel as lightly as possible, but there was little to take anyway. They were a desperately poor people in terms of items of personal value: a string of beads, a beloved trinket perhaps, or a pair of fringed buckskin gloves traded for at the agency store. Even the artistic Little Finger Nail, who would prove himself a warrior supreme to the end, would not leave behind his ledger in which he had a pictorial record of past battles with U.S. soldiers.

This was not the way the Cheyennes normally moved their camp. But the chiefs had ordered that their lodges would be left standing and lodge fires burning. Without the lodge poles, there could be no travois to slow their movement or make the group easier to track. They could cut new lodge poles in the north, and the robes of their bundles would serve for both bedding and shelter on the long trek ahead.[1]

By plan, they left the camp in small parties, some riding and some on foot, and moved up the North Canadian to Raven's Springs (now known as Left Hand Springs, near present Greenfield, Oklahoma) where the men had brought the pony herds. From long tribal habit a disciplined marching order formed, and soon the exodus began. The long, silent

column of 92 men and boys and 268 women and children moved out beneath the light of the half-moon.[2] They were followed by the herd of extra
horses. By Crow's estimate, the party had between 400 and 500 horses at the
start.[3]

Chief American Horse, who had been counseling the others to heed
agency policy, had withdrawn his eight lodges from the group despite the
dire warnings of the warriors. It had nearly cost him his life. Other Northern
Cheyenne leaders likewise chose to remain behind; these included Standing
Elk, Turkey Leg, Living Bear, and Calf Skin Shirt.[4]

Although Dull Knife still held great influence and was a principal
spokesman for the Cheyennes, Little Wolf was the main leader of the exodus and directed its course. Wild Hog was next in rank.[5] The scouts rode
ahead, warriors along each side and as a guard behind, all with rifles across
their pommels and eyes alert for anything large or small that stood to hinder
their march. Behind them thin swirls of smoke rose from the tops of the
lodges they were deserting. There was no sadness; they were going home.
No one looked back.

The Cheyennes had arrived in Indian Territory one year and four days
before, and no one had forgotten how many long days of marching it had
taken to reach the Darlington Agency. But now they were on horseback
and would not be held to the leisurely cadence of escort troops and wagons.
Everyone was aware of the peril of lagging behind. Those who fell back
would be left. As always, the welfare of the group came first, and to stop for
one would endanger the whole.[6]

Iron Teeth, a forty-four-year-old Northern Cheyenne widow who rode
with the band, said:

> At night, when we had a chance to sleep, my daughters and I made
> willow-branch shelters for ourselves. Day after day, I kept my youngest
> daughter strapped to my body, in front of me, on my horse. I led another
> horse carrying the next-youngest daughter. The oldest girl managed her
> own mount. My two sons always stayed behind, to help in fighting off the
> soldiers.[7]

The Enemy, a Northern Cheyenne woman, testified later that there had
not been enough horses for the women, and she had walked most of the
time, carrying her baby on her back. They had no tepees or travois.[8] Pug
Nose, a Southern Cheyenne, served as guide for the group.[9]

The Cheyennes would clearly have to live off the land on their march as
best they could. The chiefs knew that if no buffalo were found on the way,
they would have to take cattle from ranchers and white settlers. They cau-
tioned against killing civilians, but the warriors had their own mind on that

issue. Was it any worse to kill a white man than it was for the white man to starve a Cheyenne child?

Seemingly, the chances of successfully evading and outfighting the U.S. Army en route were so slim that only desperate people would have attempted it. In addition to the military forces of Indian Territory at Fort Reno and Camp Supply, the Cheyennes' escape to the north was threatened by troops from Fort Elliott in the Texas Panhandle; Fort Lyon in Colorado; Forts Dodge, Hays, Riley, Wallace, and Leavenworth in Kansas; Sidney Barracks in far southwestern Nebraska; and Camp Robinson. Beyond those stood military units at posts in the Dakotas, Wyoming, and Montana. Further, the army had the benefit of telegraph lines for communication and railroads for moving troops and their equipage to points of intercept in the Cheyennes' escape route.

Still, it was easy to underestimate the small band of family-encumbered Northern Cheyennes. Few white people other than experienced military men fully comprehended the fact that the Cheyennes were born warriors—disciplined in battle, daring, determined to the death. The officers sent after them later spoke in awe of the Cheyennes' fighting ability. Further, army commanders did not realize that the Cheyennes were well armed with a variety of pistols, rifles, and carbines with ample metallic cartridges procured from contraband traders. One member of the party even possessed a large-caliber, long-range buffalo gun that could outdistance anything the troops had.[10] A report from Fort Reno on September 11, obviously reflecting the views of Colonel Mizner, provided a totally invalid estimate of their armament: "What few arms they may have were secreted at the time and since their coming on the reservation, and can be of but little service in the event of an encounter with the thoroughly equipped troops of the pursuing force. . . . They are poorly provided and their capture is regarded as but the matter of a very short time."[11]

Mizner later revised his view of the Cheyennes' armament and fighting capacity. After examining the arms among the Northern Cheyennes who had not returned north, he reported that they were mostly Springfield carbines such as those captured from Custer at the Little Bighorn. He noted that the cavalrymen had little confidence in the Springfield carbine with which they were equipped. But it was not the weapon, he concluded, that gave the Cheyennes the advantage; it was their skill in using arms. "The Indian," he observed, "never wastes a bullet but fires with a purpose."[12]

Cavalry officers, on the other hand, often found it expedient to dismount their troops and take up rifle positions on the ground. In doing so, they inevitably gave up a number of battle effectives in the men assigned to tend the horses and pack mules during a fight. Normally, the dismounted cavalryman was far from well trained as an infantry skirmisher.[13] Furthermore, two-thirds of the two companies of Fort Reno Fourth Cavalry, 1st Sgt. John Feely of Company G noted, were raw recruits who had never been under fire.[14]

There was also an advantage to being pursued. By lying in wait for their pursuers, the Cheyennes held the element of surprise and could dictate the terms of battle from a superior position. The Cheyennes had proved at Fort Phil Kearny that they could effectively set a trap for an overzealous enemy. Luring the enemy into an ambush was, in fact, a standard technique of Plains Indian warfare.

Scout Thomas Donald pointed out that the Northern Cheyennes were not only better armed than the troops, but they usually had the advantage on the ground.[15] General Pope later noted these difficulties in the use of cavalry against the Cheyennes:

> The Indians have the long range arms and plenty of ammunition, and the Cavalry is armed with the Carbine, which is no match. . . . As soon as the Indians make a stand, they put themselves in rough country and in rifle pits where the Cavalry cannot charge them, nor with their Carbines fighting on foot drive them from their defenses.[16]

Sheridan observed further: "It is hard to head off or overtake Indians in an open country, well-known to them, with two or three fresh horses for each Indian to ride on in relays, the horses unincumbered by baggage of any kind, while the pursuing force has only the same horses, loaded down to some extent by rations for the man and forage for the animal."[17]

When Mizner received news from Miles of the Cheyennes' departure, he immediately dispatched 1st Lt. Abram E. Wood, an Iowan who had arrived at Fort Reno from West Point only the day before, with a wagon and five days' rations to Rendlebrock's camp. Miles, meanwhile, had sent for his agency police, ordering them to join Rendlebrock and serve as guides. Of the seventeen men in the force, seven Arapahos responded. They would catch up with Rendlebrock on the trail.[18]

Rendlebrock had indeed been fooled. Neither he nor any of his spies had known the Cheyennes were gone until Wood brought the news from Fort Reno at six o'clock that morning.[19] Hurriedly, the rations were divided and packed on their twenty pack mules. Canteens were filled at the river; horses were brought in from their pickets and saddled. Extra ammunition was issued for the Springfield carbines and for the Smith and Wesson and Schofield six-shooters, giving each man a total of 100 rounds.[20] The command would have a trail to follow, but there were two important items it did not have: a map and a compass. The lack of a medical officer would also prove critical.[21]

The two troops of the Fourth Cavalry were formed into marching order, and in little over an hour after Wood's arrival, Rendlebrock gave the order to move out. The bugler's notes carried down the line, and the Fort Reno command trotted off in double column formation on what would be a far longer, more punishing, and more precarious pursuit of the tenacious Northern Cheyennes than anyone anticipated. It would also leave behind a clamor of public complaint over government policy and military inability. Further, the ordeal would spawn bitter charges and deep recriminations among the Fort Reno officers who conducted the pursuit.

It took another hour to find the trail of the Cheyennes, who had a seven- to eight-hour head start on the troops. By Rendlebrock's account, his command marched twenty-seven miles before striking the Cheyennes' trail, "which seemed a very weak one, it having but one drag and no lodge poles at all."[22] The Cheyennes obviously hoped to throw off their pursuers by crossing over broken country where the troops would have difficulty following them. Their pony tracks first led across to the south bank of the North Canadian and followed the river eight or nine miles to Raven's Spring. There the trail recrossed the river and headed off on a northwesterly course. From the North Canadian, Gunther reported, they then "traveled through the brakes of the Kingfisher, a very rough country."[23] At 2:45 P.M., at what was likely the first rest stop for the troops forty miles northwest of Fort Reno, Rendlebrock sent a courier off with a note to the commanding officer at Camp Supply. It read: "Sir. I have the honor to state that I am in pursuit of a party of Northern Cheyennes that left the reservation at Ft. Reno last night. There are about 300 men women & children—about 85 warriors. Their present course will take them across the Supply & Fort Dodge road about Bear Creek [north of Camp Supply in Kansas]."[24]

Rendlebrock's prediction of the Cheyennes' route from this point was apparently based on the belief that they would follow up the Cimarron River to the Bear Creek juncture. At no time did Rendlebrock report back to Mizner.

Once across the headwaters of the Kingfisher, the Cheyennes' trail led more clearly over the rolling countryside that divided the southeasterly flowing North Canadian and Cimarron Rivers. Rendlebrock pushed ahead until ten o'clock that night, finally going into camp after marching fifty-two miles. The following day, September 11, the command continued on the Cheyennes' trail with the ocher buttes of the Glass Mountains rimming the horizon to the west. The troops camped that night at the mouth of Eagle Chief

Red Hills, approach to the Battle of Turkey Springs.

Creek, which feeds into the Cimarron River on a wide bend from the northwest.[25]

Here a dispute arose between Rendlebrock and his Arapaho scouts over a lost trooper. Lieutenant Wilder had left his pistol at the September 10 campsite—a grievous mistake—and sent a trooper named Angus McClintock back after it. While returning, McClintock became lost. When he failed to show up that night, Rendlebrock ordered the Arapaho scouts to go find him. They refused to do so, and the officer angrily ordered them out of his camp. Two scouts remained, however, and continued to ride ahead and guide the troops. One was an Arapaho man known as "Chalk," or "Ghost Man." The other was an Arapaho named Little Sitting Bull or, as Rendlebrock knew him, Chief Yellow Bear's son.[26]

On September 12 the command followed the Cheyenne trail up Eagle Chief Creek to Little Eagle Chief and across Turkey Creek on another long march of forty-five miles.[27] The saddle-weary troops camped that evening at a water hole west of present Alva, Oklahoma. The water proved to be heavily laced with alkali and brine, and several troopers—including Gunther— became sick from drinking it. Because of its foul taste, the horses were not watered and canteens were not refilled. The lack of water soon created a dire problem for the troops and their mounts.

The following morning Rendlebrock and his Fort Reno command broke camp and again picked up the Cheyennes' trail, following it thirteen miles to a range of red hills that created the divide between the Cimarron to the south and the Salt Fork of the Arkansas to the north.[28] At times the command was forced to move by single file or to dismount and walk through a narrow defile that wound along the top of the divide.

The Fort Reno troops were now on the spread of the Comanche Pool cattle ranch, whose seventy-five square miles of unfenced range straddled the Kansas–Indian Territory border and extended south to the Cimarron. Although its streams and features were marked imprecisely on an 1875 military map, the region was well away from any regular trails of the time and was far from being well known. Neither the troops nor the guides were familiar with the country.[29]

It was around ten o'clock that morning when the Fort Reno troops finally found the Cheyennes they were pursuing. The cavalry column had just emerged from the defile and crested a high knoll to see the dissident band moving slowly up a hillside nearly a mile ahead.[30] When they became aware of the troops, the Cheyennes halted and formed a line facing the oncoming cavalry command as it advanced to within 400 yards. At a distance beyond them, their train of women and children could be seen melting away into the hills to the northwest.

The Fort Reno cavalry now faced a Cheyenne warrior force estimated to be 130 to 150 strong, a far larger number of fighting men than they had been led to expect and over twice their own engagement strength. With thirty of his eighty-nine troops needed when dismounted to secure the cavalry mounts and pack train in a ravine behind them, Rendlebrock would be left with fewer than sixty effectives to face the Cheyennes.[31]

The mass of whooping warriors was in no way what anyone had anticipated. Many of the Cheyennes donned their war bonnets and began riding their ponies back and forth tauntingly in a display of readiness and eagerness for action. As Custer had at the Little Bighorn two years earlier, Rendlebrock's troops had found more Cheyennes than they really wanted.

At the same time the Fort Reno command was pursuing the fleeing Northern Cheyennes, the U.S. Army was enacting other measures to intercept their escape route. Fort Sill was the only military post in Indian Territory connected by telegraph lines to Fort Richardson, Texas. Mizner at Fort Reno was therefore forced to rely on couriers to Fort Sill as the quickest means of contacting Department of the Missouri headquarters at Fort Leavenworth. His Fort Sill–initiated telegram reporting the Northern Cheyenne departure of September 10 reached Gen. John Pope on September 12.[32]

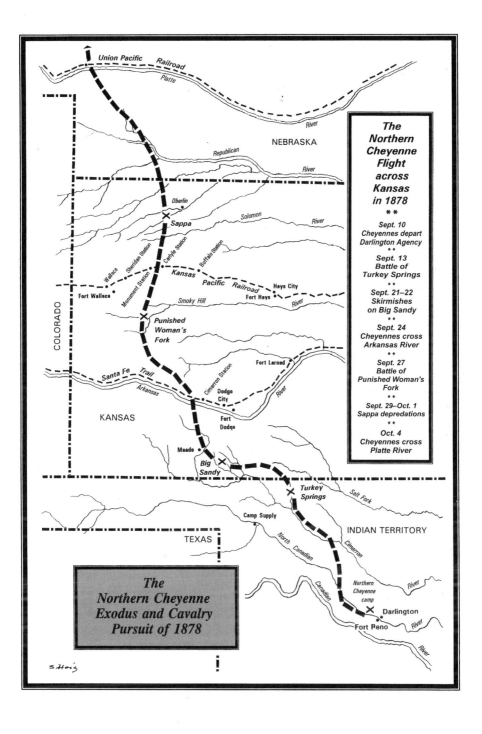

The Northern Cheyenne Exodus and Cavalry Pursuit of 1878

The Northern Cheyenne Flight across Kansas in 1878

Sept. 10
Cheyennes depart Darlington Agency

Sept. 13
Battle of Turkey Springs

Sept. 21–22
Skirmishes on Big Sandy

Sept. 24
Cheyennes cross Arkansas River

Sept. 27
Battle of Punished Woman's Fork

Sept. 29–Oct. 1
Sappa depredations

Oct. 4
Cheyennes cross Platte River

s.Haig

Mizner informed Pope that a scout (likely one Rendlebrock had dismissed) had just returned to the base with word that as of sundown the previous day the troops were steadily following the Cheyennes on a plain trail. The Fort Reno commander further proclaimed that the Arkansas River was running unusually high and might prevent the Cheyennes from crossing.

"Troops and cattlemen near Fort Dodge," he declared, "can render great assistance. Indians are desperate and will fight hard and to secure their defeat and return a considerable force should meet them when they attempt to cross the Arkansas."[33]

Pope immediately forwarded Mizner's message to General Sheridan at his divisional headquarters in Chicago. At the same time, Pope ordered Col. John W. Davidson at Fort Sill to send a troop from the Fourth Cavalry to reinforce Fort Reno. Davidson did so, but reluctantly. He argued that he might need the troops if his Kiowa and Comanche charges took a cue from the Northern Cheyennes and rose up.[34]

Pope initiated still other troop movements designed to intercept the Cheyennes. One hundred mounted infantry were rushed from Fort Leavenworth by special train for Fort Wallace to head off the Cheyennes if they crossed the railroad east or west of that post. At Fort Dodge Capt. Philip H. Remington and Company F, Nineteenth Infantry, were sent west in wagons to the small settlement of Pierceville, Kansas. In the event the Cheyennes were not stopped south of the Arkansas River, two more companies of infantry were dispatched from Fort Hays to take up positions along the Kansas Pacific Railroad between Forts Hays and Wallace. The commanding officer at Fort Lyon, Colorado, was directed to send troops to patrol east and west of that post. All troops were under orders to attack the Cheyennes wherever found unless they surrendered at once.[35]

At Fort Leavenworth General Pope had no idea how futile his troop manipulations would be or how unlikely it was that the Cheyennes would ever surrender.

8

Engagement
AT TURKEY SPRINGS

HE TWO COMPANIES OF NERVOUS FOURTH CAVALRY TROOPS and the battle-ready warriors of the Northern Cheyennes faced one another across a grassy meadow that lay between two canyons, each waiting for the other to commit to action. The day was September 13, 1878, a Friday. Two years, two months, and twenty days earlier, some of these same warriors had helped annihilate an overextended force of Seventh Cavalry on the Little Bighorn. As the troops fronted the turbulent line of whooping, war-bonneted Cheyennes who appeared to outnumber them at least two to one, everyone in the Fort Reno command realized they were a long way from their post. They alone knew of their presence and predicament on this distant and lonely field of contest in northwestern Indian Territory. There would be no allies arriving in support, no fort in which to seek refuge, no replenishing of supplies or ammunition, no medical help for those wounded in battle. All the more reason, Rendlebrock decided, for him to exercise a show of confidence. He ordered his men to dismount and advance in skirmish order.[1] The action only energized the Cheyenne warriors.

Rendlebrock was operating under two sets of orders from Mizner, one official and one unofficial. On September 5, when he first sent the Fort Reno cavalry into the field, his instructions had been to "spare no effort to bring the Indians back."[2] If Rendlebrock found the number of Cheyennes

Abram E. Wood as West Point cadet. Courtesy, Special Collections and Archives, U.S. Military Academy Library.

had been exaggerated, he would return such portion of his command that was unneeded to the post. Further, if he should have to go as far as Fort Dodge, Rendlebrock would be governed from there on by orders from department headquarters. Later, on September 8, Mizner had further instructed: "You will in no way molest these Indians so long as they remain quietly in their camp, and will carefully avoid any collision of a hostile character with them."[3]

Mizner later told an investigating committee that his orders had been specifically to bring the Cheyennes back peacefully. "I wish to draw especial attention to this point," Mizner stressed, "that he [Rendlebrock] was *particularly instructed* to induce the Indians to come back without resorting to force, if he could possibly do so."[4]

Rendlebrock's junior officers, however, testified to an off-the-cuff letter Mizner had dashed off at Darlington Agency when he learned the Cheyennes were gone. It was carried to Rendlebrock's camp by Lieutenant Wood. Although the actual message could not be found later, several junior officers testified that they had read it. There was some dispute as to its exact wording.

Lieutenant McDonald said he remembered two passages. One was for Rendlebrock to "pursue the Indians persistently and perseveringly," along with a word or two of similar intent. Another passage was: "I understand those young men [the Cheyennes] are not only ready but willing and anxious to fight. If that proves true, give them the full benefit."[5]

By Lieutenant Wilder's recollection, the letter directed Rendlebrock "to find the trail and follow it steadily, persistently and perseveringly and not to march less than 40 miles a day." Lieutenant Wood testified that the officers read the letter and commented on it, having "a great deal of fun over it." At first Wood, who later brought charges against Rendlebrock, insisted that the word *unrelentingly* was included, but he later recanted on the matter.[6] Wood said further that Mizner issued verbal orders for him to carry to Rendlebrock. The officer was to "get them [the Cheyenne] in peaceably if he could, but to use such means as were necessary to bring them to the agency, and if he gets into a fight with them, if he can avoid it, not to make an indiscriminate slaughter of the women and children."[7]

Mizner's conflicting orders had been based on the misguided premise that the Fort Reno troops were a superior force to a smaller, poorly armed group of Cheyennes. That was far from what Rendlebrock found before him. In the face of the obviously aroused and well-armed body of Cheyennes, peaceful persuasion did not appear viable. Nor did engaging such a large and imposing force without artillery or reinforcements seem a good option. The Cheyennes were displaying no desire for peaceful reconciliation.

"The Indians were now moving north and south," a Fort Reno trooper noted, "and performing various feats of horsemanship, but their chief, Dull Knife, stood square in our front, not moving with the rest."[8]

When Rendlebrock ordered his men to dismount and take up firing positions, the Cheyenne line became even more agitated. Warriors began disappearing into ravines on the left and right, while others continued to ride challengingly back and forth in front of the troops. The Cheyenne leaders—Little Wolf, Dull Knife, Wild Hog, and others such as Crow—undoubtedly preferred not to fight. But the fighting blood of the young men was hot for battle. They were more than willing to take on the troops, according to scout Donald, who said the warriors appeared "ready to clean out the soldiers."[9] With the troops now deployed in a skirmish line before them, the smell of battle—to which Cheyenne warriors were born—was in the air.

Little Wolf's memory of the battle was that the Cheyennes were eating when a sentry posted atop a hill called down that the troops were coming. He immediately harangued his young men to get their arms and horses but not to shoot first.

"I will go out and meet the troops," he said, "and try to talk to them. If they kill me I will be the first man killed. Then you can fight."[10]

Little Wolf had selected his field of conflict well. He knew there was no water source immediately behind on the trail, and his warriors firmly held the ground between the troops and any that were ahead. Further, the Fort Reno command, now dismounted, was boxed onto a plateau by ravines by which the Cheyennes could easily surround them. On this hot fall day, with temperatures soaring above ninety degrees, the burning sun was an invaluable ally to those who held the water.

Although Rendlebrock realized he had ridden into a perilous situation, he had to make at least a minimal effort to carry out the difficult orders Mizner had issued to bring the Cheyennes in peacefully. He sent Arapaho scout Chalk forward to parley with the Cheyennes.[11]

"I halted," Rendlebrock later said in his official report, "and sent the Arrapaho (Chalk) a few yards ahead to tell their Chief (Dull Knife) that I had to bring him and his people back to the Agency he had left. He said that he would not return to be starved, that he did not want to fight, but would, before he would return."[12]

"The Arapahoe went out," Gunther testified, "and was not satisfied with telling them that they should come into the reservation again, but he threw up his blankets, and made different Indian signs for them to come in, and the commanding officer would like it if there would not be any fight."[13]

Both Rendlebrock's indication that Chalk went only "a few yards ahead" and Gunther's account of the event imply that Chalk's communication with the Cheyennes may have been carried out remotely by signs without the benefit of verbal language. The use of sign language was universal among the Plains tribes and provided excellent understanding between communicating parties. Regardless of whether actual words were used, the various accounts of what transpired between the two sides agree in context: Rendlebrock wanted the Cheyennes to return to the agency; they refused and indicated they would fight before doing so.

Commanders of cavalry troops in similar situations often rode forward and parleyed directly with tribal leaders through interpreters. Rendlebrock, however, conducted no face-to-face meeting with the Cheyennes. He may have been at fault for dismounting his troops in a show of militancy that caused the Cheyennes to respond in a similar fashion, and it has been generally assumed that Rendlebrock ordered the troops to fire at Turkey Springs. But neither he nor the Cheyennes ignited the ensuing contest before any personal parley could be conducted. Instead, the fight was initiated through the unauthorized act of a junior officer: Lieutenant Wood preempted Rendlebrock and, without any instruction to do so, ordered Company G at the rear to open fire on the Cheyennes.

Wood, a native of Ohio, had risen to the rank of 1st sergeant with the Thirteenth Iowa Infantry during the Civil War, commissioned as a 2nd lieutenant in that unit shortly after the war ended. Securing an appointment to West Point, he graduated fourteenth in his class in 1872 and afterward joined the Fourth Cavalry at Fort Richardson. He was at Fort Concho when Rendlebrock was there in February 1873 but saw no Indian fighting. Wood returned to West Point in October 1876 on a two-year detail as an assistant instructor of Cavalry and was promoted to 1st lieutenant in November 1876.[14] Although his position with the command he had joined less than a week earlier was as adjutant and commissary, Wood later insisted he was "nominally in charge" of Company G, even though it was actually commanded by Wilder.[15] Wood's account of the matter is revealing:

> I saw "H" Co. dismounting to fight on foot & supposed it was to clear the front, but after deploying, the Co. halted. I waited a few moments for orders for further deployment, but getting no orders, & seeing that the Indians were filling the ravines on the right, I dismounted & took position on the right, where I learned that Capt. Rendlebrock had sent the Arapaho scout, Chalk, to parley with the Cheyennes and ask them to

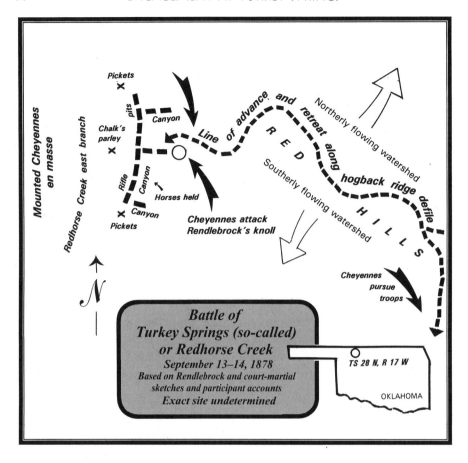

Battle of
Turkey Springs (so-called)
or Redhorse Creek
September 13–14, 1878
Based on Rendlebrock and court-martial
sketches and participant accounts
Exact site undetermined

TS 28 N, R 17 W

OKLAHOMA

return to the reservation. Chalk soon returned & I heard him tell Capt. Rendlebrock that they would rather fight than return. Upon hearing this, I ordered "G" Co., to commence firing.[16]

Wood's action preempted any further effort by Rendlebrock to carry out his orders and bring the Cheyennes in peacefully. Severely criticized later for not engaging the Cheyennes during the remainder of the pursuit, Rendlebrock was in no position to offer an official complaint over Wood's action as a loose cannon. He assumed responsibility himself for initiating the battle, although Wood's initiation of the fight was not only insubordinate but a rash move at best. With the troops dismounted in a defensive mode subject to attack by the still-mounted Cheyennes, there was little reason for Rendlebrock to have initiated the fight. His position was far too disadvantaged to exert any pressure on the Cheyennes, and the slim potential still existed for talking with the chiefs directly and trying to persuade them to return. Once the fight had commenced, however, Rendlebrock was left with no option but to continue the engagement.[17]

No sooner had the troops opened the hostilities than Cheyenne warriors emerged from ravines on both sides and in the rear to join those at the front in raking the troops with rifle fire. With bullets slicing the air about them, the Fort Reno troops frantically dug rifle pits, flattened themselves in them, and attempted to return the fire. Their carbines, however, had a more limited range than the rifles the Cheyennes possessed. The mounts and pack mules were led into a deep ravine for protection as the troops were deployed defensively in a battle line facing the main body of warriors.

The first Cheyenne assault was made against a position on the left held by ten men. Cpl. Patrick Lynch was killed and Privates Leonard and Burrows were seriously wounded during this action. Still, the troops held the position until dark. The Cheyennes attempted to capture Lynch's body, but his comrades managed to retrieve it and bury it in the ravine where the mounts were being held and the trampling of their hooves would hide the grave.[18]

The Cheyennes made other charges against a prominent knoll in the rear that commanded a view of the battle area. That position was held by Rendlebrock and Gunther, along with three or four troopers. The Cheyennes quickly realized its strategic importance and launched an attack on it. Gunther called to McDonald on the line for reinforcements, and six men were rushed forth. The Cheyennes made three charges against the knoll. The fighting was very heavy at first. One man, presumably Private Struad, and one horse were killed. Chalk, who won praise from the troops for his fighting and bravery, was severely wounded in this part of the battle.[19]

Neither Wood, who held a position on the right, nor Wilder at the rear suffered any casualties. Seven men of Company H were stationed in a ravine on the right flank. Four Cheyennes were reportedly killed and several wounded at the knoll at this point. With the troops pinned in their rifle pits and the Cheyennes unable to overrun their positions, an impasse developed. Sporadic firing continued until late evening, with neither side advancing. Not only was no medical officer available to tend the wounded troops, but there was a total void of medical supplies or attention. One trooper, once a hospital attendant, tried to dress the wounds of the men as best he could. Other men offered their handkerchiefs and even their cotton shirts as bandages.[20]

As the day wore on and the heat grew worse, thirst became more and more severe among the cavalry command, whose last water had been at the saline spring of the previous camp the morning of September 12. The stagnant pool had stood in deep holes unexposed to the sun. The command took only enough brackish water to cook with; the animals got none.[21] Both the men and their horses suffered badly through the night. One soldier later claimed the men became so thirsty they drank the urine of horses. Now the green foliage and its promise of water loomed ahead, but the Cheyennes firmly held the ground between.[22]

"We were entirely cut off from water," Wood stated, "and at 8 o'clock I was ordered with six men to see if a supply could not be gotten. We almost reached it, but were driven back and remained all night without it or anything to eat."[23]

Another reconnoitering party sent out by Rendlebrock was also forced to return to its embattled rifle positions. The Cheyennes set fire to the prairie grass at various points surrounding the troops. The fire proved no real threat, but it led an old soldier in the command to comment laconically that it "aggravated affairs, and the day being very warm and having no water, the outlook was anything but cheery."[24]

Although the Cheyenne warriors' zeal was unrestrained, their leaders' principal purpose was not necessarily to overwhelm and destroy the troops but to cripple their advance and prevent further pursuit. Rendlebrock and his officers soon realized, though, that there was no chance of carrying out the orders to bring the Cheyennes back, peacefully or otherwise. Firing stopped only when darkness fell, and the Fort Reno troops remained pinned down through a sleepless night. Vedettes—the cavalry called them "sleeping parties"—were kept on the ground the skirmishers had held during the day, while the rest of the command retired to the ravine where the stock was held. The troops had no chance to eat during the day. All this, added to the previous days' march—which had often been on foot through rough, sandy country—badly fatigued the men and debilitated many. Their ever-worsening thirst exacerbated the feeling of desperation among the troopers.[25]

During the fighting that day, Gunther had helped defend the knoll. Toward evening he began to feel ill with a fever. He was not alone; many of the men were suffering bad effects from drinking the briny water.[26] He decided to go to the ravine where the horses and pack mules were being held and see if there was any water there. The sergeant said there was none, but Gunther said he thought there might be some in his canteen on his horse. The sergeant found that, indeed, there was water in it. Gunther took a drink, but his condition continued to worsen.[27]

As he was returning to the knoll, Gunther encountered a soldier coming down into the ravine. It proved to be Sgt. E. J. Fisher, Company H, who had been in charge of the pickets around the hill. When asked where he was going, Fisher replied that it had become very cold, and he was on his way to get a saddle blanket. Gunther agreed, saying he was cold and sick himself. He suggested that Fisher let the men go down one by one and get their blankets or overcoats as they wished.[28]

When the sun rose over the Fourth Cavalry troops on the morning of September 14, their situation had deteriorated considerably. The wounded men were suffering greatly, and the need for medical attention had become critical. The officers counted their losses: two men killed and three, including Chalk, wounded. Struad was also buried in the ravine where the horses were held.[29] Rendlebrock's report of the first day's fighting also listed the loss of six badly needed horses. With no spare animals, this meant some men were left afoot.[30]

Ammunition was running precariously low, and the hunger and thirst of both men and animals were even more acute. Hanging over the outmanned group of besieged cavalrymen was the haunting memory of the defeat of Custer two years earlier, in part at the hands of some of these same Northern Cheyennes. A similar disaster was easy to imagine now. It did not help that among the Cheyennes was a warrior known as Long Hair who claimed, and other Cheyennes had supported his claim, he was the man who had killed General Custer.[31]

It had become increasingly evident that the entire force was threatened with annihilation if something was not done. Most critical was the need to reach water and, beyond that, Camp Supply, where they could rest, find medical help, and replenish their supplies and ammunition. At sunrise Rendlebrock, with the urging and full agreement of his officers, opted to withdraw.[32] As a preliminary move, he directed Lieutenant Wilder to take some men and make a diversionary move to the right in an effort to learn the Cheyennes's disposition and strength. Wilder did so, leading ten mounted troopers at a gallop along a divide that ran perpendicular to some ravines held by the Cheyennes. The detachment immediately drew fire from the ravines. One horse was hit, although not severely injured. A mounted Cheyenne party appeared, but before the two forces could contest one another, Wilder was signaled to bring his detachment in.[33]

As Wilder was making his move, Gunther was in the horse ravine supervising the building of a travois for the wounded Chalk. The trooper working on it was having difficulty putting it together, causing a delay of the retreat. Wood grew increasingly nervous. Going to the edge of the ravine, he called down to Gunther: "When in God's name will you have that ready? Time is precious, Captain. Can't you get that thing started pretty soon?"

Wood denied that he also said, "Why in the hell don't you get that travoy done? If we don't get out of here damned quick there will be another Custer massacre."[34]

Gunther, still very ill, had gone to Rendlebrock early that morning and asked for a drink of the whiskey Rendlebrock had in a flask. Rendlebrock refused, saying he would give him a drink when they made their first stand during the retreat.[35]

Rendlebrock had first decided that their best opportunity for finding water was up a ravine that led off from their battle position. He soon discovered, however, that the ravine was too clogged with dead trees to permit passage by the horses and mules.[36] He held a consultation with the other officers as to whether they should push forward or go back on their former trail. No one knew what dangers or impediments they might run into ahead, so it was unanimously agreed that the back trail was their best choice.

"Then, gentlemen," Rendlebrock said to the officers, "we will go on our back trail. I want you each one to take his post and the command will be dismounted."[37]

The eighteen pack mules under the charge of Sgt. Charles F. Wright, Company H, and a dozen men led the way.[38] Rendlebrock, mounted, followed directly behind the mules and ahead of the men with the led horses under Sergeant Fisher. Next in line were the three travois with the wounded. Rendlebrock had arranged the procession in this manner so the horses would level the ground and make the movement of the wounded in their travois less rough.[39]

Company G under Wilder, in the lead position of the dismounted troops, trailed the wounded, with Company H at the rear. Wood was assigned to cover the rear and left flank with the dismounted troops of Company G. Gunther and McDonald officered the right flank with Company H.[40] The sun had been up over the horizon nearly an hour when the horses were brought out of the ravine, and the hard-pressed command prepared to withdraw.

9
Rambunctious RETREAT

EGARDLESS OF WHETHER LIEUTENANT WOOD MENTIONED IT, it was clear to all: the dark shadow of the Little Bighorn hung over the two belea- guered troops of Fourth Cavalry. To remain pinned down without water, with dwindling ammunition, and with no hope of reinforcements would clearly spell their doom. No man among them was not ready and anxious to escape their predicament. And once the retreat began, that anxi- ety ballooned into near panic.

Rendlebrock and the horse holders, mounted and trailing four horses, led the way toward the defile by which they had arrived. Just before they entered the chasm, a problem occurred with one of the packs on the mules. Sergeant Wright dismounted and was working to fix it when Rendlebrock issued an order that the mules not be taken any farther just then. He thought there might be someone on the other side of a bluff they were approaching. Instead of ordering a horse handler to the task, Rendlebrock himself rode around the hill alone to investigate. He returned to say it was all right and the train could go ahead.[1]

Although the trail through the defile was very narrow and irregular, the mounted advance of the retreat—pack mules, Rendlebrock, horses led by handlers, and travois—remained in marching order as it passed through it and beyond the range of red sandhills.[2] But behind them a nearly chaotic

Wilber Wilder as West Point cadet. Courtesy, Special Collections and Archives, USMA Library.

situation had developed among the dismounted troops and rear guard. The Cheyennes had no intention of letting the troops escape so easily. They began pushing close on both the left and right flanks, firing at the troops from adjacent ridges.

By the time the already worn cavalrymen had dashed across the rough, sandy countryside to the defile, they had become physically fatigued. According to McDonald, the men were considerably exhausted and needing water so badly that some seemed almost out of their minds.[3] Panic began to set in as the troopers crowded into the narrow defile, and many began to call out that they could go no farther. They pleaded for the horses to be sent back. The officers, particularly McDonald and Gunther, were in no better shape.[4]

Even the strapping McDonald could hardly walk. Seeing this, Wood told him he had better mount a horse that had been brought back. At first McDonald declined in favor of one of his men. But when Wood issued a direct order, McDonald climbed on the horse and moved ahead. En route he came on Gunther, bent forward on a mount looking very pale and barely able to stay in his saddle.

Gunther, still very ill, had started out dismounted and struggled forward 1,000 yards before he requested that 1st Sgt. Thomas Gatewood bring him his horse. When McDonald saw him in the defile, Gunther was moving very slowly and obviously in great pain. McDonald asked what was wrong. Gunther told him he was so sick that he wanted McDonald to take over command of the company. He said he thought he would have to get off his horse and lie down. The two men were near the rear of the column with the Cheyennes close behind. McDonald told him he would do no such thing. Fearful that Gunther would fall from his horse, McDonald grabbed the officer's arm to steady him. Then, holding Gunther with his right hand, McDonald slapped the horse with his carbine and guided it ahead to near the front of the column.

By the time they reached the red hills, the rear guard had been diminished by men who had mounted themselves and gone on. With the Cheyennes in close pursuit and insufficient men to provide cover fire in moving from one defensive knoll to another, it became a matter of dashing from place to place. Wood soon found himself with only Company G 1st sergeant John F. Feely and three other men. The fire of this small rear guard, however, managed to keep the pursuers at a distance.

Although he was armed with a carbine and a pistol, Wood said, he had very few cartridges and was forced to point his carbine at Cheyennes to make them dodge behind the sandhills.[5] In testimony later, Wood said he

David McDonald as West Point cadet. Courtesy, Special Collections and Archives, USMA Library.

gave his carbine to a soldier, but Feely claimed Wood lost the carbine during the retreat.[6] Feely, the third-to-last man through the defile, also claimed that when he told the men to save their ammunition, which was running low, Wood countermanded him, saying the men had to fire to hold the Cheyennes off.[7] Wood acknowledged that he ordered the men to "get out of here God damned quick!"[8]

Wood remained with his men only as far as the defile. "No officer was present at the time of coming to the defile," Feely testified. "Lt. Wood had been in charge till about 300 yds. from the place when his horse was brought up by Pvt. Bolenti of G Co., and he mounted his horse and rode off." Wood issued orders, Feely said, leaving him and the three others in the rear.[9]

Sergeant Fisher supported the charge, insisting he had seen Wood mount and shout out that "he was getting out of there, as it was getting too damned hot for him." Fisher then saw the officer leave at a gallop before the men went through the defile.[10]

Afterward, in his report to General Hatch, commanding officer of the Fourth Cavalry, Wood stated: "Fortunately, no one was hit, but had there been, we would have been compelled to stay with him, & as the sequel will show, we would have been left to fate, & in Indian fighting, all army officers know what that means."[11]

But in truth, a soldier was shot by the Cheyennes after Wood deserted the rear guard. Pvt. Francis E. Burton, a farrier in Gunther's Company G who was the last man to go through the defile, was hit. A Cheyenne bullet knocked him from his saddle. No one knew if Burton had been captured alive or killed outright, and no attempt was made to rescue him. Little was ever said regarding the man, except that he was listed as a casualty of the fight. His body was never recovered, and the dire fate he may have suffered was not dwelt upon.[12]

When Wood had ordered McDonald onto a horse to go forward, he had done so for a reason. He instructed McDonald to find Rendlebrock and tell him "for God['s] sake, to halt the command & cover my passage through the defile by his fire."[13] When McDonald reached Rendlebrock, he reported that "Lt. Wood was back in the defile and the command would have to be halted long enough to make a little stand, collect the men, and let Lt. Wood come up."[14] By McDonald's account, Rendlebrock did not give him any instructions but simply moved on. Rendlebrock, however, claimed he did reply, telling McDonald to inform Wood that he was going to form at a place that he pointed to with his hand.[15]

This was supported by Sgt. Charles F. Davis of Company H who was also sent to tell Rendlebrock that Wood wanted him to stop and form a line.

Rendlebrock instructed Davis to inform Wood that it was useless to form a line in the ravines because the Cheyenne would get on the bluffs and have the advantage. As soon as he got to that ridge, he said, pointing to a place about 300 yards ahead, he would put the animals and the pack train in the ravine on the other side and stand and fight to the last.[16]

McDonald had ordered the horse holders to take mounts back to the men in the rear.[17] Each man would ride back and lead three horses. When they reached the panicky troops, Feely noted, the lead ropes were hard to untie. The men in the rear quickly cut them and jumped on the first horse they found. As a result, many of the troopers mounted animals over which they had poor control.[18]

Wood made it from the rear to the front ahead of Gunther, who arrived there still in great misery. Rendlebrock, halted at the ridge, gave Wood a drink from his flask. When Gunther came up, Wood handed him the container.[19] The whiskey made Gunther feel somewhat better, and he joined Rendlebrock in an effort to halt the orderless retreat of the troops.[20]

The Cheyennes had been firing at the fleeing troops from the nearby hills, but on seeing the troops remount they came charging down on their horses.[21] This caused the men to push forward with increased frenzy, creating even more confusion and disorder when they became logjammed in the narrow canyon. When Sergeant Feely finally made it through, he went directly to Rendlebrock for instructions. Rendlebrock again pointed to the crest of the ridge, saying he was going to make a stand there. He ordered Feely and Sergeant McGann to keep the men away from the pack train and do all they could to stop them from going ahead. Feely said Rendlebrock had "hallooed himself hoarse" in trying to reform the command.[22]

"When I got through the defile with the pack train," Rendlebrock testified, "the mounted men came rushing from the rear passing me at a pretty rapid gait. I tried my best to stop them on the plateau about 200 yards in front to make a stand there. I suppose half of the rear guard passed me if not more before I got there, they would not listen to me."[23]

Wood, Wilder, and McDonald also joined in the effort to halt the precipitous retreat and effect some organized resistance to the still active Cheyennes. The officers managed to stop and dismount enough men to form a temporary skirmish line. The makeshift rear guard fired a few shots as it fell back to a better position. Here, enough troopers were recruited to make a countercharge. Someone called out, "Let's charge; we can whip them." The men then set up a yell and galloped forward.[24] Few men had their own horses at this point, and some making the charge could not control their animals.[25] The Cheyennes retreated into ravines temporarily, but they were soon closing in again. McDonald described the ensuing action:

> The men seemed now inclined to give up the fight and go back in a wild search for water (or for some other reason). By my utmost endeavor I managed to collect about 12 or 13 men, five of whom I almost immediately afterward asked Lt. Wilder to take and keep some Indians out of a timbered ravine not very far from our left flank.[26]

With the main portion of the command still retreating in disòrder, the small force of officers and noncoms established a line of battle that fought even as it retreated from the ever-pressing Cheyennes. Although his condition had improved only temporarily, Gunther rode forward through the defensive skirmish line and turned to face the small cadre of mounted men. Of the sixteen or so enlisted men and noncoms, several were old troopers who were more responsive than the recruits to regulation battle commands. The impromptu squad included Sergeants Fisher, Gatewood, Owen O'Niell, and Feely. Gunther issued the orders as prescribed: "Men, prepare for a charge. Command Forward! Guide Center! March! Trot March! Gallop March! Charge!" The resulting sally extended 200 yards and again forced the pursuers to pull back temporarily.[27]

Gunther did not take part in the charge. He observed the action from a hilltop until his attention was drawn to two pack mules that had strayed from the main herd. Gunther ordered a corporal from his company to retrieve the mules.[28] Before the corporal could do so, however, one of the mules was captured by a Cheyenne who cut off its pack and attempted to ride it away. The mule bucked his captor off and returned to the herd, but his pack was lost.[29]

Thus far Rendlebrock had been retracing their original route from the campsite of September 12. But he spied a stand of cottonwood trees off to the right a mile and a half away that indicated there might be water there. He directed that the pack mules be taken there, and the rest of the command followed.[30] The Cheyennes made one final effort to cut them off from the location, but another charge was carried out, driving the Cheyennes back; and the command reached the spring safely.

Their ammunition supply was almost exhausted, and the cavalrymen were demoralized from having lost a bruising encounter with the Cheyennes they were pursuing. A report in the *Army and Navy Journal*, possibly written by a Fourth Cavalry noncom, summed up the retreat in as positive a light as it could:

> The Indians soon lined the hills all around, and then we mounted. Sometimes we dismounted and fought on foot, but as the horses were such

a mark, and as the Indians closed all around us, we again dismounted. We fought for six miles. The enemy formed to the amount of fifty in our front. We formed for a charge and drove them one mile; they soon formed again and were again charged and defeated. They tried to reach the water hole ahead of us but were again driven [back], losing many, and at last at noon we reached the water (a very small supply), when they began retreating in all directions.[31]

Finally, the Cheyennes withdrew, and camp was made at the spring, which was at the bottom of a ravine encased with brush interlaced with wild hemp and sunflowers. All able-bodied men were placed on picket duty around the perimeter of the camp. Upon arriving, Gunther had laid down in a shady spot, remaining there all day. Sergeant Fisher, who found him lying on his back barely able to speak or breathe, raised him to a sitting position and gave him a drink of water with some Jamaican ginger in it. Gunther managed to instruct the sergeant that if Rendlebrock was going to camp there that night, the horses should be unsaddled.[32]

One man not placed on picket was a cook, appropriately named George Cook, who was left in camp to tend the ailing Gunther.[33] Gunther had eaten nothing since the morning of the 13th, and Cook provided him with a cup of tea and a biscuit, then cleared a more level place for him to rest.[34]

Gunther was joined that night by McDonald, who came to bunk with him campaign style.[35] The two men were sleeping soundly when a shot was fired in camp. Although the incident proved harmless in itself, it became an issue in the eventual charges of cowardice Wood levied against Gunther.

The event occurred when Wood, whose blankets had been lost with the pack on the wayfaring mule, became cold during the night and got up to put on his overcoat. Cook, seeing only a form at a distance in the dark, thought it was a Cheyenne and loosed a shot from his rifle. McDonald was awakened instantly. Throwing his blanket off, he jumped over Gunther and ran with pistol in hand to investigate. As he did so, another shot and flash of gunfire went off immediately in front of him. McDonald jumped forward to see a dim figure that proved to be Cook in a stooping position with a rifle in his hands.

"Watch out, Lieutenant," Cook warned in a shrill whisper. "Right in front of you!"[36]

McDonald immediately threw himself into the grass, peering into the darkness in an effort to see the Cheyenne he supposed was there. After a minute or two he heard Wilder call out, "What is the matter?" McDonald made no reply, and Wilder soon came running over and flopped on the ground beside the two men, each peering intently into the deep shadows of the brush. McDonald began to realize that Cook had fired the shots, and when queried, the private admitted to having done so. Wood came up just as Cook was pointing to the place he had fired upon and overheard the admission.

"By God," Wood exclaimed, "he shot at me!"[37]

As this was taking place, Gunther came up with his carbine in hand, crouching in the dark to ask in a hushed voice, "What is the matter? What is it?"

McDonald explained. The much relieved but fatigued men were anxious to return to their beds, and the matter was essentially dropped with McDonald's admonition to Cook, "The next time you shoot, shoot at something you can hit."[38] Although not a particularly unusual incident in frontier camp life, Wood used the matter to indict Gunther on the charge that he did, "when a shot was fired in camp and an alarm given, behave in a cowardly manner, and keep himself hidden in the grass and bushes until the cause of the alarm had been ascertained by his juniors in rank."[39]

With the Cheyennes having withdrawn, the battle of Turkey Springs came to an end. The Fort Reno command had narrowly escaped annihilation, and their retreat had been so precipitous that, as one account reported: "There is some property lost; our officers lost all they had but their revolvers. . . . We fired two thousand rounds from our carbines, and emptied our revolvers during the charges."[40]

The cavalry unit's situation was still precarious. Three of the wounded men badly needed medical attention, rations and ammunition were almost depleted, and the condition of the remainder of the troops and their animals was very poor. They had marched 179 miles without rest, and their horses had found no forage other than prairie grass, which at times was very sparse and burned.

The command remained at the spring overnight. Willow drags were made for the two wounded soldiers and Chalk before continuing on thirty-five miles toward Camp Supply. The line of march was in the bed of the Cimarron before cutting off southwestward up Buffalo Creek. The troops made camp that night on Sleeping Bear Creek. Rendlebrock sent scout Donald on ahead bearing news of the fight and requesting help with the wounded. Donald arrived at Camp Supply at 9 A.M. September 16 and reported to Hambright, who immediately dispatched a medical officer and an army ambulance to meet the command, which limped into Camp Supply that evening.[41]

The wounded Chalk remained in the hospital at Camp Supply to recuperate. He eventually returned to Fort Reno, where he lived three years before dying and being buried in the post cemetery.[42] Seven Fourth Cavalry horses were killed during the two-day engagement, two at Turkey Springs and five during the escape, adding to several that were lost on the march. Officers estimated Cheyenne losses at about fifteen warriors and thirty wounded, with twenty ponies killed, but those numbers are questionable. Rendlebrock admitted that the true numbers were not known.[43]

The encounter with the Northern Cheyennes had been a near disaster for the Fort Reno troops. McDonald expressed the universal feeling among the command: "None of us wanted to do any more fighting. We were discouraged and as far as I was concerned I did not want to see any more of those Indians, and I thought everybody else felt the same way."[44]

But they would indeed see much more of the Cheyennes.

10

The Cheyennes
AND THE COWMEN

A NEWS ITEM FROM FORT RENO appeared in the September 12, 1878, issue of the *Leavenworth Daily Times* with the obvious intention of reassuring the Kansas citizenry regarding the Northern Cheyenne escape. It read in part:

> What few arms they may have were secreted at the time and since their coming on the reservation, and can be of but little service in the event of an encounter with the thoroughly equipped troops of the pursuing force. But little danger is apprehended from this source, however, the object of Col. Mizner being to intercept and force their return to the reservation. They are poorly provided and their capture is regarded as but the matter of a very short time. No danger is feared as to their warlike intentions by the residents and stock men in this section, as (it is believed) they will push forward with all diligence to avoid an engagement and capture by the U.S. forces.[1]

The story was naive and misleading in many ways, none more so than the reference to the safety of the stockmen. Cattlemen and cowboys in southwestern Kansas had much to fear from the Cheyenne retreat, in terms of both loss of stock and personal danger. Nor did the Northern Cheyenne warriors, who from their first breath had learned to fight for the survival of their people, hold great concern about armed conflict with U.S. troops. In truth, they welcomed the honor of engaging with those troops.

The march of the Northern Cheyennes as far as the Platte River was as one body, but at the same time, parties of young warriors—"wolves," as Mari Sandoz calls them in *Cheyenne Autumn*—rode well ahead of the others to garner cattle for food and extra horses. Only after the Cheyennes had passed did solid information begin to emerge regarding some of the incidents on the remote prairies of northern Indian Territory and southern Kansas.

"From the minor trails that intercepted the main trail," scout Donald observed, "we concluded that the young men would slip away from the main body of Indians, and go off and get stuff and come in. We estimated that there were about five hundred head of horses stolen between here [Fort Reno] and the Platte River."[2]

There were killings as well. The first instance had occurred on September 12, the day before the Turkey Springs fight, a few miles to the northwest on the Comanche Company ranch operated by the Colcord family. In 1878 the sparsely settled country of the Cherokee Outlet and southern Kansas was occupied by large, open-range cattle ranches. These ranches, many of which existed in Indian Territory on unfenced grazing land of the Cherokee Outlet, maintained their stock through a general monitoring by cowboy herders and a system of large joint roundups in the spring known as "pools." Cowherders on the open range and their stock proved to be vulnerable targets for the Cheyennes.[3]

Charles F. Colcord, later a noted Oklahoma City business leader, was such a cowboy at the time. He had been born and raised in Kentucky but moved to Texas with his family and helped his father drive cattle herds across Indian Territory to Kansas railheads. During fall and winter of 1877 and 1878, Colcord's father and two other cattle entrepreneurs consolidated their cattle, horses, men, and other resources into one organization. The new cattle company, which became known as the Comanche Pool and later the Comanche Company, covered a 75-square-mile range straddling the Kansas–Indian Territory border and extending south to the Cimarron River. The ranch included Turkey Springs. The Colcord family established their residence in three large dugouts on the Salt Fork of the Arkansas River west of present Kiowa, Kansas.[4]

On the morning of September 12, 1878, young Colcord was returning from a trip to Sun City, Kansas, 20 miles north of his home. En route he was met by a young cowhand who excitedly told him there had been an Indian attack on their range and several people had been killed. The two cowboys hurried south fearful of what they would find.

At the mouth of the Red Fork, they spied a fire in the distance and figures moving about. The cowboys first thought the group was Cheyennes celebrating around a campfire. Instead, it proved to be several Englishmen on a Western sojourn, guided by some old buffalo hunters. Colcord warned them of the danger and moved on to his home headquarters. He was much relieved to find his mother safe.

The Colcords, however, were fearful over the fate of two of their men, Reuben Bristow and Fred Clark. Bristow, Colcord's cousin, had recently come from Kentucky for a visit. The two young men had left early that morning in a wagon to gather salt at the Cimarron River saline west of present Freedom, Oklahoma. They had not returned, and it was greatly feared that they had been killed. Their fate was still unknown that night when a man came to the Colcord home and reported that a posse was being formed from the various ranches in the area to go after the Cheyennes. Colcord saddled his horse and rode to the neighboring Nelson's ranch to join the group, still not knowing the fate of Bristow and Clark.[5]

Two days later, when Colcord returned from the chase after the Cheyennes, he and some others rode south to investigate the disappearance of the two men. They soon learned the harsh truth that Bristow and Clark had been the first victims of the Northern Cheyennes. On the crest of the high divide between the Salt Fork of the Arkansas and the Cimarron River just northwest of Turkey Springs, they found the salt wagon. Its front end was lodged against a clump of willows in a ravine, and the bodies of the two salt gatherers were lying in the wagon bed. Arrows protruded from the torsos of both, and Bristow had been shot in the head.

The tracks of the mules and wagon, unshod hoofprints, and other marks in the area told a story of how Bristow had been killed and how the mules had stampeded and dragged the wagon into the ravine where the willows had halted its progress. It was apparent that the Cheyenne warriors had surrounded the wagon, loosed arrows into the two men, and taken the mules.[6]

This event in Indian Territory was prelude to others as the Cheyennes made their way westward across the unfenced ranch land of southern Kansas. The trauma the populace of western Kansas experienced during the Cheyenne retreat is interconnected with the military operation, but it also embodies a separate story. Although the resulting panic was at times founded on imaginary fears and embellished reports, the havoc rendered was often real and deadly. This controversial aspect of the Northern Cheyenne retreat has largely been overlooked or slighted outside of Kansas-related publications, but factual history cannot ignore the effects of the retreat on citizens and communities. Although newspaper accounts were often presented in the frontier's pejorative, anti-Indian perspective of the day, in the end the essential facts of most depredation charges are verifiable and provide an interesting and fuller view of this historical episode.

Grave of cowboy salt haulers. Author photo.

Western Kansas at this point in history was essentially divided into two principal segments of civilian population: cowmen and the first agrarian homesteaders. The sparsely settled country south of the Arkansas River was the domain of the cattlemen, who took the brunt of the Cheyenne raiding. Dodge City, the largest settlement in the region, became a focal point of the Cheyenne excitement. Reports of the Cheyenne retreat from Darlington and conflicts to the south reached the town, fostering alarm-generating stories in the *Dodge City Times*, whose headlines on September 21 read:

THE RED DEVILS
The Wild and Hungry Cheyennes
Commit Murder and Arson
Several Herders Murdered

Not unexpectedly, near panic resulted in Dodge, as a local scribe reported:

Thursday afternoon at 1 o'clock the Cheyennes burned a farm-house
within two miles of town. The farmer and his family saw them coming and
fled. The burning building could be seen distinctly and the Indians were
plainly visible with the aid of a glass. The greatest excitement prevailed
and women and children left their homes to gather in the streets for
protection. Guns and horses were hurriedly gathered together and pursuit
given, but the Indians soon disappeared over the hills. Engines at once
started east and west to notify the settlers of the danger, and many have
come in for protection.[7]

The truth, however—learned later—was that the farmhouse burned
because a fire was left alive in the family stove. A locomotive loaded with
citizens was rushed to the farm, and they were able to save the haystack and
stock. One of those involved in putting out the flames was the illustrious
Wyatt Earp, marshal of Dodge City. Another railroad engine and car sent to
Cimarron station twenty miles west of Dodge returned to report no sighting
of Cheyennes along the line. The Santa Fe Railroad stopped running trains
at night from Dodge during the crisis. Dodge City mayor James Kelly and
three others sent an urgent telegram to Gov. George T. Anthony: "Three
hundred Indians are driving off stock and killing herders. They are now
within six miles of our city. We are without arms, having equipped members
who have gone south. Can you send us arms and ammunition. Situation
alarming. We are powerless without arms and ammunition."[8]

Anthony forwarded the message to General Pope, whose adjutant rejected the emergency plea by answering that nothing had been heard from
Lt. Col. William H. Lewis at Fort Dodge about Cheyennes in that vicinity.[9]
This information was wired to Dodge City, whereupon a committee of citizens shot back another plea: "Indians are murdering, and burning houses
within three miles of town. All the arms we had have been sent. Can you
send us arms and ammunition immediately?"[10]

This time Anthony responded, ordering his adjutant general to rush a 200
stand of arms and ammunition by train. At the same time, he reassured Kelly
that according to General Pope, no more than seventy-five Cheyennes were
at large.[11]

The Dodge City request for firearms was soon followed by a similar one
from Hutchinson, Kansas, well to the east of Dodge. M. J. Cochran of that

city wired Anthony that hostile bands infested Barbour and Comanche Counties. Ten persons had been killed, he said, and several wounded, and many horses and cattle had been stampeded and stolen. C. G. Coutant also wired the governor from Hutchison, saying one man had been shot in the leg, another in the neck, and a child in the breast. Armed squads of settlers, he claimed, were rounding up women and children in the county and taking them to Sun City.[12]

Even in Hodgeman and Ness Counties north of Dodge, the Kansas citizenry fled their homes in great fear to gather at points of safety. A doctor later issued a claim for the $125 worth of groceries it took to feed 191 people during the scare.[13]

From Kingsley, Kansas, the Edwards County attorney wired Anthony that two cowboys had reported that the Cheyennes had destroyed their camp south of Kingsley and stampeded their cattle. Four men, he said, were known to have been killed. From Pratt County, however, A. J. Johnson replied to an inquiry from the governor that the Cheyenne scare was much smaller than reported. Still, his letter listed four men who had been killed.[14] A summation of deaths in Comanche County was made on November 11, 1878, by three citizens from that area who wrote: "We can prove seven new graves in Comanche, and two in the territory, also testify while at the same time three wounded persons stand as witnesses to their unprovoked atrocity, not a single shot being fired by the white men."[15]

An Indian Commission's itemization of thirty-two persons killed in Kansas was appended with ten others, of which several were listed as unknown.[16] Possibly, there were victims who were alone on the prairie when they were killed. Thus there were no witnesses to tell whether the victims had, as Little Wolf professed, fired on the Cheyennes first or whether they had been killed without cause.

The commission listed six persons killed in southern Kansas. An appended page added an unknown victim in Clark County and another in Barber County. Newspaper stories and memory accounts supported by complementary evidence provide record of some incidents that occurred during the Cheyenne march south of the Arkansas River.

One of these, as the newspapers reported, occurred on the Salt Fork of the Cimarron River in southern Comanche County when a Cheyenne party out scavenging for horses, food, and weapons invaded the ranch quarters of Wiley Payne. The rancher resisted, and in an ensuing fracas his brother, Walter Payne, was shot in the neck, according to one report. Another said his leg was broken and his thumb shot off. Three-year-old Charles was shot in the body and baby Lora through the shoulder. All would recover.[17]

A more deadly fracas occurred in Comanche County when a group of Cheyennes appeared at the evening camp of a cowman named Sheedy as his cowboys were sitting around their campfire. The Cheyennes asked for some food and tobacco. Having them outnumbered, the cowboys unceremoniously rejected the request. They were taken by surprise when, according to their story, one of the Cheyennes grabbed a six-gun from a cowboy and began firing. Two of the ranch crew, Frank T. Dow and John Evans, were shot dead.[18]

Cowboy Emerson Brown described a harrowing experience that took place at the ranch of Hi (Hiram) Kollar, who operated on Bluff Creek in Ford and Clark Counties. Brown, then only fifteen, was branding calves for Kollar when Hemphill's Troop I out of Camp Supply stopped to warn that the Cheyennes had broken out and were on the warpath. Hemphill told them of a young cattle herder who had been killed at the nearby ranch of Kollar's brother Henry.[19] The following day the branding crew was rounding up more calves when cowboy Anderson Hilton spotted cows moving along ahead of some horses as if they were being driven. He soon realized the horses had riders—Cheyennes who were lying off to one side to avoid being seen.[20]

Upon being discovered, the Cheyennes began shooting at Hilton. He made for the camp but had to take cover in a thicket. He was armed with a six-shooter and managed to inflict, he thought, a flesh wound on one Cheyenne. But the cowboy decided that a gunfight with six Cheyennes was not in his best interest. He fired no more and remained quiet in his hiding place until the Cheyennes left.

Brown was not armed, and Kollar had merely a six-gun. His only bullets were those in the gun's chamber. When the Cheyennes charged at them from a grove of cottonwood trees, the two men fled north to the ranch house where Kollar had a Winchester rifle. They later returned to the camp with three other men, finding everything destroyed. The attackers had shot the camp tent and wagons full of holes, evidently in case someone was hiding out in them.

Kollar and Brown went up Granger Creek to secure some saddle horses and mules grazing there. Brown spotted a mounted Cheyenne. Having the Winchester, he started to shoot; but Kollar yelled at him to save his cartridges, as he might need them later. At that moment the Cheyenne disappeared behind the far side of his pony and fled.

Kollar took his crew on to the Maily ranch near which a stage stand for the Dodge City–Camp Supply mail route was located. As they were putting their mounts in the corral, two Cheyennes crossed the creek at the stage stop a half mile east of the ranch. Seeing two horses grazing nearby, the tribesmen shot under them in hopes of stampeding them away from the ranch. Instead, the horses ran toward the house. No more Cheyennes were seen that day, but the following morning shots were heard to the south. Presently, a herder named Sebastian arrived at a hard gallop. He excitedly told a story of an encounter with the Cheyennes.

The herder said he and a man named Frazier had been with a company of soldiers and cowmen. Having no guns, they left the command and headed for the stage stand. On the way they encountered a band of twenty or more Cheyennes who fell in pursuit as the men spurred their horses to escape. Frazier's horse stumbled and fell, throwing him to the ground. He got up and ran to an arroyo where he was surrounded by Cheyennes. He had only two bullets and planned to save one for himself. The two men were saved, however, when several cowboys rode up to the stage stand and the Cheyennes retreated.

In Ford County a Cheyenne party attacked a trail herd fifteen miles from Dodge. The seven or so cowboys escaped, but George Simmonds, a black cook, was killed while trying to save the brace of mules that stampeded with the doubletree of the chuck wagon dragging behind. George W. Brown, who had been hired by the herd's owner to go out from Dodge and bring the wagon in, found Simmonds's body lying beside the wagon.[21]

On September 19 a herder for the W. C. Quinlan ranch named Con-Red was killed near the juncture of Spring Creek and Big Sandy Creek.[22] Two days later two more men—cowboys Thomas Murray and Samuel LeForce—were missing from the Quinlan camp. A newspaper story said a cowboy named Murray and a companion were killed on Bluff Creek in either southwest Ford or northwest Clark County. Two months later Murray's remains, recognizable only by his clothing, were discovered on the range by friends and buried. A scalp found in a deserted Cheyenne camp on Bluff Creek was thought to have been taken from LeForce.[23]

LeForce's remains were not found for some time. His brother, Perry LeForce, searched for him without luck. Eventually, a skeleton was found on the prairie and with it the victim's six-shooter. The chamber of the weapon was empty, indicating that perhaps the cowboy had fought to the end.[24]

The most definitive and substantial summary of the Cheyenne depredations in Kansas south of the Arkansas River was made by 1st Lt. John Harold, with the Nineteenth Infantry at Fort Dodge. Assigned to investigate the Cheyenne raid through the region below Fort Dodge, Harold left the post on October 11 with a buckboard and a four-mule wagon escorted by a sergeant and four privates.[25]

Harold and his men drove west along the Arkansas River to Cimarron station, where they picked up the still visible trail of the Cheyennes and followed it south to Meade City. From there the party backtracked the Cheyennes southeastward to near the Spring Creek juncture with Big Sandy Creek. The men stopped overnight at the Quinlan Cattle Company camp not far from where troops had encountered the Cheyennes on September 23.

Moving down Big Sandy, Harold was unable to pick up the Cheyennes' trail. After visiting at the Fraser ranch on Kiowa Creek and the Biddle and Spencer cattle camp, the investigators returned to Fraser's ranch, this time locating the trail. It was clear that Cheyenne raiding parties had operated over an area twenty miles wide. Harold next went to Kollar's ranch near the conflux of Cavalry and Bluff Creeks, then traveled fifteen miles east to Hunter's and Evans's cattle camp on the Nescatunga, and on to Payne's ranch on the Salt Fork of the Arkansas. The Colcords, he found, had moved to Kingsley, Kansas. From Payne's place the party returned north to Fort Dodge, where Harold inventoried his findings.

Harold listed ten persons killed, along with the three members of the Payne family who were wounded and two unknown strangers who Henry Kollar said had been wounded. The lieutenant also itemized the loss of property claimed by the ranchers. Missing stock included horses, mules, sheep (these from S. B. Williams on Big Sandy), and cattle, although some said they would not know their losses until the next roundup. Other items claimed by the cowmen included clothing, blankets, cooking utensils, foodstuff, harnesses, saddles, bridles, and several pistols and rifles.

North of the Arkansas River, along the route of the Kansas Pacific Railroad and above, immigrant groups were establishing the first farming communities on the raw land. Kansas land commissioner S. J. Gillmore noted the arrival of such groups in a letter to Governor Anthony on October 3, 1878:

> Many new settlers are in that district and forty-four from Iowa went to Buffalo last night, but no doubt will return immediately.... Only about two weeks ago a colony from Indiana with almost an entire freight train of goods went west on the Kansas Pacific railway to settle in Norton county and last night there were forty-four Hollanders from Iowa on the train, bound for Grove county.[26]

Some of the newcomers were Russian Mennonites who had fled to the United States to escape Cossack raiders. These peaceful farming people were prepared to face the privations of the Western frontier, but they had no idea of the danger they would soon face from a band of desperate Cheyennes.

11

The Company I
INTERCEPTION

O N SEPTEMBER 12, 1878, MAJOR HAMBRIGHT AT CAMP SUPPLY received both the September 10 note penned by Rendlebrock while on the march and a Fort Reno communication from Mizner notifying him of the outbreak.[1] Hambright immediately issued orders for Hemphill and Company I, Fourth Cavalry, to return to the field. First, however, it was necessary to get Hemphill sober. Having just returned from his erroneous expedition into Kansas on September 10, Hemphill had been assigned to serve as officer of the day for the post on September 11. When time came for him to officiate at the routine mounting of the guard, he arrived so gloriously drunk that he was incapable of performing his duties.[2]

Hemphill was instructed to proceed with dispatch to where the Cheyennes' trail crossed the Dodge road and follow it until he overtook the Cheyennes. "After overtaking the band," the order specified, "every effort will be made to turn them back peaceably, but by force if they refuse."[3] The unit was also to make contact with Rendlebrock if possible.

Hemphill received the order at 8:30 that same morning and, however much hung over, immediately set about getting his company together. The four days' rations he ordered from the post commissary were not yet loaded aboard six pack mules when the company rode out from Camp Supply. Hambright had told Hemphill not to wait, that the rations would be sent along.[4] With Amos Chapman serving as guide, 2nd Lt. Matthew Leeper,[5] and forty-six troopers, Hemphill pushed at a fast trot up the Dodge road thirty miles to Snake Creek. There he paused for an hour to rest the horses and let the men eat. He then moved on to Cimarron ranch, where he left Sgt. Jacob Schaufler and a soldier to keep an eye out for the Cheyennes. The two men were to follow him to Bear Creek ranch after daylight the next day and examine the trail for any sign of a Cheyenne crossing.[6]

It was one A.M. when Hemphill arrived at the ranch. The pack mules with the supplies reached him there. He had his men up at dawn, and after breakfast the troops scouted up Bear Creek four or five miles. He also sent a patrol to Bluff Creek and posted a sergeant and two men on the peak of a prominent knoll to keep a lookout for signs of either the Cheyennes or Rendlebrock. Company I found neither; the two were engaged in battle at Turkey Springs more than 100 miles away.

With the four-day supply of rations insufficient for scouting much farther and his horses in need of shoeing, on September 14—even as the Fort Reno troops were retreating to Camp Supply—Hemphill led his troops on to Fort Dodge. He reasoned that it was closer than returning to Camp Supply for supplies. In doing so, he found himself caught between two commanders.

Hambright was so angry that Hemphill had gone to Fort Dodge that he later issued court-martial charges against him for disobeying orders. At Fort Dodge, however, Lewis told Hemphill he had received orders from department headquarters to retain all troops coming in to that post.[7] Hemphill argued that he felt strongly that he should go back and scout the country east of the military road for the Cheyennes and Rendlebrock. Lewis agreed that perhaps it was best for Hemphill to do so. They both thought it possible, however, since there had been no further reports from Rendlebrock or word about the Cheyennes, that the latter may have given up and returned to the agency.[8]

Obtaining his rations, Hemphill led Company I back to Bluff Creek and made night camp there. He was awakened at two o'clock the next morning by a cowboy who reported that his ranch, the Henry Kollar spread at the mouth of Bluff Creek, had been raided by Cheyennes at sundown the previous day. He immediately woke his troops and told them to get a bite to eat and then saddle their horses. After writing a note to Hambright regarding the Kollar attack and sending it off by courier, Hemphill led Company I forty miles downstream to Kollar's ranch, marching nonstop and arriving at midafternoon. The troops found the deserted ranch torn up as though it had been plundered by Cheyennes. Five miles from the ranch, the troops came onto the body of one of Kollar's men and buried him.[9]

Chapman and a Private Wilson were sent to circle the Kollar ranch house in an effort to find the Cheyennes' trail. Wilson returned shortly to report that he had seen six mounted Cheyennes a few miles away. Hemphill quickly had his men resaddle their mounts, and the group charged out to where the warriors had been sighted. The group, perhaps an advance foraging party of Cheyennes, had disappeared into the sandhills that dominated the area.

Company I spent the night of September 16 at Kollar's ranch and the following morning set out on a trail that led them north of present Ashland, Kansas. There they spotted a party of five or six mounted Cheyennes. Hemphill gave pursuit. The cavalry unit was intercepted by two cowboys from the Driskell ranch twelve miles to the west on Day Creek. The cowboys said their ranch had been raided at sunrise by Cheyennes who drove off a large number of horses.

From Kollar's, Little Wolf's warriors had moved on to the Driskell ranch, just east of the Fort Dodge–Camp Supply road in southern Clark County. Two Cheyennes approached the ranch headquarters at sunrise, apparently looking for horses. They were spotted and given chase by J. W. Berryman and two other Driskell men. The ranchmen knocked one of the raiders from his pony with a six-shooter and killed him. The cowboys galloped after the other Cheyenne, who led them over a hill where they found ten or twelve other warriors sitting on their horses. Now it was the cowboys' turn to flee, but the Cheyennes did not follow or fire at them.[10]

Hemphill headed for Driskell's place immediately, reaching it after dark. Early the next morning the cowboys proudly displayed the body of the dead Cheyenne to the troops before burying him.[11] The troop was now joined by ranchers Driskell and Day and eleven of their cowboys. These men, added to Hemphill, Leeper, the troops, and Chapman, gave the command an aggregate strength of sixty-two.

Chapman picked up the raiders' trail and led the troops on it until it became too dark to do so. After going into camp and lying on the trail all night with the horses still saddled, Company I continued on, moving at a trot when the terrain and clarity of the trail permitted. At midmorning a freshly abandoned Cheyenne camp was discovered by Chapman and his scouts. Pushing ahead, the troops spied a horseman in front of them riding at a gallop. Soon after, they found the warriors they were looking for.

It was a chilling sight. Suddenly, along a ridge in the brakes of Sand Creek, an estimated 75 to 100 warriors appeared before them deployed in a battle skirmish line. The Cheyennes had been taken by surprise, and their automatic reaction was to establish a protective front behind which their

women and children could move to safety. Fresh from their victory over the
two companies of Fort Reno cavalry, Little Wolf's men held no reservations
about engaging in combat with Hemphill's even smaller force of soldiers.
Holding to his orders to try to bring the Cheyennes in peaceably, Hemphill
continued to approach them without firing. But once the troops were within
600 to 800 yards, the Cheyenne opened fire. Hemphill responded by swerv-
ing off obliquely to the right, his men now returning fire.[12] In his report on
the affair, Leeper said Hemphill led in this direction and that and finally
moved to the rear in search of high ground on which to make a stand.
Leeper thought Hemphill's behavior appeared erratic and emboldened the
Cheyennes into attacking.[13]

Opting to fight on foot, Hemphill dismounted the company and formed
a skirmish line. After giving up men to guard the pack mules and every
fourth man to hold the horses, he was left with only thirty or so men as
combatants. Little Wolf's warriors carried the fight to the troops, advancing
and driving the skirmishers back. One soldier was severely wounded and
two Company I horses slightly so before Sgt. Samuel A. Trask and several
other troopers mounted a countercharge. Trask described the action that
followed:

> We pursued them back, continuing to fire as fast as we could on a gallop
> till the Indian skirmish line arrived back to their reserve, when they came
> together as if in council. Myself and party were within about 300 yards I
> judge of this body of Indians that came together. I was behind a little knoll
> and remained there a few minutes. I dismounted from my horse and fired
> into the crowd, and as soon as I fired the other men with me fired also,
> mounted. The Indians then deployed a line with greater numbers than
> before and swept down on us. I called out to the other men to retreat to
> the company and I mounted my horse and followed up. The Indians
> charged down on the company. I don't know the distance. When I arrived
> at the company it was formed behind a small rise on the prairie, and as the
> Indians came up they delivered a fire into them.[14]

Chapman, who had lost a leg fighting the Kiowas at Buffalo Wallow in
1874, saw that the Cheyennes were about to surround the troops. He warned
Hemphill that they were much too strong and would soon have the command corralled if it did not get out of there. Hemphill wisely formed his
company and galloped north to Bluff Creek with the Cheyennes following
for a short distance before turning back to their families. The wounded man
was left at Kollar's ranch to be picked up by an army ambulance and a
medical officer. Moving on to Fort Dodge, Hemphill reported to Lewis at
three o'clock the next morning. Lewis told him where to camp and ordered

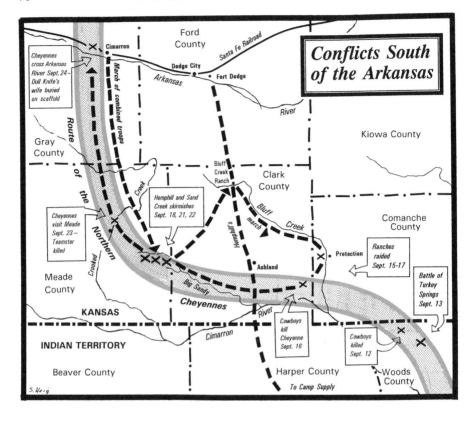

him to report back later. Hemphill's summary of the engagement again reflected the problems faced by cavalry in contesting entrenched Cheyenne
riflemen: "I tried to draw them [the Cheyennes] out, but did not succeed,
and as I could not get (after taking out my guard for the pack mules, and
No. 4s to hold the horses) over 30 or 32 men to fight over one hundred (100)
Indians, I withdrew, but not before having a skirmish with them lasting an
hour, they having the advantage of the ground."[15]

Little Wolf's account of this affair, as conveyed to George Bird Grinnell,
describes the Northern Cheyennes as moving across the prairie in search of
a place to camp when the soldiers appeared from the north. In typical fashion, the Cheyenne warriors quickly formed a defensive front ahead of the
women and children. The troops began firing, forming into one single cavalry attack line for a charge. The Cheyennes returned their fire, and after a
short battle the soldiers retreated back toward Dodge City.[16]

A newspaper story originating at Dodge City provided another account
of Hemphill's engagement:

The correspondent says the Driskell party, who left on Monday, have just returned. They, with a company of the 4th cavalry, under Capt. Hemphill, together seventy-seven strong, engaged with three hundred Indians thirty miles from Dodge at 12 o'clock Thursday. The Indians showed a degree of bravery never before displayed, and after a sharp fight drove the whites from the field. One soldier was mortally wounded. The Indian loss is unknown, but the scalp of one [undoubtedly that of the Cheyenne killed by the cowboys] was brought in.[17]

Another party of eighteen cattlemen—the posse Colcord had joined briefly—returned to Dodge City from the area to report that they had encountered 150 warriors well fortified among the rocks in the canyons of Sand Creek. They said the group waved blankets at them defiantly, daring the ranchmen to attack. But the ranchmen, who counted twenty-three camp-fires, quickly decided the Cheyennes were too much for them.[18] Returning to Dodge, the cowmen and a number of others met with Lewis and Hemphill at the fort. There they were given guns and ammunition from the 100 stand of arms that had just arrived from Kansas governor George T. Anthony.[19]

On September 17, Lewis dispatched a detail of forty-one men of the Nineteenth Infantry under Lt. Charles A. Vernon by rail westward from Fort Dodge to Pierceville with orders to intercept the Cheyennes if they attempted to cross the Arkansas River at that point. Two days later Company A, Sixteenth Infantry, arrived at Dodge on the Santa Fe from Fort Riley under the command of English-born Capt. Charles E. Morse, a Civil War veteran.

Lewis immediately ordered that unit along with Hemphill's Company I, Fourth Cavalry, to proceed by rail to Pierceville. They would be under the command of Morse, whose captain's rank preceded that of Hemphill. The cavalrymen and their horses were put aboard a special Santa Fe cattle train at Dodge City on the afternoon of September 19. Morse's company of infantry followed on another train soon after, its five heavy wagons and one ambulance taken apart and, along with mules and supplies, loaded onto another train. This same movement included thirty-five civilians eager to do some Indian fighting.[20]

Some of these were Dodge citizens; some were Driskell, Day, and Sheedy ranchmen; and some were from Colcord's cowman posse. At the Nelson ranch, Colcord had found a gathering of cowboys and ranchers telling stories of people being killed by Cheyennes, although no one knew just who had been killed. W. E. Iliff was among the Driskell-led group. He later recounted how he and seven others had ridden to Nelson's camp and joined the posse. After trailing the Cheyennes for some distance, the men had ridden into Dodge City.[21]

At Pierceville, Morse was met by Col. Charles H. Smith, who had arrived there to command Company D, Nineteenth Infantry. When Smith assured him that the Cheyennes had not crossed the Arkansas River at that point, Morse sent the train back up the line to Cimarron.[22]

Hemphill had already disembarked at Cimarron and on September 20 pushed south forty miles back to Crooked Creek in hopes of recontacting the Cheyennes. Morse and his infantry reassembled their wagons and followed behind. There on September 21, word came that 200 to 300 Cheyennes were still in force on Sand Creek. The entire command set off in that direction. En route, the cattlemen and Dodge City civilians implored Morse to separate the cavalry from the infantry and permit them to go on ahead to engage the warriors. In light of Hemphill's recent experience, Morse felt it was best to keep his command intact and refused to do so.[23]

At noon on September 21, the unit was joined by Fort Reno's Companies G and H, Fourth Cavalry, routed by the Cheyennes a week earlier at Turkey Springs. The beaten and discouraged troopers who had fervently hoped Camp Supply would mark the end of their pursuit were sorely disappointed. They would find they still had a long way to ride after a wiley and dangerous foe of whom they wanted no part.

12

Reluctant ANTAGONISTS

THERE HAD BEEN LITTLE REST OR RECUPERATION for the Fort Reno troops at Camp Supply. Although Rendlebrock and Gunther remained there with twenty-eight of the weariest men for another two days, Hambright put Wood, Wilder, and McDonald and forty men back in their saddles again on September 17—the day after their arrival. They were ordered to find Hemphill and take provisions to him.[1] Wood was the ranking officer and was in command as the detachment rode north to Cimarron ranch, arriving at dark.

The following day, with the idea that Hemphill could be somewhere to the east of the Dodge-Supply road, the troops scoured the country in that direction. Finding no sign of the Camp Supply command, Wood concluded that since Hemphill needed supplies, he had either returned to Camp Supply or gone on to Fort Dodge. That evening a courier arrived from Rendlebrock, who had been ordered into the field again by Lewis. He said he would arrive that night with the remainder of the Fort Reno command, which he did.[2]

At Bear Creek ranch, Rendlebrock learned of Hemphill's clash with the Cheyennes and that he had, as suspected, gone on to Fort Dodge. Rendlebrock decided to go there also. After a short march, however, he was met by a courier carrying orders for him to march to Sand Creek where the

Cheyennes were last seen. He turned in that direction and soon met Hemphill and Morse. Now the ranking officer, Rendlebrock assumed overall command of the combined force of cavalry, infantry, and cowmen.[3]

The Northern Cheyenne warriors were indeed still holding to the rugged ravines of Sand Creek. First contact came the evening of September 21. As the command was preparing night camp following the day's march, four or five cowboys rode on ahead to look for signs of the Cheyennes. They found more than signs, coming onto the rear guard of the Cheyennes, who began firing and driving the cowboys back toward the camp. Horses had been unsaddled and herded, supper was under way, and some members of Morse's company were fighting a prairie fire when the crack of firing was heard. Immediately, a general cry of "Indians!" went up through the camp.

When he heard the alarm, Rendlebrock's first thought was to secure the camp. He immediately ordered the wagon teams to be hitched up and horses resaddled. He directed Morse to post ten infantrymen on a skirmish line in front of the camp in the event of an attack, and pickets were established to the right and left. He looked up to see Company G, to which he had issued no orders, gallop past him out of camp. The troop had been eating, their horses grazing in a field across a small creek when the firing began. Wood, once again acting on his own, sent his company into action.

"We immediately saddled up our company," Company G 1st Sergeant Feely stated, "counted fours and moved by the right to the front."[4]

In exiting the camp, Wood galloped directly past Rendlebrock, ignoring him and making no effort to confer or ask for instructions as he plunged Company G into action. The troops soon found a sizable force of warriors driving the ranchmen back toward camp.[5] Wood dismounted his men on an opposing ridge and exchanged fire with the Cheyennes, who fell back to a hilltop and took up rifle positions. With his troops pinned down and unable to advance, he looked anxiously for reinforcements from the camp. He later described the action:

> I thought of charging them at first, but I had only about 20 fighting men
> and I thought it best to get the ridge they were on and examine the
> country beyond, while the command was coming up. This I did without
> any serious resistance and found them in prepared position on the opposite
> side of the cañon of Sand Creek, a rather deep and rugged ravine about
> 250 yds from my position.[6]

Seeing Wood depart, Rendlebrock ordered Hemphill with Company I to mount up and go out in support. Company H was held in reserve, mounted. Rendlebrock hurried forward on foot to the summit of a hill from which he could view the field of action and get a grasp of the situation.[7] Wood was angered when Company I stopped and took up a position to his rear rather than move forth to engage the Cheyennes.

"I afterwards learned that Hemphill's orders were to show himself in order that the Indians would not try to cut me off from camp," he complained to Hatch. "I was now 2 miles from camp, had the Indians in force in front and in a good position and if the command could join me, I thought the thing could be finished by dark. But I waited in vain until too late to accomplish anything when I withdrew, joined Hemphill and returned to camp after dark. I take no professional pride in this day's operation."[8]

"I've bucked against ten times stronger works many times with success," Wood would bluster later, forgetting that he had never met an Indian in combat. "I would have fought the whole force and whipped it too."[9]

But Wood had more of a problem than Rendlebrock realized at the time. When he led the Fort Reno detachment out of Camp Supply on September 17, Wood had overlooked a fundamental item of warfare. He had ordered the men to carry one day's ration in their saddlebags, but he had forgotten to have their ammunition supply replenished. Now in the midst of battle, the troopers of Company H were running out of bullets.

"They were borrowing ammunition on the line," Feely later testified. "They would run from one to another borrowing. One man went into camp mounted and brought out the cooks' ammunition—two bags."[10]

The troops remained in the field until the sun had set, then at ten P.M. withdrew, with Hemphill's Company I providing cover. Once all were back in camp, Rendlebrock ordered sleeping parties of eighteen men each to occupy posts 300 to 400 yards from the camp. He was distressed that to establish pickets he was forced to send 1st Sergeant Feely to the 1st sergeant of Captain Morse's infantry company to borrow a box of rifle ammunition. Forty rounds were distributed to each man.[11]

At sunset Rendlebrock ordered the troops to withdraw and return to camp. His refusal to engage his full complement of fighting men sorely vexed Wood, who insisted that the Cheyennes could have been whipped there and then. He later used this initial action at Sand Creek as a court-martial charge against Rendlebrock. Rendlebrock would find support from Gunther and others that the day was too far gone to effectively engage the warriors.[12] Wood was further displeased when Rendlebrock charged him with leaving camp without being ordered to do so.

"This I acknowledge," Wood admitted in reporting to General Hatch, "but our ranch followers had been attacked by the very enemy we were hunting for. I went out to protect these people and find the enemy; I did both, and chased the enemy into a position where I could not manage him, but if the command had come up, I believed then, and have not changed my mind since, that we could have beaten them easily before dark."[13]

At the start of the exchange of gunfire, the posse of ranchmen had retreated to a position behind Company G. When Feely suggested that they assist, the sergeant was told "that was not their style of fighting and [they] did not come up."[14]

Rendlebrock's inaction also peeved the ranchmen, all of whom felt his order to withdraw had permitted the Cheyennes to escape. To them, whipping the Cheyennes seemed simple. They had the Cheyennes surrounded, they had argued, and Rendlebrock should have sent to Fort Dodge for artillery to shell them into submission. But Rendlebrock dismissed the idea by saying the cavalry never considered bringing artillery out on the prairies to fight Indians.[15]

"It seemed as if the troops did not want to fight," Little Wolf observed later, "but they fired first."[16]

When morning came, it was soon discovered that the Cheyennes had moved, leaving a trail across to the south fork of Sand Creek (Little Sandy). The command followed six to seven miles with the Cheyennes in sight ahead, pausing on the way to bury a cowboy killed two days before.[17] They also crossed a trail the scouts said had been made by the Cheyenne women and children. Hemphill had a notion to follow it rather than pursue the warriors. He was unsure later whether the "squaw's trail" had even been called to Rendlebrock's attention.[18] Whichever the case was, the expedition may have missed its only hope of stopping the Cheyennes. The single thing that could have caused the Cheyenne warriors to capitulate—the army's most successful tactic in fighting warriors—would have been the capture of their women and children.[19]

The troops found that the Cheyennes had set up new defenses on the south side of the small stream behind a rock-lined bluff that provided them with a natural breastwork. Rendlebrock halted his cavalry troops on the edge of a plateau along the opposing bank three-quarters of a mile from the Cheyennes and waited for the infantry and wagons to come up. When the wagons and horses were corralled safely, one detachment of ten foot soldiers was ordered to move up an arroyo to the right; they were later reinforced by ten cavalrymen. Seeing no results from that direction, Rendlebrock sent Wilder to check on the detachment's progress. Wilder found the men had not moved from the point where they had entered the arroyo. He repeated Rendlebrock's orders and left. But later he saw that the men were still not moving forward and went to them again. This time he managed to prod them a short distance farther up.[20]

Meanwhile, another ten troopers under Sergeant Feely had been sent up a defile to the left, and twenty-five cavalrymen and some of the ranchmen were formed into a skirmish line in the center.

"I was ordered to get as near as possible to where the Indians were digging rifle pits," Feely said. "I went to the head of the ravine and the Indians opened fire on us and I remained there till called in by an orderly in the evening."[21]

The Cheyennes' position on the rocky bluff was strong, and their defensive rifle pits were well placed. Despite this, the infantry led by Captain Morse and 1st Lt. Gregory Barrett, Tenth Infantry, advanced in a curved line at the front, keeping up a constant fire that eventually drove the Cheyennes back from their breastwork to a "regularly laid stone structure about 40 feet long and about 4½ feet high."[22] There Little Wolf's men ensconced themselves even more solidly than before and prevented the infantry from advancing further. McDonald described the fortification:

> They had rifle pits and on the perpendicular side in [the] rear there were small places large enough for one person to crawl into and they were strong and protected from every side. The Indians were prepared for us. The north side could not have been attacked. From the south side there was sloping ground down to the creek and the bed of the creek was marshy and the bottom about 200 yards wide.[23]

Rendlebrock discussed the matter of making a cavalry charge with Hemphill. The Company I commander replied that he thought it would take a whole regiment to get the Cheyennes out of there.[24] But Wood was far from satisfied with the lack of aggressive action. By his account, Rendlebrock came to him seeking advice, and he gave it. He claimed he told Rendlebrock that he would move the infantry as close to the Cheyennes as possible and then charge with the cavalry. Rendlebrock denied such a conversation, saying: "I would not seek advice from him. I presume it was the first time he ever fought Indians."[25]

The troops held their positions through the day with only sporadic firing exchanged with the Cheyennes, although at long range with no apparent effect on either side. Many of the cavalry troops took the opportunity to nap behind the protective ridges. Occasionally, a trooper would have a comrade hold his horse while he went to the skirmish line to take a shot at the Cheyennes, "either for the fun of the thing, or to see how his carbine performed."[26] The cavalrymen complained that the rifle ammunition with its heavier infantry powder load was causing their carbines to kick.[27]

Around 3:30 P.M. Rendlebrock ordered Wilder to make a circuit of the Cheyennes' position to see if more could be learned about their strength and

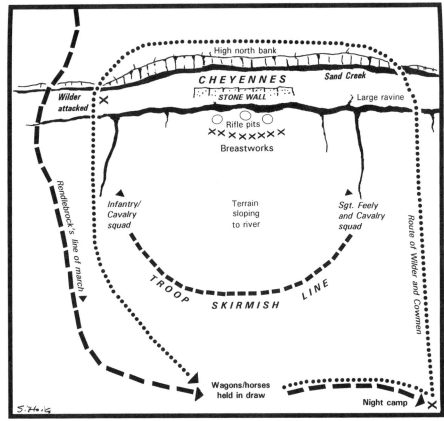

Schematic Plan of September 22 Skirmish
Based on field sketches

position. Riding out with fourteen men, Wilder met thirty ranchmen headed by J. S. Driskell. The men were looking for water. Wilder detoured from his assignment and joined in the search. Water was found within a mile of the battle scene, whereupon the cowmen joined Wilder's party. In crossing the stream below the Cheyennes' position, Wilder could see only a few mounted warriors and no other stock. He concluded that this was only a portion of the warriors left to delay the troops while the remainder of their entourage moved on.

His orders were only to "make a demonstration with nothing definite as to its purpose or extent," so Wilder gave no thought to attacking the Cheyennes from their rear. He decided that by galloping rapidly along the high bank opposite the Cheyennes' position at 600 to 700 yards distance, he could divert their fire from the attack at their front without great danger. Two of the cavalry horses were wounded during the dash, but they were not disabled.[28]

Beyond the Cheyennes' position, Wilder turned his command of troopers and cowmen back across the stream. At this point a group of mounted warriors charged Wilder's party from the river's ravine and attempted to cut it off from the command. The Cheyennes were driven back, although in his report on the affair Wilder complained that "as soon as the first shots were fired the 'cow boys' scattered."[29] The troopers and cowmen managed to make their way back to the command safely, even though the two mounts were wounded. This was the only close action for the cavalry that day. Rendlebrock later sniffed at Wilder's performance, saying: "I sent Lt. Wilder to get some information on the strength and position of the Indians but he went around flying and hardly saw an Indian and I got no information from him."[30]

Wood was even more critical of Rendlebrock. The lieutenant was convinced that the officer had passed up the best opportunity the command would have to do serious battle with the Cheyennes. He later complained:

> We had three companies of cavalry, numbering probably over 100 men and one company of infantry numbering 38 men—in all, at least 140 soldiers besides the cow men. These latter could not be depended upon unless they were cornered. With such a force and such a position to start from, I was morally certain that we could have ruined those Indians. Not only that, the weather was good, the ground was perfectly dry, and we had nearly all day for it, in comparatively open country. There was no time when this affair arose to the dignity of a fight.[31]

On this day, September 22, Rendlebrock received a message from Colonel Lewis at Fort Dodge, dated September 20. Lewis instructed Rendlebrock, "If you cannot whip the Indians try to hang on their trail and delay them. Give me full information that you can get."[32] Rendlebrock later argued that this communication now placed him under the orders of Lewis, superseding Mizner's original instructions. He clearly did not believe he could whip the warriors with inexperienced troops who were not eager to meet the Cheyennes in mortal combat. He later contended that had he charged the Cheyennes at Sand Creek he would have lost half his men, and the rest would have been massacred.[33] McDonald agreed, stating that the Cheyennes held a very strong position and that it would have been impossible to charge them because of the perpendicular bank in front of them.[34] Cowman Driskell also supported this evaluation, saying he did not think it would have been possible to attack the Cheyennes at Sand Creek without great loss and that the warriors had better arms than the cavalry, although not better than the infantry.[35]

Firing continued until about 4:30 P.M. when Rendlebrock notified his officers that he was going to move the camp to a location that offered a supply of water and wood.[36] The infantry troops were withdrawn from their combat positions and used as flankers to cover the movements of the wagon train and cavalry units. The Cheyennes provided them with a departing salvo, but no damage was done.

The command was suffering a shortage of both ammunition and food. Although the ranchmen had supplied a beef or two, the cavalry had been feeding them otherwise, and the rations of the companies were running very low. Rendlebrock gave the last piece of bread in his personal mess to a cowboy who complained that he could no longer get food from the companies.[37]

That evening Rendlebrock sent a letter to Lewis at Fort Dodge giving a brief account of the day's action and requesting supplies: "We are much in need of ammunition and rations on account of the cow men who eat with the companies and are poorly provided for. Please send them as soon as possible to our present encampment. No subsistence [meaning beef] has been found in the country."[38]

It was nearly noon the next day, September 23, before the military unit reformed and marched back to its camp of the previous day where Rendle-brock had instructed the supplies from Fort Dodge to be sent. As most had suspected, the Cheyennes were no longer there. They had slipped away once more, leaving behind thirty or so horses plus a drove of sheep a raiding party had herded off from the nearby S. B. Williams ranch on Sand Creek.[39]

Lt. John Harold arrived from Fort Dodge, escorting a supply train that brought ammunition, horseshoes, and foodstuff.[40] W. E. Iliff with the cowboy posse later charged that Rendlebrock rested in camp one day, in part to bake bread.[41]

Another contentious issue arose between Rendlebrock and Wood when the latter recommended that Lewis should be sent a letter advising him that the Cheyennes intended to turn north and cross the Arkansas River west of Dodge City. Rendlebrock rejected the action, saying he had already reported back to Lewis when Harold returned to Fort Dodge. He declared that he had information—probably from Harold, since that was the strategy of his departmental headquarters at the time—that the infantry from Fort Lyon and Fort Dodge was watching the Arkansas River and that Third Cavalry units were scouting eastern Colorado. Some of the guides had told him the Cheyennes might go up the Cimarron and cross it in eastern Colorado because there were some sheep ranches there the Indians could clean out.[42]

"No one could tell," Rendlebrock insisted, "which way the Indians would go from Sand Creek."[43]

Even as the Cheyenne warriors were delaying Rendlebrock's command, their main body arrived at the small settlement of Meade Center, Kansas, on Crooked Creek. The settlement, founded just the previous summer, consisted of only eight or ten settlers with fewer than five houses. A citizen named Cook first saw a small party of Cheyennes approaching. The dozen or so tribesmen formed a circle within a hundred yards around the town. Then the remainder of the band appeared and invaded the settlement. The settlers were caught entirely by surprise. Without horses and poorly armed, they had no chance of escape. They were much relieved to find the Cheyennes were disposed to be friendly.

A chief (unnamed) rode up before a citizen known as Captain French and threw his hat to the ground before him. This opened a parley between the two. The chief asked for something to eat and was supplied with two quarters of beef, a sack of flour, coffee, and other provisions. The beef was cooked as breakfast for the tribespeople. Frank Hough, a resident of Meade City, believed the townspeople were not harmed because "we invited them in and treated them as nice as possible and tried to make them believe we were not afraid of them."[44]

The Cheyennes had no fear of the townspeople. "They took everything they could lay their hands on," Hough claimed. "A crowd got around me and went through my pockets. They stole everything we had about the town except a ¼ of a beef we had about. They compelled me to grind their knives on the grind stones which I did without protest."[45]

Before leaving, the chief shook hands all around, then gave a signal and the body of warriors moved off. Only after they were gone did the Meade residents discover the body of Washington O'Conner in his wagon, killed by a stab wound in his neck. The Meade City settlers, sad but relieved at their own fate, buried him nearby.

George W. Brown added to the story of his friend O'Conner, telling of the latter's departure from Dodge City just prior to returning home to Meade City: "That same day two of my neighbors came to Dodge City; one was Bud Wilson, the other Wash Connor. I asked him if they had any guns and he said they had not. Bud Wilson got home all right; Connor lived three miles west. He got to within three-quarters of a mile of home, when the Indians killed him."[46]

The easily followed Cheyenne trail led west from Sand Creek before it turned due north at Meade. On September 24 the command marched forty miles to make camp on Crooked Creek. Just after sundown two sheepmen came to the camp to say they had seen the Cheyenne cavalcade—women, children, and all—pass by and had counted over 200 members. On September 25 the command marched twenty-five miles to reach the Arkansas River four miles west of Cimarron station. The troops forded the river at noon and went into camp on the north bank near Cimarron station.[47]

The Cheyennes had crossed the Arkansas River at the same place the day before, a day during which a hot, dusty gale blew so fiercely from the south that it was difficult to see or walk against it.[48] By that evening, as the Cheyennes skirted the head of Pawnee Creek and moved into Scott County, the wind had switched to the north, bringing a nighttime rainstorm and much cooler air. The wind and rain were far more disturbing to the pursuing troops than to the fleeing Cheyennes, whose widespread trail across the countryside was otherwise easy to follow.

Not long after the Cheyennes and troops had crossed the Arkansas and moved on, an elderly Cheyenne woman was found buried on a makeshift scaffold suspended above the ground on two poles four miles west of Cimarron station and two miles north of the river. Her body had been wrapped in two blankets and covered with a buffalo robe. This was likely Little Woman, the wife of Dull Knife, who according to Ben Clark was killed in camp one night when a horse trampled her as she slept.[49]

When scout Thomas Donald had arrived at Camp Supply following the Turkey Springs fight, Hambright sent a courier galloping north to Lewis at Fort Dodge with news of the engagement. This was relayed by telegraph to General Pope at Fort Leavenworth. Pope immediately notified Sheridan of the situation and itemized the troop resources available to him in stopping the Cheyennes.[50]

Although the Fort Reno troops had not been successful, Pope said, he looked for better results when they were joined by Hemphill. He was also counting on four companies of infantry under Lewis at Fort Dodge, plus another soon to arrive from Fort Riley and two from Fort Lyon, Colorado. Additionally, Lt. Col. Richard I. Dodge was being sent from Fort Hays with two companies of infantry and another company from Riley to guard the Kansas Pacific Railroad at Monument and Buffalo stations. Three mounted infantry companies and two more unmounted companies would be on the lookout from Fort Wallace. If Lewis failed to stop the Cheyennes at the Arkansas, he was instructed to follow them and join up with the troops along the rail line. There they could be moved into place with steam locomotives.[51] On September 20 Pope again wired Sheridan:

> You may count upon my using every effort and all the means I have to stop the Indians and capture them. Lewis has at his disposal along the Arkansas something over two hundred and fifty men, one half cavalry on the Kansas Pacific Road between Buffalo Station and Wallace and at Wallace are two hundred and fifty men, about one hundred of them mounted infantry.[52]

Pope also ordered Lewis to rush a soldier courier to General Hatch at Fort Elliott with an urgent request for two additional companies of Fourth Cavalry. Hambright, however, had written Hatch on September 18 to tell of Rendlebrock's engagement, adding: "I deem it most important that I should have at least one company of Cavalry from your command, and more if you can spare them, to be sent here with all dispatch."[53] Thus, even as the Fort Dodge courier was galloping south, Capt. Clarence Mauck was already marching north from Elliott with Companies B and F.

On September 20 Hambright dispatched a Cheyenne courier to Mizner with a report on the situation as known there. Hambright said he had heard nothing more from Rendlebrock. He had, however, received unofficial word from Fort Dodge that Hemphill had experienced a brush with the Cheyennes. He told also of smoke signals being seen both north and south of Camp Supply and said cattle herders had reported seeing small parties of Cheyennes herding shod horse and mules northward seven to ten miles east of the post.[54]

Although Hambright had asked for the troops to be sent with dispatch, Mauck and his two troops made an unhurried three-day march up the road the Lee and Reynolds firm had established along Wolf Creek to Camp Supply, arriving September 22.[55] There Hambright informed him of Pope's orders to join the pursuit of the Cheyennes. With new urgency, Mauck and his men galloped rapidly to Fort Dodge, where he reported to Lewis. Fate would soon bring them into conflict again with the same Northern Cheyennes whose village they had attacked on the Red Fork in November 1876.

Grinnell's interviews with Little Wolf provide an account of the Sand Creek fight from the Cheyenne side. Following their initial encounter, the Cheyennes had continued on their way and were moving up a narrow canyon when their scouts spotted the soldiers returning, this time with wagons. The band took refuge among some rock-strewn bluffs along Sand Creek, digging rifle pits along the ridges. From there they could see the soldiers place their wagons in a circle. Little Wolf said the troops and wagons, of which there were thirty or more, made the soldier force look very big.[56]

In the morning the Cheyennes attacked. According to Little Wolf, the warriors made a mounted charge down the hill and routed the cowboys (undoubtedly Wilder's detachment). But Little Wolf decided there were too many soldiers to fight and that he and his people must continue their flight to the north country.

13

Ambush at
PUNISHED WOMAN'S FORK

L IEUTENANT COLONEL LEWIS, AN 1849 GRADUATE OF WEST POINT, had fought in the Florida Seminole wars. Although born in Alabama, his family had moved to Sandy Hill, New York, in 1856, and he had remained loyal to the Union during the Civil War. While serving with the Fifth U.S. Infantry out of Fort Union, New Mexico, he had been largely responsible for the defeat of the Texas Confederate Army in the Battle of Apache Canyon by circling around the mountains and capturing the Rebels' rear guard and transportation. He was awarded a brevet major promotion for that action and later won another brevet for gallantry at Peralta, New Mexico. Lewis obtained his regular army rank of lieutenant colonel in December 1873 after having served throughout much of the West. He commanded at Camp Supply before transferring to Fort Dodge. Lewis had only recently returned from a temporary assignment in New Mexico and was ill with dysentery when he received orders from General Pope to take charge of the pursuing troops when they reached the vicinity of Dodge.[1]

Earlier, after talking with Amos Chapman at Fort Dodge, Lewis had written a letter to General Pope expressing his dismay at the conditions the Northern Cheyennes had endured at Darlington. The letter was reprinted in various newspapers and exerted some influence on the public attitude regarding the Cheyennes. It also supported War Department criticism of the Indian Bureau's handling of the Cheyennes.[2]

Despite his disability, Lewis had entrained from Dodge City to Pierceville on September 24 with one company of Nineteenth Infantry and Mauck's two troops of Fourth Cavalry. From there he wired Pope that his scouts had located the trail of the Cheyennes with 150 ponies northeast of Pierceville and that he expected soon to join forces with Rendlebrock. Pope in turn informed Sheridan of the expected junction, optimistically concluding that "their combined force should be ample to end the matter. At the worst [it] is scarcely possible Indians can cross [the] line of [the] Kansas Pacific railroad."[3]

Lewis met Rendlebrock at Cimarron station and assumed command of the consolidated force, now composed of Mauck's Companies B and F; Rendlebrock's Companies G and H, Fourth Cavalry; Hemphill's Company I, Fourth Cavalry; and Fort Dodge's Company D, Nineteenth Infantry, under Capt. James H. Bradford. Both Hemphill, a Virginian, and Bradford of Delaware were breveted Civil War veterans who had risen from the ranks. Amos Chapman led seven other scouts, one a Pawnee. They would keep the command on the Cheyenne trail, search for water, and forewarn the expedition of danger.[4]

Two of Captain Morse's heavy wagons had broken down. Much to his chagrin, at the Arkansas Lewis ordered him to turn one of his wagons over to Rendlebrock, one to Hemphill, and another to Bradford and take his company by train back to Fort Dodge.[5]

Lewis's force took up pursuit of the Cheyennes again on September 26, the easily followed a fifty-foot-wide trail leading to the north across the Kansas prairie. The scouts rode at the front, followed by an advance guard of thirty cavalrymen. Then came Lewis and his staff officers at the head of the four companies of cavalry in columns of two. Lumbering along at the rear were the wagons carrying the support equipment and provisions and, at times, soldiers of Bradford's infantry unit. It was not easy to choose between marching or riding in the jolting, springless wagons, which, Bradford noted, was extremely hard on his infantrymen.[6]

Lieutenant Wood had been placed in charge of the wagon train with orders to keep it close to the column. "This order was complied with," he later commented sourly, "as nearly as it was possible to coerce mule flesh into such [an] arrangement."[7]

A 31-mile march took the command to Pawnee Fork, where it halted to eat and rest before moving on to a dry camp that evening. The following day, much-appreciated water was found at a small lake on the prairie. After a noontime rest stop there, the column proceeded on, crossing Ladder Creek as it ran eastward before bending sharply north. There a campsite with many abandoned fires was discovered. Scout George W. Brown, who had hunted buffalo in western Kansas, later claimed he scratched about in the ashes of a campfire and found some still glowing willow embers that indicated recent occupancy of the site. Wilder, however, said they judged from the campfires that the Cheyennes were at least four hours ahead.[8] Ensuing action by Lewis was apparently based on the latter estimate.

The command approached a westerly branch of Ladder Creek known to the Cheyennes as Punished Woman's Fork. The two streams joined a short distance below the historic site of El Quartelejo, where a New Mexico Pueblo tribe had sought to escape Spanish domination and persecution around 1640. The name Punished Woman's Fork, so the Cheyennes told Seventh Cavalry officer Heber M. Creel who was assigned to study their language, came originally from the Cheyennes' use of the stream as a punishing ground for an unfaithful Cheyenne woman. The incident was said to have taken place long before the Anglo-Americans arrived. To punish her, the Dog Soldiers gave the woman up to all of the band. Afterward the tribe would wait until they arrived there to chastise any woman guilty of infidelity.[9]

It was approaching 4:45 P.M. as Lewis led his columns forward up the river valley. The scouts were 200 to 300 yards ahead, followed by Officer of the Day Hemphill and the advance guard, made up of men selected from the various units. Lewis was accompanied by his aide, 2nd Lt. Cornelius Gardener, a Netherlands-born West Pointer from Michigan. Mauck and Gunther rode at the head of the column behind the guard. The order of the five cavalry companies was G, commanded by Rendlebrock; H, under Gunther and McDonald; I, temporarily led by Leeper; F, under 2nd Lt. Alexander M. Patch, a West Pointer from Pennsylvania; and B, under New York West Pointer 2nd Lt. John W. Martin. Bradford's infantry unit was still in the rear with the wagons.[10]

Lewis halted his command at the bank of the stream. The Cheyenne trail he had been following now descended with considerable abruptness into a long, wide valley that over eons had been chiseled out of the prairie by perennial flooding of the stream. Through his binoculars, Lewis scanned the countryside ahead. From his point of entry on the elevated south bank, he held a commanding view of the valley and its adjacent bluffs for well over a mile ahead. A thick, serpentine rim of white caprock outlined the river basin, separating it from the treeless, mounded bluffs beyond. In places along the east bank, the harsh flows of past floods had produced sheer cliffs that towered over the normally gentle, tree-lined channel. Below the west rim, however, the bank sloped down to a wide, sandy flat that was clearly the choice for passage up the valley. Seeing no sign of the Cheyennes or any threatening movement whatever, Lewis motioned for the command to move forward. He and his principal officers followed the party of scouts and the advance guard down onto the floor of the valley where the Cheyenne trail extended northward along the left bank.

Lewis's party had advanced only a few hundred yards into the canyon when word came that the wagon train was finding it difficult to cross a hillside ravine. Accordingly, he ordered his bugler to sound the dismount call, and Mauck was instructed to go back to see that the train got safely down the hill.[11] Troopers all along the line were pleased to comply after having ridden forty miles that day. The men and officers took the opportunity to sit or stretch out on the soft sand and grass of the riverbank.[12]

At this vantage point, Lewis could not see that the terrain of Punished Woman's Fork proffered the makings of a classic Cheyenne entrapment. Ahead of the command, the northward-flowing channel of the stream made a ninety-degree bend to the east. At the apex of the bend another canyon cut in from the northwest. This gorge, where the main fighting would take place, eventually became known as Battle Canyon. It was composed of two dry-bedded forks, the principal one split at the far end and the smaller, secondary fork lying perpendicular to the larger one near its mouth. As these ravines narrowed to a closure at their far end, their banks became increasingly sheer and pocked with large boulders that had broken off from the caprock.

From Lewis's position, the entrance to the canyon was not discernible and, moreover, it was impossible to know that it was boxed at the extremities except for a hidden, narrow inlet. Lewis pushed ahead down the valley, not suspecting that the Cheyennes were waiting for him to follow their clear tracks along the sandy river bottom into the chasm. While both the main command and the advance guard were dismounted, Chapman and his small cadre of scouts proceeded ahead on the Cheyennes' distinct trail. They reached Battle Canyon, where once past the jutting entrance abutment they suddenly had an unobstructed view into the canyon. The scouts looked up from the tracks they were following to discover that the ravine was filled with Cheyenne ponies grazing among the boulders and scant brush. As the men suddenly realized they had ridden virtually into the lap of the enemy they sought, Cheyenne riflemen hidden behind the rocks along the entrance to the canyon opened fire.[13]

"The troops, suspecting nothing," one observer reported, "entered the [main river] cañon, and but for a glimpse of danger by the scouts would have fallen into the trap. Seeing the failure of their plans, the Indians opened fire on the head of the column."[14]

Little Wolf's strategy was to position his main fighting force among the rocks and cutbacks of the canyon, draw the troops into it, and then close the trap with riflemen posted along the canyon walls. The women and children, meanwhile, had been cloistered in a cavelike overhang at the far end of the main branch of the canyon, protected by warriors in rifle pits above and in front. The Cheyennes fortified themselves along its entrance and sides and waited for the troops to approach.[15]

With bullets whizzing past them, Chapman and the other scouts jerked their horses about and spurred them in hard gallop back toward the command. Immediately behind them, a party of thirty to thirty-five whooping Cheyennes spurted out of the canyon in hot pursuit, driving along the mid-shelf of the bank advantageously above the troops.[16] Simultaneously, other snipers began firing at the advance guard from atop the bluffs along the west bank. All along the extended line of cavalry that had been relaxing on the valley floor sudden panic and pandemonium ensued.

It was immediately clear that the command had been caught flat-footed on the open floor of Punished Woman's Fork in a totally indefensible and dangerous position. With the recent experiences with the Cheyennes fresh in their minds, the immediate response of recruits, noncoms, and officers alike was to escape the onslaught and seek protection. The entire command jumped to their feet and scrambled to remount. By common impulse they headed for cover, no one standing forth in the valley to resist the attack. A number of the horses bolted and galloped off, leaving their riders precariously afoot in the face of the Cheyenne onslaught.

At the first sound of gunfire, someone—Lieutenant McDonald said it was Hemphill—yelled out "To the bluffs!" It immediately became a general call.[17] For many, the bluffs were interpreted to mean the heights back up the canyon to the rear. As a result, most of the command fled in individual disarray up the valley to a dry rivulet that cut into the canyon entrance from the west just below the wagon train that was still struggling down the hillside. A few troopers followed their officers up the sloping west bank below the Cheyenne snipers, some taking defensive positions behind knolls and in the rain-cut gulches along the sides of the bluffs.

One of the horses that bolted and ran away was the black charger of the sixty-year-old Rendlebrock. Not only was he the oldest person in the expedition, but he was further impeded by bad feet and a heavy overcoat he had no time to shed. Horseless and with his command fleeing ahead of him, he was left on his own to run for his life ahead of the oncoming Cheyennes. The

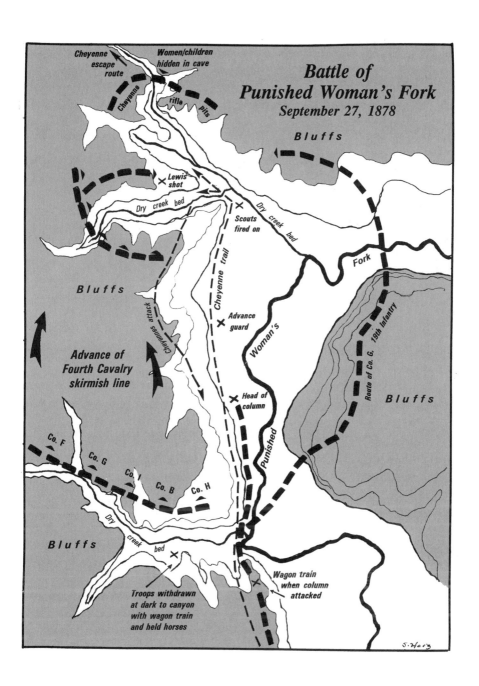

Battle of
Punished Woman's Fork
September 27, 1878

distance from his position at the head of the column to the wagon train was 400 yards, a daunting physical feat he could never have accomplished in other than a dire emergency. "The Indians came very near [to] getting me that day," Rendlebrock later confided to Gunther.[18]

Indeed, the attacking war party pursued the retreating troops well up the canyon, coming so close that one of Gunther's men who was also afoot was nearly snatched up and carried off. The military expedition was severely bewildered and disorganized by the Cheyenne attack—Gunther said it was stampeded—and none of the companies was immediately able to regroup with their full roster of men. For a time the officers as well had no plan of organized resistance, each reacting on his own until Lewis finally managed to restore military order. At the onset of the attack, Gunther, whose Company H was second in the column, quickly remounted and with a portion of his men charged for the bluffs on the left. When he reached a crevice, Gunther ordered the troops to dismount and deploy defensively. This done, they began firing at the attacking Cheyenne party in the valley.[19]

"It proved to be a fine and courageous thing because the Indians were rushing for the same point," McDonald later observed of Gunther's action, "and it was a race between us who should get there first."[20]

McDonald, also of Company H, had been lying facedown when he heard the firing to the front. Rolling over, he saw the Cheyennes driving toward the troops from the far end of the west bluff. The warriors were firing rapidly down at the scouting party and advance guard, which were retreating in great confusion back to the main command, while snipers on the bluffs were shooting at the main command itself.[21] McDonald quickly mounted his horse, joining Gunther and some men of their company in a charge for an arroyo that sliced into the side of the bluffs. Along with seven troopers, he ran forward to another small defile where they set up a fire at a party of Cheyennes galloping up the slopes in an attempt to gain the heights above the column. McDonald and his squad put up a brisk barrage that forced the Cheyennes to wheel their ponies about and return to their rock fortifications in Battle Canyon.

Other Cheyenne parties, however, had infiltrated the broken terrain atop the bluffs and were firing at whatever target presented itself. Lewis took charge in the dry creek bed, working to reorganize the now dismounted cavalry troops for a countermove against the Cheyennes. Troopers, summoned into formation by their company commanders, hastily grabbed their carbines and turned their mounts over to horse holders to be led to the rear.[22]

Prior to the attack, Lieutenant Patch had ridden forward from his position at the back of the column to join the group of officers collected at the

Valley of Punished Woman's Fork where Lewis's command was attacked by Northern Cheyennes under Little Wolf. Author photo.

front. He had dismounted when he heard the rapid firing and spied the Cheyennes chasing the scouts and advance party toward him. He saw more warriors on his left and front. Quickly remounting, he hurried back to his unit where his 1st sergeant had already ordered his men into their saddles and into sets of fours. Leading his company, Patch charged up the steep slope of the west bank where other Cheyennes had appeared in an evident attempt to surround the column. After crossing over two knolls, he found a safe place to dismount, ordered the horses taken to the rear, and with the help of his 1st and 2nd sergeants hastily formed a skirmish line. He and his men united with the line Lewis had established and moved forward across several rises "until one was gained whose elevation slightly commanded the bluff where the heaviest fire of the Indians was coming from."[23]

Lieutenant Martin, whose company held the rear position of the cavalry column, had also been lying on the ground at the head of his Company B when he heard the firing and looked up to see the Cheyennes driving along the west bluffs. As he was deciding what to do, one of his horses was struck by a bullet. Fearing that the Cheyennes might be headed for the wagon train, Martin yelled orders for his company to remount and led them to the

One of several Cheyenne rifle pits still overlooking Battle Canyon today. Author photo.

bluffs beyond the dry creek bed. There he and his men dismounted, secured their horses in a sheltered cove, and joined the other companies that were regrouping as skirmishers in the dry creek bed.[24]

The Cheyennes were clearly attempting to capture the high ground and surround the command in the valley, and Lewis's immediate objective was to establish control of the bluffs. In the safety of the dry wash, he worked to regroup the disarrayed troops, some of whom did not immediately rejoin their company.[25] He ordered the skirmishers to push forward and clear the heights. Accordingly, the four companies of dismounted cavalry formed two long, irregular skirmish lines. One line pushed out along the heights of the west bank, sweeping to the north until it eventually swung back eastward to Battle Canyon. The other advanced along the rim of the bluffs along Punished Woman's Fork, the two eventually uniting and taking up firing positions opposite the Cheyenne rifle positions across Battle Canyon.[26]

The skirmishers advanced cautiously up across the barren, shale-covered mounds of the west bank. No opposition was encountered until the line reached a draw less than 200 feet from the entrance to the canyon. There the troops began receiving heavy fire from points where Little Wolf and his men were well established behind boulders and in rifle pits along

Bluffs (at top) over which Fourth Cavalry troops advanced against entrenched Cheyennes at Punished Woman's Fork. Author photo.

the side of the canyon and atop its rock-rimmed bluffs. According to Lieutenant Martin, the Cheyennes had fortified themselves with "sixteen circular breastworks on the highest surrounding points which commanded the approaches on every side."[27]

The circle of stones, some of which still exist today, placed the troop-held heights across the canyon well within the firing range of Cheyenne riflemen. For Lewis's men, the crests of the mounds provided virtually the only protection against the Cheyennes' fire; beyond them the terrain leading to the rim of the bluffs was void of cover. Lewis, who along with Mauck had remained mounted to better command the troops, was even more visible.

Meanwhile, Mauck sent orders to the wagon train for Bradford to take his company of Nineteenth Infantry to the bluffs on the east side of the creek valley. Bradford did so, marching his men across the waist-deep channel of Punished Woman's Fork to the high cliff bank opposite the point where the head of the column had been at the onset of the Cheyennes' attack. The position, however, was too distant for their fire to be effective. At Mauck's suggestion, Lewis ordered them on ahead. The unit recrossed the stream and took up a position on a ridge that would become known as the Devil's Backbone.[28]

Mauck ordered McDonald to collect the cavalry horses and shelter them against any effort by the Cheyennes. The officer had the horses driven into a small ravine that cut into the dry creek bed from the south. From there the mounts were taken in small numbers to the creek to be watered. Some troopers led as many as twelve horses at a time while other soldiers conducted guard for the operation. Canteens were filled and sent forward to the skirmish line.[29]

The Cheyennes put up a fierce defense of their rocky fortification, and blistering fire was exchanged across the canyon. Little Wolf said that when the fight was over, the ground was stripped bare of grass where the bullets had torn it up.[30] The skirmish line faltered when the troops hesitated to advance closer to the coverless rim of the canyon. During the resulting stalemate, an exchange of rifle fire took place at long distance. There was little confirmed effect from this, although one participant claimed otherwise.

"The troops soon took possession of the adjoining hills," a correspondent to the *Leavenworth Daily Times* stated, "and succeeded in drawing the Indians from several of the pits, who running from pit to pit were shot by the soldiers, but their bodies were in every instance dragged in by their friends."[31]

With evening shadows of late September growing long and darkness approaching, the troops were hesitant to advance beyond the protecting crests of the bluffs. Lewis became impatient to push forward. He took personal charge and led a portion of Company B around the first branch of the split canyon and began moving up to the point between the two defiles. Riding to the front of the skirmish line on the high ground, he waved his sword and urged the men to press on. He was within 150 yards of the Cheyennes' positions when his horse was shot in the thigh.

"I urged the Colonel to dismount," Gardener reported, "for it seemed they were shooting at him, his horse having already been shot in the thigh. He said that he would do no good on foot, for walking was difficult there."[32]

Instead of dismounting, Lewis ordered Gardener to go back to the train, find any stragglers, and send them forth to their units. As Gardener headed off, two Fourth Cavalry troopers helped Lewis from his wounded animal. Feeling little could be accomplished by moving closer to the untraversable chasm that divided the troops and the Cheyennes, the troopers urged Lewis not to expose himself to the warriors' fire so readily.[33] Lieutenant Martin witnessed the action that followed:

> His horse had just been wounded and two soldiers were trying to hold it while he dismounted. Seeing this I ordered the company to advance and

joined him myself as quickly as possible. He ordered me to go back and bring some men forward, which I did and we took up a position behind a ridge about a hundred and fifty yards from where the main body of the Indians was, and within the first line they had fortified having in our rear one or two of the stone breastworks from which we had driven them. About a hundred yards in front was the nearest stone breastwork which they held. We had been in this position about ten minutes, Col. Lewis had taken a carbine from one of the men and fired several shots. While endeavoring to obtain a shot he exposed himself very incautiously and was shot through the upper part of the leg, the shot coming from the breastwork in front of us. I attempted to stop the bleeding by twisting a revolver in a buckskin thong tied above the wound.[34]

"I saw him rise up on his knees and fire into the breastworks in his front," Mauck stated. "While in this position he received his wound. I saw him fall over, and Lt. Martin assisting him to bind up his wound, and carry him down in the ridge and out of reach of fire. I went to see him and saw that he was severely wounded and had lost a great deal of blood."[35]

Lewis dealt with his wound coolly. "I guess it is all over with me," he observed to those bending over him.[36]

Asst. Surg. William B. Davis, a young army doctor with the expedition, was several hundred yards away with the wagon train when he was notified that Lewis had been wounded. Because the country was so rough, it took him about twenty minutes to reach the officer. By then the hemorrhage had stopped. The officer was carried about 300 yards to the army ambulance, where he was attended to. Davis removed the compress and administered stimulants and beef tea to keep Lewis alive.

Lewis was shot at around six o'clock. By virtue of rank, Mauck now assumed overall command. As dusk approached, he became concerned that the situation of the troops facing one another across the canyon 200 yards apart might cause the units to catch one another's fire. Some of Patch's Company F men complained when shots were fired over their heads from behind. Patch found Hemphill's company situated in the skirmish line to his rear and slightly to the right. Patch withdrew his men to the same line.[37]

Extremely fatigued, Rendlebrock had rested at the wagon train for nearly an hour before ordering a new horse brought up for him. He rode forward to the nearest point of the skirmish line, finding a part of his own company scattered among others on the right. He had joined those troops at a stationary hilltop position when Mauck directed him to hold that hill at all hazards. Rendlebrock asked how long, and Mauck said, "All night." So instructed, Rendlebrock ordered a corporal to go to the wagon train and get his blankets. The trooper did so, but around 9 o'clock new orders came from

Clarence Mauck. Courtesy, U.S. Army Military History Institute.

Mauck. Rendlebrock was to call Bradford and his infantrymen in from the east bank to return to camp at the wagon train. Rendlebrock complied.[38]

The Cheyenne fire continued to keep the troops pinned down. The sun was beginning to set when a storm front blew in from the north. The fierce winds brought dark, turbulent clouds. Darkness soon blanketed Punished Woman's Fork and brought the combat to a halt. The troops remained on the battle line until around nine o'clock when Mauck, believing the Cheyennes were snared in their own trap and would be forced to surrender in the morning, called in his troops.

Night camp was made in the dry creek bed where the command had entered the valley of Punished Woman's Fork. The cavalrymen bedded down, some holding their mounts through the night or taking turns while guard details from the various companies kept watch on the surrounding bluffs.[39] At break of dawn on September 28, Mauck sent his scouts, supported by Bradford's infantry troops, to reconnoiter the battle area to see if the Cheyennes had remained in their positions. One returned within the hour to report that the elusive band was gone except for some who could be seen a few miles away. These were believed to be the Cheyennes' rear guard keeping an eye on the troops. The scouts brought back dried meats and other items they had found on the battlefield.[40]

Mauck and some of the officers rode out to investigate the battle area for themselves. They found that just beyond a ridge that had cut off their view in that direction during the fight, the canyon extended out northwestward in a long, narrow draw deep enough to shield a man from view for nearly a mile. The Cheyennes had retrieved their women and children from where they were hidden in the cave—scout Brown tagged it the "Squaw's Den"—at the closed end of the ravine and evacuated the canyon through the defile.[41]

One Cheyenne warrior and seventeen ponies lay dead on the field of battle. Additionally, in making their escape during the night the Cheyennes had been forced to leave behind sixty-two live ponies with packs containing clothing and provisions. Mauck ordered that the ponies be gathered up, and he replaced his own dead, wounded, or worn-out stock with some of the ponies. He ordered that the remaining animals be shot.[42] The packs were also destroyed by the troops. Brown later described the scene the morning after the fight:

> We looked over the ground and found one dead Indian, and the next thing we did was to round up those ponies with their packs on them, that I seen in the little valley. The scouts each one roped a pony. I finally got my rope on a pony, and the next thing I did was to cut the pack off the pony's

back. I cut the pack open and found all kinds of little Indian trinkets in it.
I found a pair of buckskin gloves worth about three dollars. I took the
gloves, but left the pack on the ground.[43]

Lewis had suffered greatly through the night, although his pain was
moderated by numbness in his arms and legs. His condition was so grave
that upon reaching Chalk Creek the following day, Mauck ordered a detail
of twenty-five cavalrymen under Gardener—who had taken a near miss
through a sleeve—to escort the colonel, three wounded soldiers, and Dr.
Davis to Fort Wallace, forty miles to the northwest. En route, Lewis passed
out several times and eventually died in the ambulance.[44]

"I left the wounds open," Davis reported later, "and watched them for
four hours, taking the compress off the artery but there was not the slightest
hemorrhage. Upon examination after death [I] found a clot had formed in
the artery 1½ inches long."[45]

From Fort Wallace, Lewis's body was taken by train to Fort Leavenworth
and on to his home at Sandy Hill, New York, where in full uniform he was
laid in state in his mother's parlor prior to services at the Episcopal church
and burial in Union Cemetery.[46]

Brown, who had guided the detail across the uncharted country of western Kansas to Fort Wallace, went with Lieutenant Gardener to the commanding officer, Col. (Bvt. Maj. Gen.) Jefferson C. Davis, to give an account of the recent engagement. News of the fight and the death of Lewis
was soon flashing over the telegraph wires.[47] Gardener also carried a report
from Mauck, written at his camp on Chalk Creek on September 28. The
message was telegraphed from Wallace to General Pope at Fort Leavenworth.

> We found the Indians waiting for us about five pm in the Canons of
> Punished Woman's Fork. Col. Lewis and three men were wounded. We
> got one dead Indian, seventeen dead saddle ponys and sixty-two head of
> stock. We were prevented by dark from following up our success. I
> followed the trail this am to the point from which I detach twenty-five
> cavalry men to escort Lewis and two wounded men to Wallace. The
> Indians I think will cross the RR about Sheridan. I will be on railroad on
> their trail sometime tomorrow unless they again lay and wait for us. The
> whole outfit is together I think and will probably cross the RR tonight. If
> you desire me to follow beyond the RR I wish you would send me two light
> wagons, about eight thousand lbs. of corn and eight hundred rations.
> Please send if possible Dr. Davis or a sub to me with the detail that takes
> Col. Lewis to Wallace. I pull out on the trail immediately.[48]

Although its troops had survived an ambush in its fourth engagement
and won success in reducing the Indians' horse herd and supplies, the U.S.

Army had once again failed to stop the march of the Northern Cheyennes. And as before, the officers marveled at the Cheyennes' fighting ability. "The Indians displayed much sagacity in the choice of the location for resistance," one witness to the engagement noted, "and fought with great bravery."[49]

Like Rendlebrock, Mauck would receive his share of criticism, in part for withdrawing the troops from their engagement with the Cheyennes.[50] Any notion, however, that the troops could have held the Cheyennes in the ravine during the dark of night was as unrealistic as Mauck's thinking they would remain in place until he returned to battle them further. The battle itself—in which the troops had exchanged fire with a well-fortified enemy across a chasm that prevented further advance—had been a futile exercise in defeating, capturing, or even halting the Cheyennes. Not to have fought back would have been difficult indeed to explain to army superiors or elsewhere. But Lewis had tried to lead beyond the point of effectiveness and paid with his life.

14
Conflicted
COMMAND

N O ONE IN THE ARMY COMMAND EVER EXPLAINED, and apparently no one asked, how its limited cavalry force and infantry troops were going to stop the group of well-mounted, prairie-wise, and fiercely determined Northern Cheyennes. The cavalry bayonet and pistol charge was seldom effective in Plains Indian warfare away from the village. In the field Cheyenne warriors were experts at choosing an advantageous place of engagement and finding cover from which to defend themselves. In such encounters it was standard cavalry practice to dismount and skirmish, thus making foot soldiers of the cavalrymen. On the Western prairie the U.S. soldier was often at a distinct disadvantage to the native warrior of the Plains and was seldom, no matter how brave, as determined a fighter.

Further, the cavalry carbine—issued expressly for mounted combat— had less range than rifles and was generally ineffective against an ensconced Plains force. Regular infantry was largely a defensive weapon on the Plains, seldom employed on the open prairie unless a warrior force was pinned down or an Indian village was being attacked by surprise. It was in this latter instance, primarily through the use of cavalry, that the army won most of its principal victories over the Plains tribes.

When their home camps were attacked, warriors and boys of fighting age invariably rushed forth to conduct a delaying action so the women, old ones, and children could flee to safety. Plains Indians seldom stood and fought in the open field unless it was to their advantage or they were forced to do so. On four occasions in the ravine-slashed country of northern Indian Territory and southern Kansas, the fleeing Cheyennes had become locked in battle with cavalry troops. In each case they took up defensive positions and either outfought or held off the troops before withdrawing to continue their march.

The military Department of the Missouri under General Pope included all of Kansas under its jurisdiction. Even before the Cheyennes crossed the Arkansas, the much-decorated veteran of both the Mexican and Civil Wars had attempted to establish a second line of interception along the Kansas Pacific Railroad north of the Smoky Hill River. On September 18 he ordered Lt. Col. Richard I. Dodge to move west from Fort Hays to Monument station and take control of troops there and to the east along the railroad. Lt. Col. James Van Voast, post commander at Fort Wallace, was assigned responsibility from that post east to Monument. If the Cheyennes reached the railroad and attempted to cross, they were to be stopped "at all hazards."[1]

When the Northern Cheyenne crisis first erupted, Col. Jefferson C. Davis, a native of Indiana who rose from the ranks during the Mexican War and won six brevet promotions during the Civil War, was stationed at Fort Leavenworth with his Twenty-third Infantry Regiment. An intemperate man, he had killed his commanding officer in a duel during the Civil War. Now in his later years, Davis hoped for new military laurels to take to the reunion of the Army of the Tennessee in Indianapolis on October 30 and 31 (a month prior to his death on November 30, 1879). At his request Pope assigned him to the command of troop operations in western Kansas. On September 26 Davis and his staff entrained to Fort Wallace, where his regiment had been shipped by rail a few days earlier.

Of Davis, the *Leavenworth Daily Times* reported on September 27: "It is unnecessary to say that where Gen. Davis goes, and there is fighting to be done, that we will hear from him." Another story in the same issue, possibly issued from Fort Leavenworth, further lionized his Indian-fighting ability: "Gen. Davis is an old Indian fighter, being the officer who captured Capt. Jack, the murderer of the gallant Canby, and his murderous Modocs. If Gen. Davis and his boys of the 23rd get a good square chance at the Cheyennes there will be some warm work."[2]

Davis's appointment did not please Dodge, who had been rushed with two infantry troops from his command at Fort Hays west to Monument station on the Kansas Pacific Railroad. Almost immediately, Dodge had begun

Jefferson C. Davis. Courtesy, U.S. Army Military History Institute.

fussing with Van Voast over control of field operations along the railroad line. Before Davis arrived at Fort Wallace, Van Voast wrote to Dodge: "If the Indians are to be pursued, if I have my way, [the matter] will be turned over to you."[3]

Later, however, Van Voast disputed Dodge's insistence on using a mule pack train in the search for the Cheyennes, arguing to headquarters that his scouts had assured him he could take his command anywhere between Wallace and the Union Pacific Railroad in wagons. Mules, he contended, would have to be constantly guarded against theft by the Cheyennes.[4]

Even as he was arguing these matters, Van Voast was making preparations for capturing the Cheyennes. When the Twenty-third Infantry with 100 mounted troops under the immediate command of Maj. Alexander J. Dallas arrived at Wallace, they reported that warriors had attacked a party of emigrants near Sheridan station. On September 13, the day the Fort Reno troops were engaged with the Cheyennes at Turkey Springs, 1st Lt. George H. Palmer and his company went by rail to Sheridan station on the Kansas Pacific line, finding nothing amiss. Taking five men on an engine with him to Gopher siding, he found an abandoned wagon but no sign of Cheyennes. Rejoining his unit, Palmer marched to Gleason's ranch, where he was met by a portion of the Twenty-third Regiment from Wallace. The remainder of the regiment under Dallas united with them at Sheridan, whereupon the entire command returned to Fort Wallace, learning the news of Rendlebrock's engagement with the Cheyennes.[5]

Emulating the actions of the Department of the Platte on the Union Pacific Railroad, Van Voast loaded a Kansas Pacific train with materials for a campaign: rations, forage, wagons, ambulances, packsaddles, and other items. A locomotive was kept standing ready under a full head of steam, and three companies of Twenty-third Mounted Infantry went into wait near Wallace station. Other troops were stationed at every point on the railroad, and scouts were sent out in every direction. But all this went for naught when Davis arrived on September 28. Davis immediately ordered the railroad cars to be unloaded, leaving Van Voast to complain to the *Hays City Sentinel* that "had not his plans been altered by higher powers, the Cheyennes would have inevitably been captured."[6]

Davis also ordered Major Dallas and his Twenty-third Infantry, then reconnoitering for the Cheyennes thirty-five miles south of Wallace, to return to the fort. When Lieutenant Gardner arrived with Lewis's body and news of the fight on Punished Woman's Fork, Davis wired Pope at the Leavenworth headquarters: "I now know where the Indians are and can begin to operate intelligently. Prospect good for capturing the Indians."[7]

In line with his new strategy, Davis withdrew the troops stationed at Carlyle station under Lt. William H. Vinal. Davis also ordered Dodge at Monument station to move south and scour the country along Poison Creek, another Ladder Creek tributary paralleling Punished Woman's Fork about two miles to the south. This took both Vinal's and Dodge's troops away from their position of guarding the Kansas Pacific line.

Dodge saw Pope's appointment of Davis as a hindrance to his own military ambitions. "Pope would be foolish," he complained in his journal, "to put me aside for Davis if he could help it. I know all this country, the Indian trails and where they are likely to go."[8]

Although Dodge felt he was better qualified than Davis and resented being ordered to reconnoiter to the south, he became lost from his command while searching ahead for water and was forced to fire shots in the air in order to be found.[9]

Davis had miscalculated the speed of the fast-moving Northern Cheyennes, who swept to the east of Dodge's command, pausing only briefly at the Saline River. As Dodge was groping about on Poison Creek on the night of September 28, the Cheyennes reached the railroad line west of Carlyle station just a few miles from Monument station. Only by the chance discovery of a railroad section hand was it learned the Cheyennes had crossed the Kansas Pacific line and were on their way to the Solomon River. They had done so at night totally unobserved and without opposition.[10]

The following morning, September 29, the day after his arrival at Wallace, Davis commandeered a Kansas Pacific train to take him and Palmer's infantrymen to Monument, returning that same afternoon. Davis learned there that the Cheyennes had crossed the railroad between the two very posts he had evacuated.

In truth, neither Davis nor Dodge effected any impediment to the flight of the Cheyennes. Dodge later argued that Davis was more of a hindrance than a help in stopping the tribal entourage. Davis held the same opinion of Dodge's performance.

"To my very thorough disgust," Dodge wrote in his "Diary of Events" report, "I find that the Indians crossed R.R. at Carlisle on the very night that I left the R.R. and that they must have passed my Comd on their way north about or north of the Smoky and not more than five miles at the very outside to the east of me."[11]

Davis hurriedly redirected the troops under his command. Dallas was sent north from Fort Wallace to search the lower Beaver and Republican Fork with the aim of forming a junction with Dodge. Capt. Duncan M. Vance, also at Wallace, was directed to scour the headwaters of the Little

Beaver with seventy unmounted infantry and twenty-five cavalry troops and then move down the river.[12]

"They are all ordered to push," Davis wired Pope. "Certainly some of those commands ought to catch the Indians."[13]

None of them would do so.

Taking up the wagon transportation provided at Fort Wallace by Van Voast, Dallas led his three companies of mounted Twenty-third Infantry to the North Fork of the Smoky Hill on September 30, reaching the head of the South Sappa on October 1. Although he had been given orders to unite with Dodge's command, no point of juncture had been established. With no water to be found on the South Sappa, Dallas marched on to the North Sappa. Still finding no water, he continued on to Beaver Creek. There he was joined by Vance. Together the two scouted easterly down the Beaver for some distance.

Vance's detachment included 102 men of the Sixteenth Infantry, the five companies commanded by 1st Lieutenant Palmer, 2nd Lt. Leven C. Allen, Capt. Clayton Hale, and 1st Lieutenant Vinal. They were accompanied by the twenty-nine Fourth Cavalry troops who had brought in Lewis's body, Assistant Surgeon Davis, and scouts George Brown and Andrew Phillips. Transportation included two army ambulances and five wagons loaded with ten days' rations, forage, and twelve tents. On their way to Beaver Creek, the infantrymen took turns in the wagons, the three reliefs each riding an hour at a time.[14]

Vance stayed in touch with Dallas by courier. When the two commands camped near one another on October 2, it was agreed that Vance would scout on down the Beaver and Dallas would push north to the Republican and follow it to its juncture with its North Fork. While bivouacked at the fork of the two streams, Vance's camp was visited by several Kansas cowmen who had been trailing the Cheyennes. From them he learned that the Cheyennes had crossed Beaver Creek three miles below the mouth of the Little Beaver. He realized that he was too far behind to be of help. Nonetheless, he marched on until he encountered Mauck's trail, following it along the North Fork of the Republican and going into camp with Dallas. While he was camped there, a courier reached him with new orders from Davis. Vance was instructed to return to Wallace if he had no immediate prospects of striking the Cheyennes. He did so, arriving back at the post on October 8, having marched 220 miles.[15]

Lieutenant Palmer later expressed the critical feeling of officers at Fort Wallace toward both Mauck and Gardener for not sending immediate notice ahead of the fight at Punished Woman's Fork. "A messenger on a good horse," he argued, "could have brought us the news in 8 hours at most which would have enabled our troops to move in the proper direction and place themselves in front of the Indians some hours before they could have possibly reached the rail road."[16]

Dallas waited on the Beaver for his scouts to report. One of his guides came in to announce the discovery of the Cheyennes' trail five miles to the northeast. Dallas quickly headed there and began following the trail up the Republican River to Indian Creek, then on to Frenchman's Creek. Evidence of the Cheyennes' flight was scattered along the route.

"Over 30 abandoned ponies," he reported, "some with packs upon them, were found. The rising ground south of Stinking Water Creek was strewn with abandoned food, clothing, travois, etc."[17]

Dallas continued on to the South Platte, arriving at Ogallala station at night on October 5. From there he pushed on across the sandhills to Camp Sheridan, Nebraska. He and his men rested four days before marching south to Sidney, Nebraska, where they entrained for their home base at Fort Leavenworth. Regimental returns recorded the command's total march of 1,094 miles in their futile search for the Cheyennes.[18]

Behind them in the meantime, Dodge had been recalled from south of the Smoky Hill and ordered to march north to the Sappa with his four companies of dismounted infantry to pick up Mauck's trail. Returning to the railroad at Sheridan station, Dodge sent nine sick soldiers to Fort Wallace on a train, watered his animals, and filled his water kegs and canteens before heading north behind Mauck. Water on the trail was hard to find. His infantrymen, now footsore and "used up," were permitted to ride in the already overloaded wagons by details.

The Cheyennes' trail led them onto a high, dry prairie. Mauck's trail was discovered on October 2 at Little Prairie Dog Creek. Dodge's command also encountered their first evidence of Cheyenne depredations in a gutted ranch house whose occupant had fled ahead of the Cheyennes. Pushing on to the South Sappa, Dodge found the entire valley in chaos.

"Murder, rapes, arson and pillage," he wrote in his diary. "No man escaped except those who hid in the bushes bordering the stream. Every female of ten years and upward, who fell in the Indians['] hands, was violated. The Indians killed no women or children nor did they scalp any men."[19]

Pushing northward to the head of Driftwood Creek on October 5, Dodge, too, met the Kansas cowmen Vance had encountered, now returning from their pursuit of the Cheyennes. The men reported that Mauck had left the Republican three days earlier and that Dallas and Vance had been there two days before. Vance's men, Dodge noted, were in wagons and thus made better time than he could.

On October 4 Dodge reached the Beaver. There he encountered the cowman posse driving some ponies the Cheyennes had left behind. The men told him Mauck had left the Republican River two days before and Van Voast and Dallas the day before. Realizing that his foot command could not possibly catch up with either Mauck's cavalry or the Fort Wallace infantry unit, Dodge began a return march back to Monument.[20]

"I am therefore hopelessly out of the race," Dodge wrote. "While the command lunched, I held long and anxious communication with myself on the subject. I can do no possible good by continuing to advance."[21] He eventually persuaded himself that "it takes far more courage to turn back than to go forward, but I finally determined to turn back."[22]

Shortly after he had turned his troops around, a courier reached him carrying new orders from Davis. Dodge was to join Dallas and assume command of that column as well as his own. With Dallas now fifty miles to the north, Dodge considered the order impossible to obey. Ignoring Davis's command, he continued southward to Monument station. There he learned that Davis had left Wallace and returned to Fort Leavenworth. Dodge telegraphed a report of his march to him there.

Although the force under Lewis and Mauck had failed to win a military victory at Punished Woman's Fork, the brief fight was nonetheless a serious blow to the Cheyennes. The warriors had not only failed to delay the advance of the troops, as they had at Turkey Springs, but in addition to any casualties they may have suffered, they had lost desperately needed mounts and supplies. Their line of march north of the Smoky Hill River took them away from the dry, barren prairie into productive farming country along the several small streams that meandered west to east across Sheridan County, Kansas. There they saw great opportunity to make up for their losses.

The Cheyennes knew they had done little to stymie the pursuit of the troops behind them. Mauck had arrived at Carlyle station on September 29, camping there half a day to rest and reoutfit, then resumed the chase of the beleaguered but relentless band. The Cheyennes' route, he found, now led northeastward. Dodge described their trail from the Smoky Hill.

"After crossing they moved singly or abreast," he wrote in his diary, "no two ponies went out behind the other. They covered a broad space of from 3 to 8 miles, except where they cross streams of fire guards, there was no trail to be seen."[23]

From Carlyle, Mauck's command had marched another eighteen miles before going into camp for the night. Supplies reached him there. Presumably, these were the two light wagons, 8,000 pounds of corn, and 800 rations he had requested from Pope.[24]

The Cheyennes' trail continued on a northeasterly course, cutting across the South Fork and North Fork of the Solomon and Prairie Dog Creek in Sheridan County before swinging back northwestward across the South, Middle, and North Forks of Sappa Creek in Decatur County and on across the Beaver and Little Beaver in Rawlins County.

From the Beaver, the Cheyennes moved on to the Republican River, fording it near the mouth of Frenchman's Fork. Their plight was apparent in the played-out horses and abandoned packs found along their path. Mauck reported from the Republican River on October 2 that the Cheyenne had crossed that stream five miles east of its forks near present McCook, Nebraska, at nine o'clock that same morning: "They have stolen nearly two hundred and fifty horses in the last three days and have abandoned about sixty on the trail."[25]

Sol Rees, a scout for Mauck, told of finding jaded ponies, Cheyenne packs, and garments taken from settlers' homes scattered along the trail. He also claimed he and Amos Chapman came onto a worn-out Cheyenne man who had fallen behind in the march. The old man was placed in an army wagon and taken along but was eventually murdered by some of the soldiers.[26]

At Frenchman's Fork on October 3, Mauck had his first sighting of the Cheyennes since Punished Woman's Fork—through binoculars from approximately ten miles behind. Instead of pushing on immediately, however, the fatigued command, having had nothing to eat and no water for their horses since the morning of the previous day, halted for a break at midafternoon. That was the last Mauck and his troops would see of the Cheyennes. When the command took up the pursuit again, darkness soon made the Cheyennes' trail impossible to follow. After halting for the night, Mauck took to the trail again early the following morning and that night reached the Union Pacific Railroad at Ogallala, Nebraska, where he went into camp. There he received orders to join Maj. Thomas T. Thornburgh, who had taken up the chase with three companies of mounted troops from Sidney Barracks.[27]

When it was learned that the Cheyennes had crossed the Union Pacific line, near hysteria caused many women and children at Ogallala to board the Union Pacific train for Omaha and other places of safety. Men armed themselves, saddled their horses, and stood ready to defend their town. Only a few days earlier, an announcement from Fort Leavenworth had confidently proclaimed:

> One thing is sure, however, that the Indians will never cross the Union Pacific road as at all points along that line, and particularly at Sidney, troops are posted waiting but the order to move. A number of companies of

cavalry and mounted infantry have been lying at Sidney ever since the first news of the outbreak was announced. The troops at Sidney also have several Gatling guns with them. A long train, for the accommodation of the soldiers, and their horses with an engine attached with full steam constantly on, is lying at the Sidney depot, waiting for the word.[28]

But the Cheyennes had moved too fast for the army despite its command of railroads, communication by telegraph, and Gatling gun firepower. Dodge blamed Davis for sending him south to Poison Creek and not keeping him on the railroad.[29] Davis was equally critical of Dodge for turning back despite orders to continue on and take command of troops under Dallas, commenting, "He was out nine days, marched twenty-five miles a day, and accomplished nothing so far as I can see."[30]

Davis was also highly critical of Mauck. In his summary report on October 17, he concluded that Mauck's tardy arrival at the Kansas Pacific Railroad showed he had fallen behind the Cheyennes not less than twelve hours in time and thirty miles in distance. He also criticized the officer for not sending a courier to Wallace at the close of the engagement at Punished Woman's Fork. He suggested further that Mauck's operations were so highly censorable that they demanded a thorough investigation.[31]

Rendlebrock received considerable blame for his failure to corner and defeat the Northern Cheyennes. The officer's critics included the cowmen and civilians from Dodge City, his fellow officers, and his commanding officer, Mizner. In a report to departmental headquarters, Mizner brought a litany of charges against Rendlebrock. In disregard of orders, he had camped too far from the Northern Cheyenne village on the North Canadian to effectively monitor their activity. He had failed to report on their movements "but quietly remained in camp."[32]

Further, Mizner charged, Rendlebrock had abandoned the pursuit of the Cheyennes at Turkey Springs, thereby leaving a small force of cavalry sent expressly to reinforce him (Hemphill's unit) at the mercy of a superior force of Cheyennes. Rendlebrock, Mizner concluded, had shown a lack of energy, zeal, and efficiency.

But militarily, there was plenty of blame to go around in addition to Rendlebrock: Mizner for not being more aware of the developing situation at Darlington, departmental headquarters at Leavenworth for underestimating the fighting ability and determination of the Cheyennes, and the field commanders for their failure to engage the warriors more effectively. Lieutenant Palmer opined:

> It seems miraculous that two or three brigadiers, four or five colonels, majors, and about a thousand men in good positions with wagons, rail road

and telegraphs were unable to stop the march of this party of 50 [an underestimate] warriors who carried their women and children with them and rode broke down ponies from the Indian Territory away into Nebraska. When the Indians crossed the rail road on our line, Col. Dodge was wandering around on the Smokey, south of Sheridan, Dallas with all the mounted men was about 40 miles south of Wallace, and the 16th Infry were at Fort Wallace and at this time the Indians crossed at Carlyle 50 miles east of Wallace. We can now see that our troops should *all* have been on the railroad and all east of Sheridan with cars ready to carry them to where the Indians crossed.[33]

Although Palmer's criticism of the strategy of both ranking and field officers—hindsighted though it was—had considerable merit, he underestimated the strength, fighting capacity, and mobility of the Cheyennes and overestimated the capacity of either the infantry or cavalry to stop them. A significant factor that drew little attention from those critical of Rendlebrock and Mauck for not engaging the Cheyennes more effectively was noted by a correspondent from Fort Reno. He observed that the Cheyennes had the equivalent of three remounts during their flight, whereas the Fourth Cavalry units had only the one set of cavalry horses that were unquestionably severely played out by the long pursuit—much of it without their normal forage. To any cavalryman actively engaged with an enemy, the condition of his mount was paramount. The horses, like the men who survived over three weeks on two hardtacks a day, traveled a very long way without respite or adequate subsistence.[34]

In spite of the supposed might of the U.S. Army, the Cheyennes achieved the seemingly impossible and made it back to their home range north of the Platte. But it would not end there. A tragic fate lay ahead for many of them.

15

Death ALONG THE SAPPA

"MY FRIENDS, WE MUST TRY TO GET THROUGH HERE without so much fighting or we may all get killed," Little Wolf told his people following the fight at Punished Woman's Fork. "We must go faster."[1]

In dire need of horses, harness, and food after the loss at Punished Woman's Fork, the Cheyennes—the warrior element, by all available record—committed some of the worst depredations of their flight homeward after crossing the Solomon River. In their hurried pursuit through the area, the commands of Mauck and Dodge saw some of the havoc but not all. Rendlebrock described the carnage:

> On the evening of the 29th they [the Cheyennes] entered a colony of Russian Mennonites and slaughtered about forty men, but didn't hurt the women and children. Most of the killing was done on the two Sappas, Prairie Dog and Beaver Creeks. We saw a great many pitiful sights, and once at night came on three small children asleep on the prairie in their night clothes, four miles from any house. We fed them and turned them over to a good farmer.[2]

Dodge, whose command followed along behind, recorded the scene similarly in his diary of events:

Oct. 4th—Pushed on early. In four miles passed the Beaver. A beautiful valley dotted with ranches and cultivated fields. Not a living soul to be seen. At last a party of one man and four women came to us. Three of the women, mother, daughter, and daughter-in- law live in a large ranch near by. The three husbands had been butchered inside of the ranch, and the women respectively violated. This is Bohemian Colony and the people are unarmed and unprepared. Twenty-five men killed and two missing on the Sappa, twelve men killed and one missing on the Beaver. Over fifty women violated in all.[3]

Gunther also testified to finding the children at a homestead in the Sappa valley:

There I saw in one place, about fifty yards from a house three bodies; they were lying as close to each other as the length of this table. It looked to me as if they had been at work down in the field, near by the house, and had started to run for the house, when the Indians had cut them off and killed them. . . . Within six hundred yards, of where we found these bodies, we found three little children, who were in their night clothes.[4]

Reports of killings, rapes of women, theft of livestock, and burning of houses along Prairie Dog Creek and the Sappa River in Decatur County flooded into Kansas newspapers.[5] Although some reporting was exaggerated, many of the deaths and depredations listed in the stories were later verified by army and state of Kansas investigations and by witness accounts. A summation of the victims issued in July 1879 contained twenty-six victims in Sheridan, Decatur, Norton, and Rawlins Counties during September 30 and October 1, 1878. An addendum listed several more who died of wounds received during the raid, claiming a total of at least forty-one dead in Kansas.[6]

Some writers have linked the assaults committed against settlers and property along the Sappa to an attack by U.S. troops on a Cheyenne village there four years earlier. In April 1875 a force of Sixth Cavalry under Lt. Austin Henely was ordered into the field from Fort Wallace, Kansas. The troops were to look for and intercept some Southern Cheyennes who were fleeing from Indian Territory following their uprising and defeat by U.S. forces under Nelson Miles. Henely discovered a Cheyenne camp of about 200 tribespeople under Bull Elk camped along the banks of the Sappa, attacked it, and massacred 19 men and 8 women and children.[7]

A Northern Cheyenne woman told an investigating board of officers that it was mainly Little Wolf's men who committed the Kansas depredations in 1878.[8] Old Crow also said that most of the murders on the trail were committed by men with Little Wolf, adding: "None of those who may have committed murders ever told me anything about it. I used to keep advising them to behave themselves as they went through the country, telling them that all we wanted to do was to get north; that we wanted to commit no depredations; and the young men who committed depredations and did mischief never told me anything about it; they concealed it from me."⁹

Little Wolf told Grinnell:

> We tried to avoid settlements as much as possible. We did not want to be seen or known of. I often harangued my young men, telling them not to kill citizens, but to let them alone. I told them that they should kill all the soldiers that they could, for they were trying to kill us, but not to trouble the citizens. I know they killed some citizens, but I think not many. They did not tell me much of what they did, because they knew I would not like it.¹⁰

Newspaper reports, personal accounts, and official investigations in Kansas gave the public a dire view of the ordeal. A newspaper special from Buffalo station reported:

> The Indians crossed the Kansas Pacific on Sunday morning, after killing Col. Lewis in the battle of the 27th. They crossed twenty miles south of Monument, struck northwest to the cattle trail on the north fork of the Solomon River, and attacked the herders of Smith & Savage, driving them away and stampeding the cattle. They destroyed the Sheridan post office and ranch of F. Bayles besides several others in the vicinity, going northwest to Prairie Dog Creek. On Monday [September 30] they cleaned out J. L. Peck's store and postoffice and the ranches of A. Robinson and James Gaummer on Sappa Creek.¹¹

Two boys at Sheridan post office were shot at, but both managed to escape. One hurried to Oberlin to give the alarm that they had been fired upon by a large party of warriors, but the idea of danger from Cheyennes seemed far-fetched at that time, and his warning was ignored.

From their camp on the Sappa, the Northern Cheyenne warriors fanned out in raiding parties. Near the Rawlins County line on the North Sappa, one band of twelve warriors came upon the covered wagon of William Laing, fifty-three. Laing, who had migrated from Scotland by way of Ontario, Canada, was on his way to Kirwin, Kansas, to pay for some land he had preempted. He was accompanied by his youngest son, Freeman, fifteen, and two daughters of their neighbor I. R. Van Cleave's, Eva and Lou. Both Laing and the boy were shot to death in the wagon. The raiders looted the wagon— feasting on the provisions—confiscated the wagon's canvas cover, then cut the horses loose from their harnesses. It was widely reported in newspapers that the two girls were taken to the Cheyennes' camp where they were raped and their clothing and jewelry taken before they were freed and permitted to go to the home of Jacob Keefer (Keifer). Some accounts, however, dispute that the two girls were abused in any way.[12]

It was nearly sundown when the raiders arrived at the Laing homestead on North Sappa. They found the two eldest Laing sons, John, twenty, and William Jr., seventeen, just ending a day's work in the field. The boys' three sisters—Mary, twelve or thirteen; Elizabeth, nine or eleven; and Julia, seven or eight—had come out to ride back in the work wagon. The two boys were immediately shot and killed and the terrified girls sent scurrying back to their cabin. They had just informed their mother, Julia Laing, of what had happened when the Cheyennes invaded the cabin. Evidence indicates that Mrs. Laing and at least the two older girls were raped and the cabin set on fire before the victims managed to escape through the resulting smoke and darkness of night, fleeing eight miles without clothes.[13]

Another band attacked the Keefer home when Thomas Lynch, a drover, was having breakfast there. Keefer was away at the time, but Lynch successfully defended the house with his pistol. In the process, he reportedly wounded a Cheyenne who was wearing an apron taken from a neighbor's daughter.[14] On September 29 and 30 at least nine men were killed on the Sappa and Prairie Dog Creek. One was George Abbott, who was seeking a stray horse when he was shot down by the Cheyennes. The tribesmen then slaughtered more than sixty of his cattle.[15]

Capt. William G. Wedemeyer, Sixteenth Infantry, was assigned by the commanding officer of Fort Wallace to investigate and report on the Northern Cheyenne depredations. He conducted a survey of the havoc the Northern Cheyennes wrought through Sheridan and Decatur Counties. During October 1878, less than a month after the raid, Wedemeyer proceeded to Buffalo station, Kansas, and from there rode north to settlements along the South Fork of the Sappa River, the North Fork, and the Beaver. His report itemized the people killed, as well as property losses. Sixteen people are listed as having been killed on September 30 and twelve on October 1, a total of twenty-eight with one man still missing.[16]

Wedemeyer picked up the trail of the Cheyennes at Buffalo station on the Kansas Pacific line. There he learned that drover Ed Miskelly had been killed on the cattle trail north of the Sappa, that another cowherder named Alexander Foster had been killed, and that thirty cow ponies belonging to rancher N. Dowling were taken in Decatur County on September 30.

Gus Cook, a former buffalo hunter and drover, later described the Foster killing. Foster had just relieved Cook from riding night herd on the

South Sappa. Cook had gone back to the mess wagon to get breakfast and change horses. While there, another herder came galloping in to report that he had seen a lot of Cheyennes down in the draw. As the cowboys were getting their guns out of the mess wagon, they heard several shots. Cook told his story in cowboy fashion:

> A fellow by the name of Charley Green and myself got on our horses and started for Foster. The Indians had killed him, had shot him three times, one through the head and the body and hand. They were going through his outfit, cutting up his saddle and taking the pieces they wanted. Our horses were going right down to them. We rode in between the Indians and the horses and jumped off and pulled down on the Indians; most of them got on their horses, some went up and some went down the big draw and came out at the first little draw they struck that came out of the same side we were on. We did not lose any time in getting back on our horses and starting the loose horses back towards the wagon.
>
> We ran the horses up the spur as fast as we could, but the Indians got up the draw on either side of the two little draws, which were not over 300 yards apart. They were shooting at us from behind and from either side and hollowing as only an Indian can. I was thoroughly scared, my hair stood straight. I was sorry on my account that I had not stayed with the girl I left behind me. I also promised if I got to Dog Creek again that I would attend church regularly.[17]

From Buffalo station, Wedemeyer proceeded to the North Fork of the Solomon where he found the deserted home of F. Bayless ransacked. Furniture was partly burned, and dishes, utensils, and feathers from beds were scattered all about. Bayless had fled with his family, as had his neighbor Jackson Leatherman, his wife, and eight children. Their house was ravaged, as were several other homes on the North Fork that had been invaded and from which property had been taken. A man named John Young had been wounded and later died.

Continuing on, Wedemeyer assessed the damage along Prairie Dog Creek, listing household goods, provisions, stock, chickens, clothing, and other items that had been taken by the Cheyennes but no deaths. Along both branches of the Sappa, however, it was a different story. There Wedemeyer learned that the husbands of both Margaret Smith and Sarah Hudson had been killed and that horses, mules, harness, and other items had been taken from both homesteads. Watson Smith was making hay in the field with his father, James, Sarah Hudson's husband, and some others when they were attacked.

"The Indians rode up to us where we were making hay and commenced shooting at us," Watson recounted. "My [father] stood in front

of me—the Indian in back of me—he shot over my head—I saw my
father fall—saw him after he was dead. He was shot by both bullets and
arrows."[18]

Joseph Raab, who was also there, gave further details:

> One of these bands descended upon the haymakers on the Hudson claim
> and immediately began to unharness Smith's team by cutting the harness.
> They wanted the horses to take the place of their own poor ponies. Smith
> had a rake in his hand. He tried to drive them away and they shot him.
> That scared Hudson's team and they started to run. He took after them
> and the Indians shot him through the heart. Smith had two bullet and two
> arrow wounds. Smith crawled to a bunch of willows nearby where we
> found him the next day.[19]

Both Smith and Hudson died. Their bodies were discovered by H. D.
Colvin, who lived nearby. On the morning of September 30, Colvin was
plowing at his homestead near the small settlement of Oberlin, Kansas, in
Decatur County. His two daughters were playing in the stable, and his wife
had just joined him when four horsemen were seen riding down a nearby
draw. They all had blankets over their shoulders, their hair hanging loosely
down their backs. As they rode, their short stirrups brought their knees
almost as high as their saddle pommel.

Colvin continued his work, but when he saw other mounted Cheyennes
nearby, he took his family into their log cabin, pulled the curtains over the
windows, and knocked loopholes out of the chinking between the logs. Colvin
was armed with an old cap-and-ball navy revolver, a double-barrel shotgun,
and a squirrel gun that refused to stay cocked. He had only enough powder
for one load of the revolver.

> After some time the Indians rode up a pocket draw east of the house and
> on coming almost to the top of the hill dismounted, leaving some of the
> horses and five of them came down toward the house. Four of them kept
> in a crouching position and the fifth, a young chief with fancy headdress,
> was jumping around backwards and forwards but all the time coming
> nearer. I waited as long as I dared, fearing a rush and taking a good aim
> with the revolver, I fired at him. Just as I pulled the trigger he gave a spring
> backward and I shot him through the arm. They all broke and ran for their
> horses.[20]

At midafternoon several white men rode up to the homestead. They
warned Colvin that he had better take his family to safety. The homesteader
threw a sack of grain and some bedding in the wagon and headed in to the
settlement. On the way the group came upon the body of Hudson. The

corpse was loaded into the wagon and taken to Oberlin, where a large number of other settlers had gathered for protection. The following morning,
October 1, Colvin met Watson Smith, who told of having been with Hudson
and James Smith when the Cheyennes attacked them.

Watson Smith said he ran and escaped, but he did not know if his
father had been killed. Colvin, the boy, and several others went out and
found Smith still alive. He had been shot several times, however, and was
extremely weak from loss of blood. They took the wounded man to his house,
where he died that night.

Colvin's party rode down Sappa Creek to see if other settlers had fallen
victim to the Cheyennes. At Keefer's place they met Mauck and his command. After conversation with the officers, Colvin's group continued on.

> We soon found the bodies of [Moses] Abernathy and [Marcellus] Felt and
> loaded them into the wagon. About a mile further we found Fred Walters'
> wagon with the oxen turned around and tied to the wagon. We could find
> no trace of Walters although we looked for quite some time. We went on
> as far as Pete Drohen[']s and were looking around at the wreck the
> Indians had made of the household goods when Brant Street came down
> the road from the rock on the S. side of the creek where he and his family
> had been hiding with John Humphrey, who had been shot but gotten
> away and joined Street. We went over and helped Street hitch up his
> oxen, load his family in together with Humphrey and started toward
> Oberlin. Humphrey died a week or so later. Coming on down the creek we
> soon found the bodies of Old Man Humphrey, Westphalen, and his son,
> Lull and Irwin [Iroin].[21]

The Westphalens had immigrated from Germany to Nebraska and only
recently to Kansas. In addition to the death of her husband and son, Dora
Westphalen suffered an arrow in her shoulder while resisting her attackers.
She gathered her other seven children and hid with them in the tall grass
all night until she was certain the Cheyennes were gone. After the attack,
she took her remaining children and returned to Nebraska with her brother-
in-law and his family.[22]

Cowboy Billy O'Toole was near the Humphrey homestead when the
Cheyennes rode up. He and seven others—Mrs. Humphrey, J. J. Keefer,
Robert Bridle and his wife, and some young girls—hid in thick underbrush
as the warriors charged the house, "filling the valley with their war whoops."[23]
After looting and ravaging the house, the Cheyennes went into camp near
the house and had a meal of the chickens, hogs, and canned preserves they
had confiscated. When they had moved on late that afternoon, O'Toole
and the others made their way cautiously to the Keefer ranch, where a

number of people had gathered in the wake of the Cheyenne raid. There O'Toole joined forty other Kansas cowmen in forming a posse to pursue the Cheyennes. They caught up with them near the Laing homestead and exchanged fire. During the skirmish, he claimed, the men surrounded three Cheyennes and managed to kill two of them, one a wounded warrior estimated to be about age eighteen.

While on the North Fork of the Sappa, Mauck learned that a party of sixty citizens was on the trail ahead of him. A short time later he met the entire posse returning, having turned back at the Beaver. With some difficulty he persuaded one of them to accompany him. Just below the forks of the Beaver, Mauck came onto a Mennonite settlement where several men had been killed and their families driven to the prairie. He placed the women and children in the care of the posse member and continued on.[24]

Various stories were told of what happened with the cowboy posse. A. N. Keith, a horse wrangler for a trail herd passing through Kansas, said that on the Beaver the men found a blind and toothless Cheyenne elder who had been left behind to die. The old man pulled his blanket over his face as the men discussed what to do with him. Suddenly, one of their party grabbed a lodgepole and, using it as a club, hit the old man in the head and killed him. Keith blamed the soldiers and their wagons for holding up the cowboy posse.

"If the cowboys had gone alone," he complained, "the Indians would never have gotten to the Platte river."[25]

Another account says the posse was fired on by three Cheyennes—an old man, an old woman, and a boy. The old woman and the boy escaped, but the old man was shot and killed. It was said that Sol Rees, whom Mauck had met at Keefer's place and hired as a guide at five dollars a day, took the old man's scalp, and it hung in the Pioneer Drug Store at Oberlin for many years.[26]

In addition to her husband, Eliza Humphrey lost three horses, harnesses and saddles, clothing, provisions, and other items. Several of her neighbors—Patrick Drohens, G. B. Street, L. Fuller, and Nathan Ryder—were also robbed. A number of murders, rapes, and other atrocities were committed along the Sappa and Beaver Creeks.[27]

Soon after the Cheyenne invasion, minister C. E. Towne of Kirwin, Kansas, issued an impassioned plea that help be provided for the widows and orphans of the raid. "They [the women] are in dreadfully destitute circumstances," he wrote. "They have lost their husbands, their property, their all."[28] Widow Barbara Springler and her four children, he said, had no bedclothes and were forced to sleep on the cold ground. The children had

"Last Indian Raid in Kansas" marker at Oberlin, Kansas, overlooking graves of Sappa victims. Author photo.

become ill from subsisting on grasshoppers and wild cactus. It was feared that with no medicine and medical help, two would soon die. The minister provided a list of the twenty-eight persons killed and those wounded.

In retribution for their forced removal from and treatment in Indian Territory, the Northern Cheyennes had made a number of innocent citizens pay with their property, personal welfare, and their lives. On September 30, 1911, a monument to the settlers killed during this "last Indian raid in Kansas" was dedicated at Oberlin, Kansas. On it are the names of nineteen Decatur County citizens who perished during the Northern Cheyenne retreat. Beneath the monument are the gravestones of the victims.[29]

16
Capture
OF DULL KNIFE

COWBOY WILLIAM STREET OF OBERLIN WAS EATING SUPPER with a cattle outfit near Atwood, Kansas, on October 1 when an orderly from Mauck's command arrived. Mauck was in search of someone to carry dispatches to the railroad. Street, who had recently joined other cowboys in driving off a party of Indians attempting to open the gate of the ranch's horse corral, was chosen. He accompanied the orderly to Mauck's camp. The officer penned some dispatches by candlelight, and Street headed north on a 130-mile ride to the Union Pacific telegraph station at Ogallala, Nebraska. There he was interviewed by Maj. Thomas T. Thornburgh, Fourth Infantry, commanding at Sidney Barracks, as to where he thought the Cheyennes would cross the Platte River. When Street guessed it would be between Ogallala and Big Springs, Thornburgh asked him to see if he could locate the Cheyennes and then notify him.[1]

By his account, early the next morning Street climbed the railroad windmill tower and spied the Cheyennes crossing the South Platte River east of Ogallala. He quickly telegraphed Thornburgh, who had a ten-wheeler engine under full steam with artillery mounted on flat cars, stock cars for horses, troops, and wagons all standing ready at Sidney.[2] While Thornburgh was loading and moving his force to Ogallala, Street and a party of cowboys trailed the Cheyennes to beyond the North Platte where they came onto five Cheyennes butchering a beef. They fled, and the cowboys followed but soon turned back when a larger Cheyenne force was encountered.[3]

Thornburgh disembarked at Ogallala on October 4 and set off in pursuit with three companies of Fourth Infantry and one troop of Fifth Cavalry that arrived from Julesburg under Lt. George B. Davis. Mauck's saddle-weary and spent Fourth Cavalry troops arrived at Ogallala just behind him, receiving orders from General Crook to push forward without waiting for supplies to arrive by train. Mauck would have to rely on Thornburgh's supplies and whatever beef he could find in the country.[4]

Thornburgh picked up the Cheyennes' trail but soon found that in typical fashion it kept breaking off in several directions. He followed one of the trails to Ash Creek. There he left a message on a stick in the trail telling Mauck he had no guides and only Street with tracking experience. He asked Mauck to send him some trailers if he could.[5]

Thornburgh found himself engulfed by the sandhills of western Nebraska. Street described the region as a "waterless waste of sand-hills and grassy swales that was little known to and seldom visited by the white man."[6] Sending his wagons and many of his infantrymen back, Thornburgh pushed on with 135 mounted troops. At one point the troops came close to the Cheyennes, only to be deprived of contact by a heavy souplike fog. When the fog lifted, the Cheyennes were gone, their trail dividing into one that headed east of north and the other west of north. Thornburgh chose the stronger of the two to follow, only to be thrown off again when the Cheyennes found a herd of cattle and drove them for a time before stampeding them in all directions.[7]

The Cheyennes' trail was eventually rediscovered, and pursuit continued. Thornburgh and his troops were close enough to smell the cow-chip smoke of the Cheyennes' campfire. Played-out ponies with packs still on were found abandoned along the trail. In one place rifle pits had been dug out in the sand as if the Cheyennes had considered making a stand. From there they scattered in all directions. In severe need of water, Thornburgh swung back southwestward to the mouth of the Blue River and followed it north.

On October 8 Thornburgh was running low on supplies when he came onto the trail of another military unit operating in the region. It proved to be the Third Cavalry command of Maj. (Bvt. Lt. Col.) Caleb H. Carlton.[8] Carlton, an Ohio West Pointer commanding at Camp Robinson, had recently returned from a reconnoitering expedition on Montana's Little Missouri River. At urgent orders from the Department of the Platte, on October 3 Carlton had marched south from Camp Robinson down Sidney Road. At Snake Creek he received word that the Cheyennes had crossed the railroad near Ogallala. Turning abruptly eastward, Carlton followed the Snake River for three days,

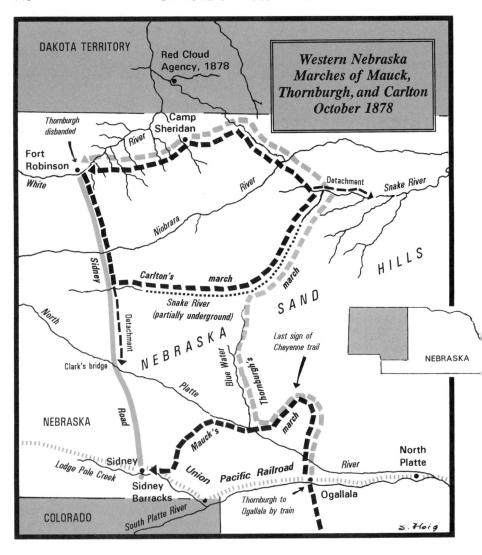

finding either alkali water pools or no water at all for either his men or the
stock traversing the hot, heavy sand. Thornburgh discovered his trail in the
barren hill country of present Grant County, Nebraska. Thornburgh's aide-
de-camp Lt. John Bourke reported:

> This day (7th) took up Colonel Carlton's trail going East. On 9th after a
> hard march over sand ridges, struck Snake river near its head; communi-
> cated with Col. Carlton who sent us some supplies from those of his own
> command. Oct. 10th Joined Carlton's command in camp on Niobrara, at

mouth of Antelope Creek. Oct. 11th united commands and moved to head of Big White Clay Creek 30 mi., and Oct. 12th marched 16 mi. to Camp Sheridan. Officers, men and horses suffered severely from want of food and water and from severe marching. The Cheyenne warriors turned into the Sand Hills knowing the troops to be ignorant of that country and hoping there to detain pursuit, until their women and children by some other trail could escape to the north. . . . To pursue the Cheyennes in such a country and under the unfavorable circumstances of our march was just exactly what the Cheyennes wanted us to do.[9]

During the march a courier arrived from Sidney Barracks carrying a telegraphic message from Sheridan at department headquarters. Sheridan said Spotted Tail and his Brulé Lakotas had left their agency and were burning grass in all directions. He feared a general outbreak was under way. Although his information was false, Sheridan directed Thornburgh, Carlton, and Mauck to "use your good judgment as to the intent of the pursuit of the Cheyennes if it leads in the direction of these disaffected Indians."[10] With their troops and animals suffering badly for lack of food and water, the two commanders gave up their search and marched north to Camp Sheridan. After holding a council with the Sioux there and eliciting Red Cloud's promise not to shelter the Cheyennes, Thornburgh and his command continued to Camp Robinson where they were disbanded and reassigned under orders from Crook.[11]

"The whereabouts of the Indians was still a mystery," Carlton reported. "They had undoubtedly eluded Major Thornburgh's men by scattering in the sand-hills two weeks before. Since then the country along the Niobrara has been well scouted both north and south of that stream; but in vain."[12]

Mauck meanwhile had marched from Ogallala on October 5, coming onto some of Thornburgh's wagons left abandoned with a few men when the teams gave out at the North Platte. Taking rations from the wagons, he continued on to a former campsite of Thornburgh's command. Nearby, his scouts found the stick in the trail bearing Thornburgh's note. Now forty miles from Ogallala, Mauck went into camp without wood or water. Sheridan's telegram reached him there. Taking the message to mean that it was "impolitic and useless" to follow the Northern Cheyennes further, Mauck abandoned the pursuit and headed for Sidney Barracks, where he could obtain forage and supplies.[13]

The Cheyennes had fought off U.S. troops at Turkey Springs, Big Sandy Creek, and Punished Woman's Fork. They had successfully evaded attempts to intercept them at Bear Creek, the Santa Fe rail line along the Arkansas River, the Kansas Pacific rail line along the Smoky Hill, and the Union Pacific rail line along the Platte. Neither the military forces of the Department of the Missouri under Gen. John Pope nor those of the Department of the Platte under Gen. George Crook had been able to halt or capture them. Now troops from various posts within the northern departments were ordered into the field.

During October 6–21 Capt. Peter D. Vroom left Camp Sheridan with two companies of Third Cavalry, totaling 107 men, and marched southwest up the South Fork of the White River to its head. The unit marched 370 miles without finding any trails or signs of Cheyennes. From October 7–15 Capt. Henry W. Wessells Jr. covered much of the same territory, leaving Camp Rains at the Spotted Tail Agency with a troop of Third Cavalry and fourteen Sioux scouts to scour the country westward as far as Flint Butte. He likewise found no sign of the Cheyennes.[14]

Col. William H. Wood and three companies of Eleventh Infantry and one of Fifth Infantry—a total of 180 officers and men and 10 Indians—from Fort Sully near present Pierre, South Dakota, scouted westward along the Cheyenne River. He hoped to intercept or pursue the Cheyennes when they moved north along the west side of the Black Hills and crossed the Pierre-Deadwood road. With an absence of telegraph lines along the road, Wood was dependent on scouts, couriers, mule trains, and Indian passers-by for information. On the evening of October 7, a courier from the Cheyenne Agency at Fort Sully brought him two communications from Vroom. One dated September 28 said the Cheyennes at Red Cloud Agency were making a peaceful move north to their new agency; another dated October 6, reflecting Sheridan's telegram to Vroom, reported erroneously that they had destroyed everything at their agency before leaving.[15]

Wood pressed on up the Cheyenne River. On October 12 he met a mail carrier who brought rumors of a recent fight between troops and hostile Indians at Bear Butte in the Badlands. Two days later Wood encountered some Sans Arc Lakotas returning from serving as witnesses at the U.S. District Court in Rapid City. They stated they had heard nothing of any such fight. One, Chief Crow Feather, said he had only recently visited the Spotted Tail Agency where Chief Spotted Tail had declared that he and his people would fight the Cheyennes if they appeared there. He said, too, that his young men had told him the Cheyennes had crossed Hat Creek and were moving west of the Black Hills toward the Bighorn country. Finally, on October 20 Wood broke camp and headed back to Fort Sully through a driving snowstorm.

Maj. Joseph G. Tilford led nine companies of Seventh Cavalry from Camp Sturgis and Camp Ruhlen down the White River to hunt out the sandhills south and southeast of Camp Sheridan. Maj. Eugene M. Baker was sent from Fort Keogh with three companies of Second Cavalry to guard against the Cheyennes crossing the Yellowstone. Capt. Thomas J. Gregg departed from Fort Custer on the Bighorn River in southern Montana with three companies of Second Cavalry and searched eastward to Rosebud Creek. On October 24 Capt. James W. Powell and three companies of Sixth Infantry embarked from Fort Buford at the mouth of the Yellowstone on the steamer *General Sheridan* and moved up the river to a place known as Wolf Point. None of these scouting ventures produced any sign of the Cheyennes.[16]

By Little Wolf's account, the Cheyennes had continued on from the North Platte to the Niobrara (Running Water) River. There Dull Knife harangued through the camp, saying that now that they had reached their own ground, they would no longer fight. They should, he said, go on to the Red Cloud Agency.[17] As a result, Dull Knife's party, many of whom were related to the Lakotas, cut off a few at a time, some by day and some by night. Eventually, they all reunited in the direction of where they believed the Red Cloud Agency was located.[18] Unknown to them, however, the agency was no longer at Robinson, which was now designated as a fort. During October 1877, while the Northern Cheyennes were in Indian Territory, the government had moved the agency, buildings and all, to Dakota Territory.

Little Wolf had opposed splitting the band. He felt their chances were better if they remained together and worked their way up to the Powder River country of Montana or perhaps on into Canada. He and his group would remain through the winter among the endless Nebraska sandhills, living off the abundant antelope and deer. They kept a good lookout for the soldiers, but none appeared.[19]

On October 21 Carlton took to the field again. This time he was accompanied by twenty Oglala Sioux scouts under American Horse and Rocky Bear. The column marched southward up Chadron Creek and went into camp at noon twenty-five miles from the fort. The following day Carlton sent Capt. John B. Johnson, a thirty-five-year-old Massachusetts Civil War veteran who had once served as agent for the Cheyennes, with a detachment of eighty-five Third Cavalry troops on its reconnaissance up Chadron Creek for ten miles, where he came onto Dull Knife's band. They were led by Oglala scouts Lone Bear and Eagle Pipe.

The winter storm that had hit Wood's infantry command was spitting a mixture of rain and snow behind them as they approached a pass that cut upward into a range of hills. The scouts suddenly spotted a dark mass pushing toward them into the teeth of the storm. They quickly realized this was a band on the move, possibly the elusive Northern Cheyennes they were searching for.

The band was strung out as it emerged from the hills, but when it spied the troops it quickly consolidated. The women and old ones immediately herded the ponies and pack animals into a defendable draw. As the bitterly cold wind whipped sleet and snow into their faces, warriors of the band made ready to fight. Singing their war songs, they donned their war bonnets and brandished their weapons over their heads. Their leaders, however, made signs that they wanted to talk.[20]

The Oglala scouts along with interpreter Joe Larabie were sent forward to parley, and they soon learned the identity of the band. It was indeed a segment of the fugitive Cheyennes under Dull Knife along with Wild Hog and Crow. They agreed to meet with Johnson. This encounter on October 22, 1878, ended a long and difficult search by the U.S. Army for one portion of the fleeing Northern Cheyennes. The band, Johnson learned, had been headed for the new Red Cloud Reservation to join the Lakotas under Spotted Tail. As a result, they had separated from the group headed by Little Wolf and continued north across the Niobrara—and into the path of troops who were searching for them.[21]

Although still defiant, the famished Cheyennes had practically no ammunition or food. A count later showed there were 149 tribespeople consisting of 46 warriors, 61 women, and 42 children.[22] Johnson ordered his men to dismount and form a skirmish line. With thirty-five men assigned to guard the pack train and serve as horse holders, he was left with only fifty fighting men. He calculated that Cheyenne women could be counted among their fighting strength along with the warriors and that the ragged band was potentially a formidable foe. When the Oglala scouts and Larabie went forward to parley, they were met by the Cheyenne headmen. These included Dull Knife, Old Crow, and Wild Hog, plus another "Herculean warrior" known as The Sioux because of his fluency in that tongue.

Although The Sioux did much of the talking for the group, Wild Hog appeared to hold the most influence. Larabie conveyed Johnson's demand that the Cheyennes surrender. The demand was eventually agreed to, but only after the Cheyenne leaders had expressed their passionate determination not to return to Indian Territory. They pleaded to be taken to Spotted Tail's reservation. With the hour becoming late and the winter storm growing worse, no effort was made to disarm the Cheyennes or take their horses. Johnson reported:

> They were hurried off to where the main body of soldiers could be employed to guard them. By the time they were gotten in, night closed; and in the midst of a raging storm they huddled into a thicket at the water's edge, and the troops mounted guard over them. That night they

were provided with some old canvas for sheltering the sobbing children;
but it was wisely determined not to issue them any rations until after they
could be dismounted the next morning.[23]

Carlton was away from the camp at the time. With the storm still raging
the next morning, Johnson surrounded the freezing tribespeople with troops
and ordered them to give up their guns and horses. The Cheyennes refused
to comply. The troops prepared to attack, and for a moment a deadly fight
appeared imminent. But the chiefs realized they were severely overpowered
and that undoubtedly many women and children would be killed in a fight.
They capitulated and ordered that their weapons be handed over. The warriors piled them at Johnson's feet.[24]

They turned over some of their weapons but none of their ammunition.
In all, the Cheyennes produced only a dozen firearms, among them old muzzle
loaders, along with numerous bows and arrows.[25] Johnson believed more
guns were likely hidden away, but he felt the only way he could know would
be to shoot the Cheyennes down in cold blood, possibly with losses to his own
troops. Later it would be known that some pistols were hidden in the bosoms
of Cheyenne women and rifles were hung down their backs. Other weapons
were taken apart and worn as ornaments by the women and children until
they could be put back together again. For now, Johnson did not push further for more weapons, but 131 ponies and 9 mules were taken in and driven
off to Camp Robinson. The horses were in bad shape, and en route Lt. George
F. Chase, an Illinois West Pointer, was ordered to shoot fourteen animals
that could not keep up with the herd. The Cheyennes gave some to the
Oglala scouts, evidently with the hope that they would be returned later.[26]

The troops also found evidence of the Sappa raids among the Cheyennes' effects. A sergeant came to 1st Lt. J. C. Thompson, Third Cavalry,
with two Cheyenne bundles he had found left behind. They contained two
silver napkin rings with the names Frankie and Jessie engraved on them, a
blood-stained white apron, women's linen underwear, a handkerchief with
a name sewed on it, quilts, clothing, a boy's saddle, some dolls' clothes, and
other items.[27]

Rations were issued to the starved band. Carlton, who had returned to
take charge at the Chadron Creek camp, concluded that he would take the
Cheyennes to Camp Robinson pending orders from departmental headquarters. He was not ready for the reaction when the Cheyennes were told their
destination was not the Dakota Red Cloud Agency. Cheyenne spokesmen
made highly emotional speeches, begged, argued, and harangued, declar-
ing that going to Camp Robinson meant going back to Indian Territory.
Rather than go there, they vowed, they would die where they were.

As these protests were being made, other Cheyennes began digging holes in the frozen, snow-covered ground and erecting log barricades among the bushes. The weather was intensely cold, and both the Cheyennes and soldiers were suffering badly. Although hungry, frozen, and facing hopeless odds, the severely destitute Cheyennes—some clothed against the bitter cold with only thin sheets—were still prepared to fight. Frustrated at this stubborn, virtually suicidal determination, Carlton sent an urgent request to Camp Sheridan for a 12-pound Napoleon gun. This was rushed forward by Lt. Ernest A. Garlington, Seventh Cavalry, while Lts. Winfield S. Edgerly, George D. Wallace, and William H. Baldwin provided support with two companies of Seventh Cavalry that had been scouting westward from Camp Sheridan. Chase, who had gone on to Camp Robinson, arrived back that night with an additional howitzer.[28]

When daylight arrived on October 25, the Cheyennes found themselves surrounded by troops who had dug their own rifle pits around the perimeter of the Cheyennes' location. Carlton talked to the chiefs once more. He told them that because of the women and children, he would not fire unless they tried to escape. But he said they could either move to Camp Robinson, where he could supply rations, or face starvation. The band finally gave in when the Oglala scouts convinced them that for now they could get more to eat at Camp Robinson than at the new Red Cloud Agency.[29] Although they were still determined not to return south, the Cheyennes capitulated and agreed to go to the fort.

But the Cheyennes' fighting spirit was by no means squelched. As they were being loaded into wagons for the 28-mile trip to Camp Robinson, Wild Hog delivered a fiery harangue that caused the warriors to begin singing their war songs. For a while it appeared an altercation was about to erupt. The disturbance was eventually quieted, however, and the shivering caravan moved on to the fort, reaching it late on October 26.[30]

Camp Robinson—named for Civil War veteran 1st Lt. Levi H. Robinson, Fourteenth Infantry, of Vermont, who was killed by unknown Indians in Wyoming in 1874—had begun as a military camp in connection with the Red Cloud Agency on March 4, 1874. It sat nestled in a valley between the White River to the south and the towering Pine Ridge rock escarpment that sheltered it on the north. By 1878 the post's parade ground was surrounded by officers' quarters on the north, a long barrack on both the east and the west, and various offices, storehouses, corrals, and stables to the south. A road led south from the post proper, crossing the southeasterly flowing Soldier Creek to a bridge over the White River and to a sawmill on its south bank.

The Cheyennes were incarcerated in a vacant log barrack on the south side of the parade ground. The barrack featured a central squad room that ran the length of the building with a narrow mess room on the south and an open porch on the north. At each end of the mess hall were 12-by-12-foot rooms occupying the corners of that side of the building, one planned as a kitchen and the other as a washroom. Similarly, the corners on the porch side featured two enclosed rooms, originally designated as a storeroom and a 1st sergeant's room.[31]

The washroom on the southwest corner became the main entrance into the barrack. Each of the four corner rooms was equipped with wood-burning stoves, and one central stove heated the squad room. At the rear of the barrack, a plank fence six to seven feet high connected the barrack and the small adjutant's building to the west, producing an enclosed area of approximately 30 by 135 feet.

Troops under Lieutenant Chase were posted as guards around the building. The day following their arrival, Chase again demanded that the Cheyennes turn in all their guns. Although another eight or nine weapons were produced, the officer ordered all of the prisoners to go to one room of the barrack while he inspected their packs and other property. He found some bows and arrows, along with powder, lead, and caps. He removed them and ordered his guards to keep a close watch for other arms. At other times, Chase claimed, he inspected the persons of tribesmen. They willingly threw off their blankets, saying they would happily leave all their effects behind if they were permitted to go to Red Cloud Agency where they could live in peace. They pleaded with Chase to notify General Crook of their wishes.[32]

A sergeant in charge of the Cheyennes' kitchen reported that he had seen a pistol drop from a woman's clothing. Chase discussed this with Dull Knife, who secured the weapon and turned it over. The woman said the gun had belonged to her husband, who was killed on the way up, and that it was merely a keepsake.[33] But this caused Chase to post two guards inside the building night and day and to order that there be enough light in the room at all times so activity could be monitored. No one except officers and the interpreter were to be permitted inside the building without Chase's written permission.[34]

Soldier cooks were detailed to prepare and provide three meals a day for the hungry Cheyennes, including rations of sugar, salt, and coffee issued twice a day. Five minutes before a meal was to be served, a soldier would enter the central room of the barrack and beat on a tin boiler. The Cheyennes would take their places along the walls of the room while the cooks

George F. Chase. Courtesy, Special Collections and Archives, USMA Library.

issued the meal. The women were given access to the post slaughterhouse, where they obtained much of the butcher not taken by the garrison.[35]

Although the Cheyenne men were confined to the fenced enclosure, the women were permitted to go to nearby Soldier Creek or the White River under guard to obtain water. The water closet and sink were far from adequate to serve the needs of the Cheyennes, but small parties of women and children were allowed to go out near the stables to answer the call of nature. After Wessells took command at Camp Robinson on December 4, he assigned the women to police the parade grounds and unload wagons of grain.[36]

To pass the time during the day, the Cheyenne men sat in groups playing cards or smoking, the women in making moccasins or doing beadwork. With the exception of some of the young men, most were good-natured and appeared content—until the issue of their returning south came up.[37] They were very anxious about their pending fate. Acting Surg. C. V. Pettys said that almost every day one would ask him through an interpreter what would be done with them.[38] A few guards with sidearms were posted in the 1st sergeant's room, and the building and enclosure were patrolled by perimeter guards day and night.

The military was unsure just what the government wanted to do with the Cheyennes as they were held in the barrack through November and into December waiting to learn their fate. The Cheyennes were searched again for weapons. The soldiers found a few more guns but not some hidden under the floorboards. The Cheyennes were happy because they were in their home county, but they were greatly worried that the army might try to send them back south. Dull Knife and Hog implored Carlton to send them to the Dakota Red Cloud Agency, but the officer said he had no authority to do so. The chiefs were as adamant as ever: they would never go south again.

During this period the Cheyennes were treated well. They were fed, given presents of tobacco and candy for the children, and kept warm and rested. Big Beaver stated that for the first two months of captivity at Camp Robinson, the Cheyennes had a good time with plenty to eat and nothing to fear. "Old people would go down to the stream," he said, "and gather us willow bark and y[oung] people upon mountains but all would be back by dinnertime."[39]

In the evenings soldiers and officers with their wives would come to see the younger members of the band dance. A courier was sent to the Pine Ridge Agency, asking the Lakotas there to supply moccasins for their Cheyenne friends. The Lakotas responded generously, furnishing 104 pairs, more than enough for the entire body of prisoners.[40]

The Cheyennes' only requirement was that they all be back for the evening meal. But Dull Knife's son Bull Hump learned that his wife was at the Pine Ridge Agency and went to see her. His absence was soon discovered by a soldier cook who found one cup too many at mealtime. Bull Hump was caught and brought back. Following this, the Cheyennes were locked up in the barracks and denied liberties.[41]

Upon learning that the Cheyennes were being held at Camp Robinson, Oglala chief Red Cloud requested permission to visit friends and relatives among the group. He feared they would kill themselves rather than return south, and he recommended that their knives be taken from them.[42] Permission for the visit was granted, and on November 8 Red Cloud arrived at Camp Robinson accompanied by Red Dog, Little Wound, and other Oglala chiefs. Under strict military supervision, Chase allowed the delegation to enter the prison barrack. Tears ran down the faces of warriors and women alike as they met and embraced one another.[43]

Indicative of the Northern Cheyenne–Lakota relationship, the daughter of Oglala scout Two Lance, who was married to a Northern Cheyenne, was among the prisoners. As a favor to Two Lance, Carlton had turned her and her children over to him en route from Chadron Creek to Camp Robinson. Another woman among the Cheyennes was a sister of Oglala chief Red Bear. Even Red Cloud had relatives in the group.[44]

A joint council had been arranged with the two tribes. Red Cloud and his Oglalas joined Lieutenant Chase and other officers at one end of the long barrack room, and the Northern Cheyennes seated themselves in a semicircle at the other end.

"The great father told me to treat the white men in my country well," Red Cloud said to the Cheyennes. "I have done right by them. We have gained our land and our homes, and my people are to have them forever. You young men who stand around me, make your hearts strong. If you have sisters or mothers in here, look at them and you will gain by it."[45]

Red Dog repeated Red Cloud's admonition: "You young men look to your fathers, mothers, and your little ones. They look very hard [in bad condition]. Have pity on them and do right."[46]

On November 17 Carlton wrote to departmental headquarters from his camp near Camp Robinson that he had five parties of Oglala scouts in the field looking for Little Wolf and his party. The Oglalas had reported no trace of the elusive Cheyennes, but during the search they lost forty-five ponies. Carlton suspected that the Oglalas might know where Little Wolf was hiding and that the missing ponies may have been given to the Cheyennes.[47]

Carlton reported that in late October Little Wolf's son and a companion had visited a Cheyenne man who lived in a tepee near Camp Robinson. The man had a wife and children among the prisoners. Little Wolf's son escaped, but his companion was captured by two Oglala scouts and taken to Camp Robinson. Guided by the prisoner, Carlton led a command out the following morning. He found three strongly fortified camps in the bluffs; but the occupants, having been forewarned by Little Wolf's son, were gone.[48] The Sioux scouts had told them that Red Cloud Agency had been moved to Pine Ridge. Little Wolf said later that he might have gone there but did not know where it was located.[49]

As these events were taking place to the north, an old Cheyenne woman and her son were found by some cowboys near the Snake tributary of the North Platte and taken to Sidney Barracks. The two Cheyennes had come a long way from Indian Territory, but their pony had finally played out, and they had been left behind. Taking refuge in a cave, the pair faced starvation. Finally, they took a lariat and choked the pony to death. They had lived off its raw, rotting flesh for several days before the cowboys discovered them. When Ben Clark interviewed them at Sidney Barracks, they told him fifteen of their people had been killed in fights with the soldiers.[50]

The two Cheyennes had likely been with Little Wolf's party that divided from that of Dull Knife, Hog, and Old Crow. Apparently, the woman was speaking of Little Wolf's people when she said the Cheyennes intended to join Two Moon's band at Fort Keogh. Little Wolf and his followers would surrender there if they were promised they could stay. If not, they would join the Sioux in Canada. During all this, Dull Knife's people languished in the prison barracks. But not even the appeal by the Oglalas had changed the minds of Dull Knife and the others. They had been through too much.

"They will never return to the Indian Territory," the editor of the *Omaha Daily Herald* wrote to the secretary of the interior, "unless tied hand and foot and dragged there like dead cattle. It means starvation to them. I implore you for justice and humanity to those wronged red men. Let them stay in their own country."[51]

Such appeals went unheard in Washington. Just before Christmas, Wessells received his orders: he was to move the Cheyennes back to Indian Territory. There were no instructions as to how he was to do this, simply that he should do it "without difficulty."[52] But he was not to let the Cheyennes know until everything was ready.

17

By Force of STARVATION

THE NORTHERN CHEYENNE ESCAPE FROM DARLINGTON had ignited an old contest between the Department of the Army and the Department of the Interior over who should be in charge of Indian affairs. In his annual report for 1878, General Sheridan attacked the operations of the Bureau of Indian Affairs under E. A. Hayt and the Department of Interior under Secretary Carl Schurz, charging corruption and gross incompetence in providing for the tribes. When Schurz defended his department publicly and demanded that Sheridan offer proof of his charges, the fiery general accused him of "disingenuousness." Bad management of Indian affairs, he declared, had resulted in the massacre of officers, soldiers, and citizens on the frontier.

"The question of justice and right to the Indian," the general wrote with some disingenuousness of his own, "is past, and cannot be recalled. We have occupied his country, taken away from him his lordly domain, destroyed his herds of game, penned him up on reservations and reduced him to poverty. For humanity's sake, then, let's give him enough to eat."[1]

Schurz was particularly incensed by Sheridan's charge that the Northern Cheyenne escape had occurred because they had been starved at Darlington. Schurz answered by citing agent Miles's claim that 2,100 head of cattle and 100,000 pounds of flour had been left over at the agency at the end of 1877. The Cheyennes, Miles reported to him, had remained quietly on the reservation, and none had gone hungry.[2]

In fact, Miles claimed, he was surprised to discover in review that the Cheyennes had received more rations than required by treaty. He had, he admitted, withheld coffee and sugar from them. But that was done lawfully, his reasoning went, not as a matter of punishing the Cheyennes but as withholding an award. Those items, he explained, were intended to be inducements for the performance of useful labor, as indicated by a federal act of 1875.[3]

At Camp Robinson, putting the Cheyennes back on the overland trail during the middle of winter also became an issue between the two departments. The Indian Bureau claimed it had requested that the military do so on November 16, when the weather was still mild and pleasant. Instead, the bureau charged, the officers in charge of the Cheyennes in captivity—apparently meaning Johnson and Wessells—vacillated until the end of the year and into the dead of winter.[4] Wherever the blame lay, stark events at the post would soon cast doubts on Sheridan's claim of military judiciousness and his appeal to the nation's sense of humanity.

This triggered still another contentious matter: the failure to supply clothing for the Northern Cheyennes for their removal back to the south. The army insisted that a request for such had been made in November but that the Indian Bureau had done nothing to provide the clothing.

"Cold weather having set in," Sheridan's office told the *New York Times*, "the journey could not be undertaken until the prisoners were provided with clothing at a season when the temperature was often 15 degrees below zero."[5]

Hayt countered that the request for clothing was not made until December 30. The request was authorized on January 6, and on January 7 Captain Johnson was asked to indicate the number of men, women, boys, and girls for whom clothing was needed. Johnson responded, and on January 9 the garments were ordered. The much-needed clothing did not reach the freezing Cheyennes at Camp Robinson in time to meet the army's schedule for their return.[6]

During their stay at Camp Robinson, the Cheyennes were under the charge of various commanders: Major Carlton, Lieutenant Thompson, Captain Johnson, and Captain Wessells, who took command on December 4, 1878.[7] Prisoners though they were, the Northern Cheyennes were not particularly unhappy through November and December. They had escaped the sordid conditions of Indian Territory; the cooler, thinner air of the north country made them feel good. And importantly, the Camp Robinson military fed them well—except they wanted more meat. When the Cheyennes told Lieutenant Chase they were especially fond of soup, he got them beef bones from the camp butcher. Occasionally, officers at the fort would stop by, sometimes with their wives and families, to hold amiable conversations with Dull Knife, Wild Hog, and others. Almost every day the Cheyennes asked what would be done with them. They vowed they would not return to Indian Territory even under the threat of death to them all.[8] Still the Indian Bureau issued no reprieve. The government was intransigent: the Cheyennes would be sent back.

"I may say that my own opinion coincides with that expressed by General Sheridan," Secretary of Interior Schurz wrote, "as to the policy of returning the prisoners to the Indian Territory when he says that 'unless they are sent back the whole reservation system will receive a shock which will endanger its stability.' "[9]

The option of letting the Northern Cheyennes remain in their native habitat was never considered. Further, the military was already under severe criticism because of its inability to stop the Northern Cheyenne exodus. As one Third Cavalry officer noted, if the Cheyennes should escape now, it would be considered "a disgrace on the army."[10]

In late December the necessary measures were set in motion to return them to Indian Territory. An overland march to the rail depot at Sidney was arranged, and wagons were prepared. On January 2, 1879, four companies of Third Cavalry (A, E, F, and L) under Vroom and Chase arrived at the lower cavalry camp just east of Fort (as of January 1, 1879) Robinson on their way to Fort McPherson, Nebraska. Officially named Camp Canby after Gen. Edward R.S. Canby, who was murdered by California's Modocs in 1873, the camp was dubbed "Mudville" by the troops. Vroom's command was assigned to serve as an escort for the Cheyennes and as a precaution against trouble.[11]

Saying nothing about his orders, Wessells made several efforts to persuade the Cheyennes to return south. They continued to reject the idea. Wessells could kill them there, they said, but they would not go back. Finally, on Thursday, January 3, when all was ready, Wessells sent for Dull Knife, Wild Hog, Old Crow, and Tangled Hair to meet with him in the adjutant's office. New orders had just been received, Wessells told them, and they would have to return to the southern agency immediately.[12]

The Cheyenne leaders pleaded their case, stalling for time. They pointed out that their people were in no condition to be on the trail in frigid temperatures and deep snow with scant clothing. The women and children could make the trip far better, the chiefs argued, when the weather was warm in the spring. But Wessells was deaf to any argument that conflicted

Henry W. Wessells II. *Harper's Weekly,* September 16, 1899.

with his orders. He told the chiefs to discuss the matter with their people, and he would see them again the next day.

Wessells met again with Wild Hog, whom he considered "a leader in the whole thing," on Friday, January 4, and asked what their decision had been. Wild Hog replied that they had agreed they would do anything except return south. The Cheyennes' obstinacy angered Wessells. He wanted to have this matter resolved quickly, if possible by January 10. Vroom's horses were rapidly depleting the small supply of hay available at Fort Robinson. January 10 was the day on which he was to begin a four-month leave of absence to have a dental problem attended to.[13]

Deciding that drastic measures were necessary, Wessells issued an order that same day. Their meal that night would be the Cheyennes' last, he told them. All food would be cut off from the prisoners, and no more wood would be delivered for the stove in the barracks. He hoped the Cheyennes would be driven to subservience by hunger and freezing temperatures. The two soldiers who were cooking meals for the Cheyennes were withdrawn.[14]

Four days passed without food or wood, and the Cheyennes failed to capitulate. Wessells issued another edict: there would be no more water. Wessells testified later that it was his idea to cut off their rations and fuel, but he had notified General Crook of his actions.[15] The officer was never officially censured for these harsh measures, which some Fort Robinson officers considered excessive.

"I am very sorry that you are being starved and used in this way," 1st Lt. Charles A. Johnson told Wild Hog. "It makes me feel bad to see you suffering the way you are; I would not have you suffer so if I could help it."[16]

When maltreatment of the captives was reported outside Fort Robinson and military circles, some newspapers reacted editorially. The Chicago Inter-Ocean expressed its outrage: "They were kept in the lodge used as a prison, without fire or food, and practically without clothing. This was inhuman and disgraceful, but an act of treachery and perfidy followed that far exceeded it."[17]

On Monday, January 6, an even heavier—to them perhaps the worst possible—blow was delivered. Through his interpreter, Wessells informed the Cheyennes that the government had decided to send some of them to Fort Leavenworth for trial, and the remainder would be returned to the Indian Territory agency. This news was especially threatening to the young men.[18]

A deep, heartfelt moan rose from the captives, but for several moments not a word was said. In addition to their dread of being returned to Indian Territory, some said the young men feared the new edict meant the white man intended to execute them by hanging. They knew that after one of its so-called trials, the U.S. government sometimes put ropes around the necks of tribe members and let them fall to their deaths.[19] Finally, Dull Knife, undaunted and resolute as ever, spoke.

"Neither my people nor myself will return," he vowed. "We now stand on soil that by right belongs to us; we cannot live in the Indian Territory. We want to go to Red Cloud or Spotted Tail's home and live in peace with the whites."[20]

Wessells made still another move. On the evening of January 8, he made plans to seize Wild Hog, whom he considered the leading spirit of the Cheyennes' resistance. He was quiet about his plot until the next morning when he informed 2nd Lt. George W. Baxter, Third Cavalry, to prepare H Company for any emergency that might develop. He then called for four troopers who were to come to the adjutant's office behind Wild Hog and be prepared to act when he gave the signal. He later sent for two more men.[21]

When told to come to the adjutant's office by himself, Wild Hog suspected treachery. He asked that Wessells meet him in the barracks where everyone could hear what the officer had to say. He relented and went to the office only when Old Crow agreed to accompany him. Wessells demanded that the two men say immediately what they were going to do about going south. Wild Hog repeated that he wished to put the move off until spring when the weather was warmer. He told Wessells to see how they were clothed.

"There was nothing on us hardly," he said later. "The snow was that deep (about two feet); the weather was exceedingly cold."[22]

Wild Hog said also that he had been trying to give his children to the Sioux so they would not starve to death if he did. Even as he spoke, Wessells gave the signal for the guards to grab the two Cheyennes and place them in irons. When the hefty Wild Hog resisted, Wessells joined Lieutenant Cummings and two troopers in wrestling him to the floor. During the fracas, Wild Hog managed to pull a knife from his belt. He insisted later that he was attempting to commit suicide by plunging it into his belly. But the knife was deflected. The blade cut Private Ferguson of Company E on the hand but still slashed Wild Hog in the side before the men were able to place handcuffs and leg irons on him. Old Crow, who had been sitting quietly in a chair under guard, was also ironed.[23] As this was taking place two Cheyennes, Strong Left Hand and an old man, came into the room. "If you are going to iron them," the two said, "iron us too."[24]

The guards did so. While they were waiting for an army ambulance in which to convey the prisoners to Captain Vroom's camp, Wild Hog and Old Crow pleaded that their families be permitted to go with them. Wessells agreed to this request. Wild Hog's wife was called out of the barracks, but when she went back to get her things, the young men refused to let her leave.

"Some soldiers came to the door," Tangled Hair testified, "and said, 'We want your women and children to come out'; but the young men surrounded their women and children, and would not allow them to go out. Then we all consulted together and decided that, rather than be shot down in there, we would break out."[25]

"Let us never go out and give up to these people," the young men declared, "to be taken back south to the country we have run away from. We have given up our horses and our arms, and everything we have and now they are starving us to death. We may as well die here as to be taken back south to die."[26]

As Wild Hog and Old Crow were being placed in irons, a Cheyenne woman looked through a window to see the men being shackled. She quickly ran to the barracks and told the others what had happened.[27] The response was immediate. The women wailed, and young men shouted their defiance and prepared for war. They began ripping up the floorboards to retrieve the weapons they had cached there. They used boards and stove parts to barricade the doors and block the windows and to fashion war clubs. For now, the fear was that the troops might shoot through the windows, so rifle pits were dug in the ground where the floor had been pulled up. The Cheyenne men began singing and dancing in preparing their war medicine.[28]

A Cheyenne who said he wished to give up attempted to come out of the barracks. But he was grabbed by others and forced back inside. Other tribesmen began crowding out of the door as if to escape. Wild Hog's son came out of the barracks with a sheet over his head and cried out to guards, "Get out of the way; here we come!"[29]

The attempt to bolt was halted when a squad of soldiers trained their carbines on the group. Wessells stood in front of the barracks door and ordered Rowland to call out to those inside. His message was that he wanted all who were willing to go south to come forth, promising that none would be hurt but would be fed well. No one came out.[30] By midafternoon an ominous silence dominated the barracks. To those outside, the building with its covered windows loomed as a danger zone. Even interpreter Rowland was afraid to go into the building. Everyone believed the prisoners had hunting knives and would use them.[31]

Around 4 P.M., 1st Lt. James F. Simpson, who was officer of the day, began to fear trouble and asked Wessells to increase the guard around the barracks. Six more sentinels were assigned; there were now three at each end of the structure, one in front, one directly in the rear, and two at the west end near the adjutant's office. In addition to the men walking post, seven men were posted inside at the northwest corner of the prison barracks. Others retired to the guardhouse for the night. Shortly before dark, the outside entrance on the southeast corner was nailed shut with heavy planks and strapped with three heavy chains. Both front doors leading to the veranda on the north were likewise secured with planks and iron bars.[32]

Pvt. Arthur G. Ross, who was on guard between 5 and 7 P.M., heard the Cheyennes working at the windows—loosening them so they could be easily pushed out, he thought. He reported this to the corporal of the guard. He was so certain there was going to be trouble that night that when he returned to the guardhouse he did not unload his carbine and place it in the rack. Instead, he stood the gun up in the corner of the room, warning others that it was loaded and they were not to touch it.[33]

Just before dark, Wessells brought Wild Hog and Old Crow, still in chains, up from the lower camp to the barracks. Both had agreed that if their wives and families were released to them, they would tell their people they must go south. At the same time, Company H, Third Cavalry, which had been held in ready south of the prison barracks, was marched under arms to the parade ground near the building. Company C, Third Cavalry, likewise had been ordered to form in a skirmish line between their quarters and the barracks. The sight of the two companies of soldiers with guns near the building excited the young men, who feared even more that the soldiers were going to shoot them.[34]

Wild Hog talked with the others through the cracks between the logs of the barracks' wall and advised them to surrender. No one inside would do so, but after a delay the families of the two chiefs were permitted to leave. Wessells then called for Dull Knife to come out. The stately old chief answered through a chink in the barracks wall. He would prefer to come out, he said, but his young men were against it, and he would not leave his people.[35]

Wild Hog and Old Crow learned that the young men were preparing to break out that night. The chiefs informed interpreter Rowland, and he in turn passed the information on to the officers. Private Ross said he heard Lieutenant Chase tell Wessells as much. Lieutenant Johnson was not surprised to hear of the plan to break out. The actions inside the barracks had convinced him that the prisoners would not stay there much longer. Rowland, too, was so concerned that he moved out of the prison barracks where he had been sleeping. In his report to department headquarters on January 12, Wessells said nothing of being warned that the Cheyenne were about to attempt a breakout.[36]

The Northern Cheyenne captives were not of one mind. They essentially were represented by three adult groups: the old chiefs, the women, and the young men. Following the arrest of Wild Hog and Old Crow, the young men took charge and determined the fate of the rest, as testimony by the Cheyenne prisoners reveals. The warriors gathered in a corner room of the barracks and held councils that excluded the old men and the women.[37]

Pumpkin Seed's Son, a boy of about thirteen, said some of the women wanted to come out of the barracks, but the young men would not let them do so. Two Cheyenne women, Red Feather and The Enemy, testified that the young men had agreed not to let the women know of their plans to escape. They said most of the women were in bed when the first shots were fired.[38]

One Cheyenne woman said that when offered the opportunity to allow the children to be fed, Dull Knife was willing but the young men said no. According to another, the young men declared, "One starve, all starve." Dull Knife and Wild Hog, she said, had tried to keep the young men quiet, but the young men had made up their minds to escape the day of Wild Hog's arrest. Another woman testified that she did not know anything of the plan to break out until the first shot was fired by Little Finger Nail. Pumpkin Seed's Son said some of the women tied up their traps (bundles) when they first saw an increase in the sentinels.[39]

Although hunger among the prisoners was real and starvation a distinct threat, some of the women had saved a little tallow. When Wessells had sent them to unload grain from incoming wagon trains in squads of ten or fifteen, the women would pick up corn, take it back to the barracks, and parch it.[40] Wessells contended that his restrictions on food and fuel "did not seem to do much good because they had fires right along and food that they had staved away in bags."[41]

Like the women, the older men were excluded from the conclave of young warriors. Old Crow stated that the young men had no confidence in him because of his service as a scout for the military, and they had threatened his life on occasion. Blacksmith agreed that the young men concealed their plans from the old men and indicated that the old men were afraid of the warriors.[42]

The guard at the barracks was changed every two hours. Pvt. Michael O'Hearn was on guard duty that day on the south side from 1 to 3 P.M. and later from 7 to 9 P.M. He could see the Cheyennes through the cracks in the windows they had boarded up as they passed back and forth in the barracks. Some of the young men motioned at him with the spiked war clubs they had made.[43]

Preparations were being made for a daring, almost suicidal effort to escape. Of the 130 Cheyenne captives, 44 males were old enough to fight. But there were not enough guns for all. Their armament was later enumerated by the military as consisting of fifteen rifles, two revolvers, and various knives.[44] Some of the weapons were reconstructed from gun parts worn as ornaments by the women and children.[45] Others were retrieved from where they had been cached beneath the floors. The supply of ammunition was limited. Makeshift clubs were manufactured from floorboards and from the iron stove that no longer produced heat—futile weapons indeed against the military's rifles and pistols. To get more weapons, the Cheyennes would take firearms from soldiers they killed. Parfleches were piled up under the windows so the warriors could easily step out. Toward sunset the young men dressed themselves in their best attire and kissed each other for what they realized would be the last time.[46]

One hope for making their escape work was the possibility of capturing horses at nearby ranches. For this purpose, some of the women and older men were said to have carried lariats, saddles, and bridles among their bundles of effects. Deadman's Ranch, five miles to the south, was closest. It was operated by Edgar Beecher Bronson, a nephew of Henry Ward Beecher. He had been friendly with the Cheyennes, particularly Little Finger Nail whose artistry and singing he greatly admired. As one of the principal leaders of the revolt, Little Finger Nail would soon prove a determined and capable warrior.[47]

"I thought the Indians might break out during the night," Wessells told the Board of Officers investigating the Fort Robinson affair, "but having received them as prisoners of war, I supposed them to be almost entirely disarmed. I thought that possibly they might have 4 or 5 pistols, but the larger guard with them besides the main guard, could readily manage them until the two companies fell in."[48]

Later, military critics suggested he could have done several things: increased the guard even more, placed iron bars over the windows, situated artillery to cover any line of escape—moves that might have prevented the ensuing loss of life among both the Cheyennes and the troops. Others outside the military strongly questioned the propriety and lack of humaneness in his attempts to starve and freeze the captives into submission.

The Northern Cheyennes had time and again, with both words and actions, made it unequivocally clear that they would never again forsake their beloved homeland. Not even the painful memories of Mackenzie's driving them out into the merciless, frozen hills of Montana two winters before would make them remain quietly imprisoned to face starvation.

18

Fort Robinson
OUTBREAK

O N THE NIGHT OF JANUARY 9, THE GLOW OF A PALE MOON REFLECTED on a field of foot-deep snow that blanketed Fort Robinson. The post lay in frozen silence from the wintry grip of minus-zero temperatures. The only movements were those of seven sentinels, rifles to the shoulders of their heavy buffalo coats, walking their posts outside the Cheyennes' prison barracks. Shortly before ten o'clock it began.[1]

A Cheyenne warrior—either Little Shield or Little Finger Nail[2]—jammed the barrel of his carbine through a window at the southeast corner of the barracks. The breaking glass startled the guard, Pvt. Frank Schmidt of Company A, who was posted there. As he whirled about, the Cheyenne aimed his weapon and fired. The bullet struck Schmidt's belt buckle and passed downward through his abdomen.

Mortally wounded, Schmidt let out a loud scream as he threw up his arms and fell back in the snow. Simultaneously, the warrior knocked out the window sash and jumped through to grab the soldier's carbine. Schmidt died within five minutes.[3]

This action was the signal for other, similar moves in a well-planned break for freedom. Behind the curtained windows of their prison barracks, the Cheyennes had arranged a coordinated attack on the guards. Simultaneous with the shooting of Schmidt, Pvt. Peter Hulse on post near the adjutant's office was hit in the right thigh by a pistol shot from inside the barracks. He died after suffering greatly from the wound for fifteen days.[4] Pvt. Daniel Timmany was nearing the end of his beat on the south side of the building when he heard a sudden crashing sound. He whirled about to see a Cheyenne leap from a window at the east end with a war whoop. The warrior loosed a pistol shot at Timmany, hitting him in the upper right arm. The ball missed the bone and caused no lasting damage. Other Cheyennes followed through the window and ran to the front of the building. Still another shot from the barracks struck guard Pvt. Edward Glavin in the ball of his right thumb.[5]

Corporal-of-the-guard Edward Pulver was in the prison guard room when he heard something that "sounded like a lot of glass and pans falling."[6] He ran out onto the porch to investigate and was about two feet from the barracks when he was struck in the arm by a Cheyenne bullet. It caused a wound much like Timmany's. Behind Pulver, the other six guards slammed the porch door shut and scrambled to exit the room through the window.[7]

As they did so a Cheyenne in the squad room thrust a rifle barrel between the logs of the partition and fired. The ball struck the revolver of Pvt. James E. McHale, breaking it and driving a metal fragment into his right thigh. He would recover.[8] Another Cheyenne on the porch fired a shot at random through the closed door of the squad room. The bullet struck Pvt. James Emory, passing through his right thigh. He, too, would recover.[9]

Pvt. Louis Young was adjacent to the center area of the barracks when the Cheyennes broke through the windows of the porch and began firing. Young saw Pulver stagger but not fall. The Cheyennes fired about a dozen shots, four in Young's direction, all missing their mark. He was startled but not surprised by the eruption, having heard Lieutenant Chase tell Wessells of Wild Hog's warning that an escape attempt was imminent. Young ran onto the parade ground and began returning fire.[10] Pvt. Julius P. Janzohn had been posted inside the fence on the south side of the barracks. He, too, had heard the prison occupants tearing up the floor on his morning tour, but all had been quiet during his 5 to 7 P.M. post. He was in the guard room getting ready to go on duty at 10 P.M. when the outbreak erupted. The firing continued from the barracks for five minutes as the Cheyennes were making their escape. The guards returned volleys into the building as the Cheyennes made a mass exit through the doors and windows of their barracks prison.[11] While the others were fleeing, a squad of five Cheyenne riflemen took up a defensive position at the northeast corner of the building and exchanged fire with the guards.

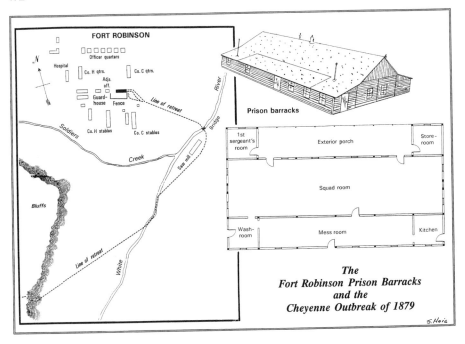

The
Fort Robinson Prison Barracks
and the
Cheyenne Outbreak of 1879

Sgt. John J. Mitchell, acting quartermaster of Company C, was at the stable when the Cheyennes made their break. He had a close view of the Cheyenne rear guard as it formed a defensive line even with the Company H stables. He saw the five Cheyennes, the first out, stop and face the pursuing troops. When soldiers opened fire at the people dashing toward the river, the five men began jumping up and down and sounding war whoops in an effort to draw the fire to themselves. Three of the five were killed, and the other two had their legs shot out from under them. One of the men, Tangle Hair, dragged himself across the snow to Company C barracks, where a soldier secured medical help for him.[12]

"The next day I found 50 Carbine brass reloading shells," Mitchell said. "While these [five men] were firing all the rest were running behind them. They covered the retreat."[13] The Fort Robinson officers later noted that these five protectors displayed "the most devoted heroism [and] met death in the performance of this duty."[14]

The rifles of the five held the soldiers at bay temporarily while the other Cheyennes raced pell-mell down the road leading to the sawmill bridge over the White River—men carrying toddlers under their arms, women struggling through the snow with bags of effects, old and young stumbling frantically along. Some of those fleeing were shot intentionally; some were hit by fire aimed at the rear guard.

As officer of the day, 1st Lt. James F. Simpson had checked the sentinel posts at nine o'clock before retiring to the adjutant's office. When he heard the shots, he ran out to find a soldier, Peter Hulse, lying on the ground in front of the building moaning. Flashes of gunfire were coming from the windows under the porch. He yelled for the guard to fall in, discovering that Corporal Pulver had been shot in the arm. Simpson told him to go to the hospital. Company C, meanwhile, had spilled into formation at the south end of their barracks, some in their underclothes and some barefoot. Simpson considered going to them, but the gunfire from the porch was too heavy to risk doing so.[15]

Sgt. Michael F. Lannigan of Company C had retired for the evening, taking his clothes off to go to bed. When he heard the shooting he jumped up and quickly put on his pants and boots, then ran to grab his carbine from the gun rack. Still shirtless, he strapped on his gun belt as he ran outside. There he saw the Cheyennes fleeing over the open ground east of the prison barracks. The men of Company C fell out in disorder behind Lannigan and began shooting at the Cheyennes. Big Beaver (Young Pumpkin Seed as a boy) recalled that the soldiers, many in long underwear, looked all white.[16] With the troops confused and the company badly disorganized, there was so much cross fire that it was impossible for Lannigan to tell who was shooting where. Wessells came running up and yelled at the men: "Follow them up and kill them! Don't let them get away!"[17]

Wessells had also just fallen into bed when the shooting began. He jumped up, pulling on his pants, a pair of Arctic boots without bothering with socks, his overcoat, and a hat. He ran to where Company C was huddled in the cold, awaiting orders.[18]

"I got Company C, Third Cavalry, to follow," he reported to headquarters at Fort Omaha. "The Indians fired at us repeatedly with carbines, and we killed five bucks in a few moments."[19]

The Company C troops followed the Cheyennes in no regular order, every man firing on his own. There was no method to discern which were warriors and which were not. In the chaos of the moment, the soldiers made no effort to discriminate; they shot at whichever dark object presented itself. Before the Cheyennes reached the river, at least twenty had been killed. Eight were warriors; the rest women, children, and babies.[20]

One of the victims was Old Sitting Man, who already had an injured leg. When he hit the ground jumping out of the window, his leg buckled and broke, making it impossible for him to go on. He sat by the barracks singing his death song. A soldier put his rifle against the old man's head and blew his brains out over the snow.[21] A newspaper reporter described the carnage in the vernacular of the day:

> Captain Wessells had Company C out quickly from their quarters, which run in an oblique direction to the prison house of the Cheyennes, and volley after volley was poured into the fleeing desperadoes and as earnestly returned by the Indians, who sped toward the saw mill, which lies south, and their bleeding bodies, mangled and torn, bucks, squaws and papooses all together, literally strewed the road they had selected for their much hoped for deliverance. This lasted for miles out into the darkness until the neighboring hills, rising like giant icebergs, were reached, and many a one stumbled and fell just as the mountain fastnesses were reached, where pursuit would be impracticable and safety gained.[22]

When they reached the river, the Company C men, fatigued and frozen, were sent back to the base with the women and children they had captured, many of whom were wounded. There the troopers were immediately ordered to saddle up and return to action.[23]

Iron Teeth, whose husband had been killed on the Red Fork, now suffered even more losses.[24] In preparing for the outbreak, she gave her twenty-two-year-old son the pistol she had hidden from the soldiers. He used it to smash a window and, with his youngest sister strapped on his back, jumped out into the snow. Iron Teeth and her older daughter followed. The family remained together at first, but at the river the son went off in one direction with the young girl while Iron Teeth and the older daughter went another and found a cave to hide in.

The two women remained in the cave for several days, nibbling on a small chunk of dried meat and eating snow for water. Eventually, they were found by the soldiers and taken back to Fort Robinson. There, as the recaptured people were brought in, Iron Teeth watched anxiously for her son and youngest daughter. Finally, she saw the girl. Iron Teeth asked her about her brother.

> It appeared she did not hear me, so I asked again. This time she burst out crying. Then I knew he had been killed. She told me how it had been done. They had hidden that night in a deep pit. The next morning the soldiers had come near to them. The brother had said to her, "Lie down, and I will cover you with leaves and dirt. Then I will climb out and fight the soldiers. They will kill me, but they will not know you are here. When they go away, you can come out and hunt for our mother." The next day she came out, but the soldiers caught her.[25]

Some warriors attempted to make a stand at the sawmill south of the White River bridge, but they had little ammunition and were soon overwhelmed and killed by the advancing line of troops. One of the victims was an elderly Cheyenne woman who had taken refuge behind a tree stump near the mill. Wessells spied her and instantly decided she was a warrior. Unarmed himself, he yelled for a soldier to shoot. The woman, whom Wessells later described as eighty years old and unable to keep up with the others, was hit six times and killed.[26]

Those who miraculously escaped the troops' bullets followed the path of the leading warriors across the bridge, swinging around the sawmill westward and recrossing the White River. Some who managed to reach the river were so famished from thirst that even as bullets flew all around them, they threw themselves down beside the icy stream and drank until they were almost too waterlogged to continue.

Others, while crossing the stream, broke through the ice crust and fell into the frigid water. Already emaciated from hunger and thirst, they were now hampered by numbed legs and feet and clothing that was soaking wet, heavy, and quickly freezing stiff. This made them even easier prey for the troops of Company E, Third Cavalry, under Captain Vroom and Lieutenant Chase, who had come from Camp Canby to take over from the dismounted soldiers. Warriors who might have otherwise made it to safety held back for the struggling women and became victims of the continuing fire of the troops.[27]

When he was awakened by Lieutenant Chase, Vroom had ordered him to put his men under arms and wait for further orders. When the firing grew heavier, Chase went to Vroom again, this time being told to lead Company A in a dismounted skirmish line across the valley east of the post in the direction of the firing. Vroom then directed 2nd Lt. George A. Dodd with Company E to move in the direction of the Sidney road and 2nd Lt. George W. Baxter to remain in camp with Troop F. Company L was quickly mounted, and Vroom led it to the post at a gallop. Learning that Wessells was already out with Companies C and H, Vroom pushed up the moon-shadowed trail a Cheyenne party had left in the snow.

Chase at first thought the Cheyennes would be trying to escape down river. Finding they had gone in the opposite direction, he continued up the White River valley until 3½ miles west of the post he encountered a warrior hiding in the brush and killed him. At this point Chase was joined by Vroom, who ordered him to send his men back—some to return mounted—and gave him a horse so he could continue on. With four or five men, Chase moved up the river valley, seeing no sign of the Cheyennes. Vroom and his men meanwhile had dismounted and were pushing forward as skirmishers along the north bank. When Vroom sent word that the Cheyennes were

immediately to his front and pushing up the slopes that led to the sheer
bluffs, Chase dismounted and joined him.

It was said that the Cheyennes, who had hunted this country long before the army built Fort Robinson, knew of the towering bluffs just northwest of the post from earlier years. Even so, the sheer stone walls were clearly
visible to the Cheyennes at Fort Robinson during their captivity. It was easy
to see that the steep slopes leading to the vertical stone cliffs were inacces-
sible by horseback. To most, the cliffs seemed impenetrable, but rancher
Edgar Bronson claimed the Cheyennes were aware of a hidden passage in
the cliffs by which the summit could be reached.

"Almost daily for months," Bronson wrote, "had I ridden beneath these
bluffs, and would readily have sworn not even a mountain goat could as-
cend to its summit; but, hidden away in an angle of the cliff lay a slope
accessible to footmen, and this the Indians knew and sought."[28]

According to Big Beaver, when they first arrived the young men were
permitted to go off into the hills as long as they all reported in at supper
time.[29] Beaver said that at the start of the outbreak, he heard one of the
young warriors shout for everyone to make for the point of bluffs—"that's
where our bodies will lie!"[30] Others, however, said they were not told where
to run but simply followed behind the first group to escape the building.

Some of the warriors who had reached the top of the rock cliff began to
pour heavy fire down on the troops, causing the two officers to initiate a
retreat back to cover 500 yards away. As the troops were pulling back, they
discovered a number of Cheyenne women and children who had taken refuge among some rocks and trees. They were fired upon; several were killed
and others taken prisoner.[31] Chase testified:

> I called to them to give up, which they refused to do and I ordered them
> shot, passing on and leaving them either killed or wounded. I advanced
> with four men to within a few yards of a very steep rock about 75 feet high
> and almost perpendicular through which there was an opening and
> through this opening I could see the Indians going. I ordered the men to
> fire on these Indians.[32]

Among the victims were Big Antelope (or White Antelope), his wife,
and their baby. Big Antelope's wife was struck in the leg by a bullet and fell
to the ground. In an effort to rescue her, Big Antelope ran to her and handed
her their baby, which he had been carrying. He then turned and faced the
troops with his only weapon, a knife. He was quickly driven into the ground
by a shot from a soldier. His wife stumbled through the snow to reach him,
but she was cut down by another volley. The troops, thinking they were all
dead, hurried up the slope. Afterward, Big Antelope and the baby were

found lifeless and frozen, but his wife was still breathing. She was taken to the base hospital but soon succumbed. Before doing so she told the interpreter that Big Antelope had stabbed her, then stabbed himself and died. An examination of the bodies revealed that in addition to having been shot several times, Big Antelope had six stab wounds close together on his right breast, and his wife had also been both shot and stabbed.[33]

One of the women killed on the slope was a daughter of Dull Knife.[34] She had paused to pick up a child whose mother had been killed and was among five women who were so fatigued that they had fallen to the ground to rest until they could gain strength enough to go on. But the soldiers had shot them where they sat.

The girl was erroneously identified by some as the youngest daughter of Dull Knife, whom officers at the post called "the Princess." The Princess, however, is known to have arrived at Pine Ridge Agency following the outbreak with the other surviving women and children.[35] The daughter killed on the slope was not Dull Knife's only loss during the outbreak. His grandson Little Hump had stopped on the trail to defend a party of women and children. Mortally wounded, he lay helpless in the snow. When rancher Bronson rode up, Little Hump made a last desperate swing at his leg with a knife and fell back in the snow dead.[36]

Most of those who died on the slope were women and children. The soldiers had been merciless in their moonlight slaughter, but some rare instances of humaneness were shown during the breakout. Wessells came upon a small child less than two years old lying in the snow. He picked up the baby and carried it to a safe place.[37] Ireland-born Capt. Joseph Lawson, who in November had visited the prisoners with his wife and daughter, joined the others in pursuing the Cheyennes to the river. He ordered some of the soldiers to pick children up out of the snow and take them back to the post. Returning to his command and mounting his Company E, Lawson reported to Wessells, who shortly before midnight ordered him to scout the south bank of the White River eastward in the direction of Crow Butte. Upon returning, he and his troops were sent westward along the river where they found a trail in the snow. At the end of the trail, one of Lawson's men made a surprising discovery. Sitting in the snow was a seven- or eight-year-old Cheyenne girl playing with a deck of cards.[38]

Angeline Johnson, wife of Lt. C. A. Johnson, briefly cared for a Cheyenne baby who had been shot in the leg at the same time the baby's mother was killed. She fed and did what she could for the child, and the post doctor came and set the leg. The small victim was turned over to a recaptured Cheyenne woman, but the baby soon died.[39]

Wessells and the Company C men followed the Cheyennes toward the sawmill. After crossing the White River bridge, however, he had mistakenly headed off to the left. Finding no Cheyennes there, he returned to the post, where he mounted Company H and led them to the bluffs, from where firing could be heard. Rejoining Vroom and Chase, he ordered the latter to take the captured women and children back to the post.[40]

In case the Cheyennes were making an effort to reach Red Cloud Agency, Wessells directed Vroom to take Company L out at least ten miles on the Hat Creek road that ran northwest along the bluffs. Vroom did so, combing the road until sometime after 2 A.M. Finding no tracks in the snow and having heard nothing more from Wessells, he returned to camp.[41]

Wessells, meanwhile, led a detachment of seven men up the north bank of the White River. Picking up a moccasin trail, he followed it and encountered three warriors. In a brief skirmish, two of them were killed. When the third Cheyenne charged Wessells and his men, a recruit who was holding the horses panicked and let them loose. Without mounts, Wessells gave up the fight and trudged six miles back toward the post before the horses were caught. He assigned 1st Lt. Emmet Crawford, who had recently come to Fort Robinson as a member of a general court-martial, with thirteen enlisted men to search for any Cheyennes that might be hiding out in the bluffs. Crawford remained there until daylight.[42]

Chase, whose own company was badly fatigued, had taken Company F and scouted eastward down the White River beyond Camp Canby. He found the country so badly broken and covered with deep snow that he returned to the fort, arriving at daybreak. He then remounted his Company C and led them back to the bluffs of the previous night's action.[43]

James Rowland testified that during their captivity the Cheyennes were generally treated well by the soldiers, except that the women feared the soldiers at night. But during the outbreak it was a different story. One Cheyenne woman told Rowland she was lying in the snow wounded when some soldiers tried to shoot her in the face. She dodged, and they shot her finger off.[44]

The morning following the breakout, Lt. Joseph F. Cummings ordered three wagons to be hitched and with a detail of guardhouse prisoner soldiers went out to gather up the dead and wounded Cheyennes. He first worked his way from the prison barracks to the sawmill, the soldiers picking up the stiff corpses from where frozen patches of blood stained the snow and piling them in the wagons. When a wagon was full, Cummings had it taken to the sawmill. There the corpses of the Cheyennes were laid out on the ground and arranged in rows, one of men and another of women and children. The detail worked its way to the bluffs, finding blankets, lariats, and pools of blood in the snow. As he approached the bluffs, Cummings was hailed by two civilians on horseback.[45]

The men were Henry Clifford, who lived between the fort and the old agency, and a friend called Scotty. They had ridden up to look over the battleground. Clifford was married to a Sioux and sometimes served as an interpreter at the fort. He was asked to examine the dead bodies and see if Dull Knife was among them. He did so but did not find the chief. The two men continued on to the edge of the bluffs, where they found seven or eight frozen bodies in the snow. These were the women and children Vroom and Chase had ordered to be shot the night before. Higher up on the slopes they found the corpses of two slain warriors, three women, and a child. Further on, two more bodies were discovered, one in a ravine and one under a tree.[46]

The two men were about to return home when Clifford saw a trail in the snow. Following it, he soon came upon an old man lying in a hole with a baby girl strapped on his back. Clifford drew his pistol, but the man spoke in the Sioux tongue, saying he was Sioux and pleading not to be killed. Clifford ordered the man to remain where he was while he sent Scotty to bring Lieutenant Cummings. When Cummings arrived, the man was told to come out. From him they learned that two women and a girl were hiding in a hole nearby. Clifford had the Sioux call them out, promising they would not be harmed. The five captives were placed in a wagon and taken back to the fort along with the frozen corpses Cummings and his detail had collected.[47]

The fuller tragedy of these victims might never be known. Cummings testified that on the night of the outbreak, while returning to the post with the wounded prisoners, he heard firing in that direction. Shortly afterward he met a party of about a dozen citizens with guns in their hands, one of whom was J. W. Dear, a licensed trader at the former agency site. "As there was no soldiers there," Cummings said, "I was convinced that these citizens were killing wounded Indians. I found no more alive after meeting them."[48]

Lieutenant Simpson also told of seeing three white citizens in a buckboard searching the yet-undisturbed bodies of the dead Cheyennes at the bluffs. One was heard to say, "I've got a pipe. That's what I've been looking for."[49] Another man was seeking the victims' blankets. Simpson identified the buckboard as the mail hack of the Sidney and Black Hills Stage Line. It was a dark night, and the men were well bundled against the cold, but Simpson believed the driver was Edward Cook, division superintendent of the line.[50]

Cummings collected the dead Cheyennes at the sawmill, and on the evening of January 12 he had the accumulated corpses buried in a pit near the mill: fourteen men, nine women, and four children. Four of these had been among the twenty-three wounded treated by Asst. Surg. C. V. Pettys. Some of the Cheyennes, Cummings found, had been shot in the face at close range. He was further dismayed when he discovered that many of the corpses had been scalped—some twice—and that the bodies of Cheyenne women had been exposed by having their dresses pulled up over their heads. Even the blankets laid over the corpses had been stolen. Two private citizens at the fort were suspected of having committed the mutilation, indecencies, and thievery. The two men denied such, and no charges were ever brought against them or any of the troops.[51]

During the morning of January 10, Wessells rushed a quick telegraphic report off to Sheridan:

> The Cheyennes at ten P.M. made a break from their building. Thirty-five were recaptured, about thirty killed; eighteen had previously surrendered, making a total of fifty-three in our hands now, including Hog, Crow, and Left Hand, three head men. It is reported to me that Dull Knife is dead, but I am not sure. We will have many more before dark as the trailing is good and five companies are out.[52]

Dull Knife was not dead, somehow managing to escape to the Pine Ridge Agency in the Dakotas. Some at Fort Robinson agreed with Lieutenant Crawford, who wrote that Dull Knife, with his wife and one child, had been "taken from near the post to Red Cloud Agency by a half breed Cheyenne in a wagon unbeknown to the officers at the post."[53] Big Beaver, however, told George Bird Grinnell that instead of following the others up the slope, Dull Knife and his small party had turned off along the base of the bluff until they found a small cave in the rock wall. Here they hid for ten days, suffering great hunger and cold until finally they felt it was safe enough to strike out for the Pine Ridge Agency to the north.[54]

At division headquarters in Chicago, General Sheridan interpreted Wessells's report to his own satisfaction, wiring the secretary of war in Washington, D.C.: "They [the Indians] doubtless will all be captured, and with the highest regard for humanity in doing so."[55] So far, Sheridan observed, only thirty had been killed.

19

Without SURRENDER

O N THE MORNING OF JANUARY 10, WESSELLS SENT COMPANY L WEST up the Hat Creek road, Company A south up the Sidney road, Company C to the east on a Cheyenne trail leading toward Crow Butte, and Company E west up the White River. Meanwhile, he and Vroom, with Company H, returned to where they had left the Cheyennes the day before. Wessells separated from Vroom, taking several men to hunt out Soldier Creek as it snaked through the pine-decked bluffs in the direction of the Fort Laramie road. On a ridge along the stream, he discovered a trail in the snow leading further into the hills. He sent for Vroom to join him. Vroom described the action that followed:

> I joined Captain Wessells as soon as possible, and we followed the trail.
> Near the head of this creek, there was a knoll upon which the Indians had
> taken position and they had made several trails leading around the base of
> this hill and into the creek bottom. They allowed the whole company to
> get into the bottom and then opened fire upon us. One man of my
> company was mortally wounded, several horses were shot and the men
> took shelter in the creek bottom. We remained there for some time and
> Lieutenant Chase arrived with "A" Company, having heard the firing and
> followed the trail.[1]

The wounded man, Pvt. W. H. Good of Company L, Third Cavalry, was knocked from his horse by a shot from a high bluff and badly wounded. His comrades laid him on the ice of a small stream. He observed wryly to those attending him that he had gotten a Cheyenne yesterday, but they had gotten him today. He was placed on a travois to be taken back to Fort Robinson, but he died en route three hours after being shot.[2]

While Vroom was taking Good back to the post, Wessells attempted to circle the Cheyennes' position and dislodge them. He was unsuccessful and remained there with Company A until dark, when they returned to the base. He was satisfied to have the Cheyennes move on, Wessells reported, because he felt they could not go far in the deep snow.[3]

Another soldier casualty occurred on January 10 several miles east of Fort Robinson. Second Lt. George W. Baxter, later the territorial governor of Wyoming, was searching for Cheyenne trails with a detachment of fifteen Company H men in the vicinity of Crow Butte. The party found a young Cheyenne boy and took him prisoner. Two hours later they discovered the trail of a lone person leading into the bluffs behind Crow Butte. Following it, they came onto a campfire that was still burning, but no Cheyennes. Leaving Pvt. W. W. Everett and another soldier to guard the location, Baxter led the remainder of the detachment to search the other side of the bluff. Baxter had just reached the top of the rise when Everett spied a warrior lying in a small gulley. He was covered with a clay-colored blanket. Thinking the man would surrender peacefully as the boy had done, Everett dismounted and walked toward him, making signs and calling for him to give up. Instead, the Cheyenne rose up and fired, hitting Everett in the stomach. Baxter and his detachment galloped back down the bluff and surrounded and fired on the man, killing him. Everett was taken back to the post hospital, where he died the following morning.[4]

During the early afternoon of January 10, 2nd Lt. Joseph F. Cummings, Third Cavalry, took seven dismounted men and followed a trail to the top of some bluffs west of the post. Dividing his party, he sent a corporal and another soldier to search out a deep ravine. Presently, he heard the corporal shout excitedly, "We'll have to shoot!" This was followed by four shots. Cummings hurried down into the ravine, calling for his men not to kill anyone unless they had to.[5]

His admonishment came too late. Arriving at the scene, he found the two soldiers standing guard over a middle-aged Cheyenne woman, a male about eighteen, a girl about fifteen, and a small child. At the mouth of a cave lay two young warriors. Both had been shot in the head. When Cummings asked if it had been necessary to kill them, the corporal showed him a Springfield carbine with a loaded cartridge, a belt with thirty-eight rounds of copper cartridges, and an old pattern six-shot Colts revolver that used paper cartridges, plus a pouch of bullets, a bag of powder, and a few caps. He said he had called out to the Cheyennes "How, How" and "Washti, Washti." The woman had attempted to come out of the cave, but the two warriors had pulled her back. The soldiers insisted that the warriors had raised their weapons before they were shot. The younger Cheyenne surrendered by tossing a knife into the snow.[6]

On January 11 Wessells went back to where he had left the Cheyennes and found them still in place. As he approached their position with Company C, farrier Peter W. Painter was wounded by a shot fired from ambush. The shot grazed the back of his shoulder, making an open flesh wound from which he soon recovered.[7] The Fort Robinson troops suffered another casualty that day, but not from Cheyenne fire. Pvt. Bernard Kelley of Capt. Joseph Lawson's Troop E was accidentally shot by a sergeant from his company. The sergeant's carbine discharged while he was placing it into the boot on his saddle. Kelley was taken back to the base hospital, where surgeons Moseley and Pettys were forced to amputate his left leg at the hip. He survived the operation; but when he raised his head and shoulders to look down at where his leg had been, he fell back and died.[8]

Also on January 11 the Cheyennes shot and killed a Company E mount. Fearful that the warriors would obtain the dead horse for food, Lawson ordered a ten-man detail to burn the animal to cinders.[9]

Wessells remained in the field all day but did not attack. He eventually retired back to Fort Robinson for the night, leaving three companies to maintain a watch. Returning early on January 12, he found the Cheyennes had moved during the night. A large trail leading toward the Hat Creek road was discovered. Company C under Simpson and Company A under Chase took up pursuit. In following a smaller trail that branched off from the main one, Sgt. James Taggart of the advance guard spotted four or five Cheyennes around a small campfire in the bottom of a ravine. When he fired at them, the warriors ran and jumped into a hole. Chase ordered a detail of four Company A men under Cpl. Henry P. Orr to circle the ravine while he advanced from the opposite side with Taggart and a few men. While attempting to flank the Cheyennes, Orr was shot through the left arm and chest. He died without uttering a sound.[10]

Simpson rode up and took charge. He ordered Sgt. Gottlob Bigalsky and a detail of twelve men to surround the Cheyennes' position while he and Chase continued on the main trail. The detail was instructed to prevent the Cheyennes from getting Orr's body or his weapon. Bigalsky and his men succeeded, but the Indians in the hole managed to slip away.

With thirty-five men of the two companies remaining, Simpson and Chase followed the main Cheyenne trail to within five miles of the Hat Creek road. There the trail disappeared into an area where a large number of cattle had grazed recently. Staying in the general direction down a canyon, however, the troops found moccasin tracks leading out into the open country of the Hat Creek valley. The trail had been lost and found again on several occasions when Chase, riding at the lead, was crossing from one ravine to another. Suddenly, Cheyenne riflemen appeared over the rim of the ravine and opened fire. Chase immediately yelled back to the troops, "It's an ambush! Get under cover!"[11]

He attempted to jerk his horse about and retreat, but the startled animal did not respond. Fortunately for Chase, Taggart and four soldiers were also in advance off to his left. They quickly dismounted and set up a cover fire that gave the officer time to control his mount and get back to the troops. During the skirmish, one Fort Robinson trooper and three horses were wounded.

The question now arose as to whether the troops should charge the Cheyennes or wait for reinforcements. They decided on the latter option, and a courier was sent galloping off to Fort Robinson. Companies A and C remained under cover in a gulch for the remainder of the day and night. They were joined by Company L under Vroom at one o'clock on the morning of January 13 and by Wessells with Companies F and H at midmorning. Two pieces of brass Napoleon artillery arrived from Robinson around noon.

Wessells took command, redeploying the troops but making no attempt to attack the Cheyennes' position. Instead he chose to shell them. Under the direction of Baxter and Chase, forty rounds of artillery were thrown at the entrenched Cheyennes, who had dug holes and constructed barricades.[12] Although the artillery pieces were moved to various points, they were not effective in dislodging the Cheyennes. The artillery bombardment continued until the supply of ammunition was exhausted.

"Here I thought something of charging the Indians," Wessells admitted, "but I felt certain I could get a good chance at some time later, that they were bound to go to Red Cloud Agency, so I thought it would be risking too many [men] and did not do it."[13]

Instead, Wessells ordered the four companies into camp for the night. On the morning of January 14, the troops found the Cheyennes had once again left during the night. They did not go northward onto the plains toward Red Cloud as Wessells had anticipated but moved farther into the protecting hills. With his men poorly equipped for field duty in winter weather and short of provisions, Wessells returned to Fort Robinson to pick up pack mules and two wagons with supplies that included tents for the troops, who had been without cover during the intense cold.[14]

At Fort Robinson Wessells recruited two guides: half-Lakota John Shangreau and his Lakota uncle, Woman's Dress, who had arrived from Pine Ridge Agency just after the Cheyennes' break for freedom. Shangreau had accepted the job of scouting for himself and Woman's Dress for five dollars a day and the use of a horse for each.[15]

The two scouts picked up the Cheyennes' trail and led the Fort Robinson force twenty miles northwest of the post among the range of bluffs the tribe had been known to frequent in earlier times. Reaching the place where he had last seen the Cheyenne party, Wessells went into camp. He took up the trail again the morning of January 17, and at sundown camped on a small creek the Cheyennes called "The Crazy Man Jumped Off the Bank."[16]

Shangreau, Woman's Dress, and seven soldiers were sent forward to reconnoiter. The men came onto a recent Cheyenne campsite, its fires still smoking with the smoldering remaining bones and hide of a slain beef the famished party had eaten there. A curious flat trail leading to the site through the snow befuddled the soldiers. Shangreau explained that after butchering the beef, the Cheyennes had placed the meat on the hide and dragged it to their camp.

Certain that the Cheyennes were close by, the party dismounted and continued by foot, leading their horses up the steep, rocky slope. The trail extended diagonally upward to the promontory point of a ridge. Well aware that the Cheyennes might have established a rifle pit ahead and could be lying in ambush, the men moved cautiously.[17]

Their suspicions were correct. Shangreau was advancing when he suddenly found himself looking into a paint-streaked face looming above a boulder. At that instant a rattling volley of gunfire erupted down from the redoubt held by the Cheyennes. Shangreau quickly took shelter behind a big pine tree and exchanged fire with the warriors, hitting one. Then he realized that the others in his party had fled, leaving him alone to face the attack. He quickly decided it was time for him to leave also, and he scrambled down the steep hill with bullets bouncing off the rocks all around him. He escaped without being hit, but in retreating he passed the body of one of the soldiers who had been shot and killed.

The body was that of Pvt. Amos J. Barbour of Company H. The remainder of the scouting party returned to camp, making no attempt to recover Barbour's body, which was well within the range of Cheyenne fire. During the night, the warriors scalped Barbour's corpse and threw it over a cliff into a deep ravine.[18]

Shangreau was annoyed that Wessells chose not to attack the Cheyennes' position. This meant the scouts would have to do the perilous work of following and locating them all over again. The next afternoon Wessells finally led an eight-man squad on a mounted charge against the Cheyennes with revolvers in hand. By then the Cheyennes were long gone. Barbour's corpse was recovered, but the warriors had taken the trooper's horse, carbine, pistol, ammunition, and clothes.[19] Shangreau discovered the dead soldier's scalp laying on a boulder. He handed it to Wessells, who at first thought it was a piece of dog skin. When Shangreau told him what it was, the officer angrily threw it aside. The body was carried to camp on a pack mule and taken back to the post for burial.[20]

The Cheyennes retreated from their redoubt, moving along the range of bluffs that extended westward from Robinson. Learning that a large number of stage company horses were corralled at Bluff station, a stage stop between Fort Laramie and Deadwood twenty-seven miles west of Robinson, Wessells ordered Troop E to proceed ahead. The station sat nestled in a grassy meadow beside a small spring-fed rivulet that flowed down through Monroe Canyon and out of the bluffs onto the prairie basin. There the waters coursed northward into Warbonnet Creek and thence into Hat Creek.

Maj. (Bvt. Col.) Andrew W. Evans, whom Crook had ordered forth from Fort Laramie to take command at Fort Robinson, arrived by stagecoach at Bluff station early on January 19. Evans, a veteran of the Civil War, had fought Indians in Indian Territory, New Mexico, and Arizona. He was joined at Bluff station later that day by Wessells, whose command had been bolstered by the arrival of Troops B and D from Fort Robinson. Scouts reported they had discovered a Cheyenne trail that led out north and back again three miles from where the bluffs fell off sharply. Another beef, they said, had been slaughtered and butchered on the sandy flatland between Squaw and South Antelope Creeks.[21]

From this discovery, Evans reasoned that the Cheyennes were hiding in the hills during the day and venturing out onto the open prairie at night to secure food. He sent Lawson with his Troop E to reconnoiter the area. The detachment was unable to cross the rough, mountainous country on the course directed, however, and returned to Bluff station.

The following day, January 20, Evans ordered Wessells and Lawson to march "under the cliffs"—north of the bluffs, that is—toward Hat Creek with Companies H and E, Third Cavalry, in search of the Cheyennes' trail. They took the command's wagons and pack mules that carried their supplies, equipment, and extra ammunition.

View from Coliseum Butte overlooking flatlands and Antelope Creek to the north. Photo, B. J. Dunn.

At the same time, Evans led Companies B and D on a scout to the summit of a towering plateau four or five miles northwest of Bluff station. This was Coliseum Butte, whose towering, sheer-cliffed plateau presented a grand view of the undulating prairie that stretched far northward for 100 miles toward the Black Hills of South Dakota. The ancient tribal fortress, its rocky rim indented with prehistoric fire pits, presented such a command of the surrounding terrain that it had long been a choice platform for tribes of the region to send and receive smoke signals.[22]

Approaching a position where Shangreau suspected the Cheyennes were entrenched, Evans ordered the troops and scouts to dismount and advance on foot, leading their mounts. Within 100 yards of the point, they were met by rifle fire. Evans's horse was hit and killed. A skirmish ensued, during which the troops dismounted and took up a position against the Cheyennes, exchanging fire in a standoff through the rest of the day.[23]

The Cheyennes left their fires burning through the night and kept two preteenage boys behind to occupy the troops. The remainder of their party slipped down from the precipice by some passageway unknown to whites and headed north up South Antelope Creek. Evans, thinking he had the entire Cheyenne party corralled in their fortification, remained in place. The two Cheyenne youngsters with whom Evans was engaged eventually withdrew to rejoin their party and take part in the bloody fight that soon took place. Evans was left guarding an empty bastion with his two companies of troops.[24]

Troops A and F under Chase and Baxter arrived back from Robinson and reconnoitered northward along the Hat Creek road. Chase with two companies searched ahead for the Cheyenne trail. Shangreau and Woman's Dress, scouting in advance of the troops, soon reported that the Cheyennes' trail was scattered over the prairie where they could not follow it because there was no snow on the ground there.

Chase pursued, deploying his two companies into a skirmish line with five- to seven-yard intervals between the men. The troops were ordered to carefully examine the area over which they passed and to reassemble every three miles. During this advance Sergeant Bigalsky came onto a Cheyenne trail leading southward in the bottom of a draw.[25] Wessells arrived and took up pursuit, but the trail was soon lost again.

Evans, still believing he was engaged with the Cheyennes on Coliseum Butte, sent orders for Wessells and Chase to bring their force to the butte and camp at its foot to cut off the Cheyennes' escape route out onto the plain. Although Wessells and his officers felt strongly that the Cheyennes were ahead of them, they returned to the bluff as ordered and camped under its north cliff. That night a campfire was spotted in a ravine a mile or so distant. A squad was sent to investigate, discovering the fires to be those of a detachment that had been sent out from Wessells's Company H and become lost in the dark. The men of the detachment told of having discovered the trail of several Cheyennes ten miles from the bluff. It led in the same direction as the one seen earlier by Chase's men.[26]

Wessells issued orders for Companies A, E, and H to march as early as possible the following morning with all the rations their horses could carry. January 22 broke clear and pleasant as Wessells followed the Cheyennes' trail down South Antelope Creek with his entire command. Shortly before ten o'clock, Woman's Dress crested a rise just beyond the juncture of South Antelope and Antelope Creeks and was hammered in the arm by a bullet.[27] At the same time, Shangreau's mule was hit in the neck and driven to the ground. Almost simultaneously, a ball slammed into the chest of Pvt. Henry A. Du Blois. His horse was also struck.

Instantly, several warriors charged from their concealment in an attempt to grab Du Blois's rifle and the wounded horse. Shangreau yanked his

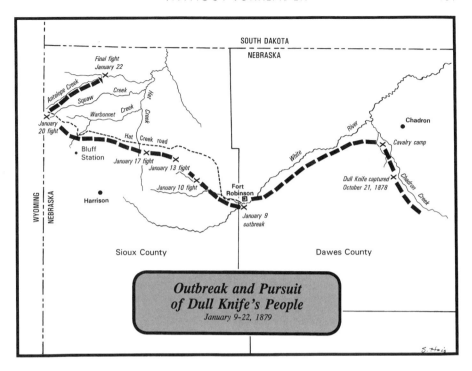

**Outbreak and Pursuit
of Dull Knife's People**
January 9-22, 1879

pistol from its holster, but another shot from a Cheyenne gun smashed the pistol's stock to bits and made the weapon useless. He attempted to crawl to the wounded soldier, but the Cheyennes' fire was too intense.

Hearing the firing, Wessells galloped forward, coming upon the wounded Woman's Dress. The officer immediately ordered Company A at the lead of the column to dismount, advance, and open fire on the Cheyennes in an attempt to protect Du Blois. He yelled to his troops, "Try to save that man!"[28] Du Blois was rescued, although severely wounded. He was placed on a travois for transportation to the post but died two hours before reaching Fort Robinson on January 24.[29]

The Cheyenne party of thirty-two—eighteen men and boys, eleven women and girls, and three children—had eluded and outfought the troops for thirteen desperate days. They were no longer able to evade or outrun the pressing troops. Still, they would not surrender. In a final act of suicidal resistance, they took refuge in an oblong pit washed out of the sandy north bank of Antelope Creek. The pit—estimated at 10 to 12 feet wide, 30 to 50 feet long, and 6 feet deep—presented a narrow opening onto the waterless bed of Antelope Creek. Situated at the head of a northward bend in the

Death pit (in foreground) where the Cheyennes made their final stand. Author photo.

river, the pit overlooked a broad flood plain. A ravine marking the dry channel of the stream traced along the foot of the sand bluffs that banked the river on the north. The undulating bank and ravine presented the only cover for troops in the otherwise flat, treeless terrain above or below the pit.

The Cheyenne women and children burrowed deeper into the bottom of the hole, and the men dug out firing positions along the sides of the pit to establish a perimeter of defense around the bank. Clearly, the Cheyennes, men and women alike, were prepared to hold out to the death.

Wessells rejected any attempt to attack the Cheyenne position until Company F and the wagons could be brought as reinforcements. Meanwhile, the three companies dismounted and took up carbine positions 150 yards south of the pit, exchanging occasional gunfire with the Cheyennes. Company F was ten miles back, and it took them until 2:30 P.M. to reach the scene.

When they arrived, Wessells deployed his dismounted command in a skirmish line three to four paces apart and began moving forward in a semi-circle formation. Company A moved up over the north bank to a position north of the pit, and Lawson with Company E closed in toward the mouth of the pit. Baxter with Company F was sent northeast of the pit, and Wessells led Company H to the northwest.[30] Discounting the horse holders, Wessells retained 100 men to actively attack the embattled Cheyennes.[31]

By plan, Chase was to move his men to a position from where he could charge the pit in a coordinated move with Wessells's Company H. As the troops of Company A were repositioning, the Cheyennes made them pay. A carbine ball struck Sgt. James Taggart in the neck and killed him instantly. Upon attaining the new position, Chase quickly found that it was partially vulnerable to the Cheyenne fire. Deciding not to wait for Company H to obtain its launch position, Chase ordered an immediate charge against the pit.[32]

Firing as they went, he and his troops pushed up over the bank and advanced to within twelve yards of the pit, firing into it. The Cheyennes rose up and returned the fire. Farrier George Brown had reached the edge of the Cheyenne entrenchment and discharged his carbine when he was hit. He uttered several loud screams and tried to throw off his cartridge belt before falling dead at the rim of the pit.[33]

Seeing Chase advance with Company A, Wessells hurried forward with his men. The two units surrounded the Cheyenne refuge and from a distance of five yards or so poured volley after volley into the hole. During this action Pvt. George Nelson was shot in the stomach and killed instantly.[34]

Wessells twice ordered the firing to cease while he called to the Cheyennes to come out and surrender. Both times he was answered by shots from the bowels of the pit. The gun smoke became so thick around the position that the soldiers were forced to wait for the air to clear before firing again. Much of the firing was done blindly. The entrapped Cheyennes continued to answer the fire sporadically. During one lull in the attack, their firing ceased, and the troops could hear them chanting inside their death hole. The troops' firepower had been so severe that it seemed almost useless to continue.

Thinking that the Cheyennes would surely surrender, Wessells and Chase, accompanied by Sgt. Willard D. Reed, who knew some Lakota words, crept to the edge of the pit. The soldier called out "Washie," believing it meant "Give up!"[35] The answer was an instant Cheyenne volley. A ball creased Wessells's left forehead, knocking him unconscious. As he toppled forward, Chase grabbed him and dragged him out of the Cheyennes' firing range. The bullet had passed along the officer's scalp, making a painful but not serious wound.[36]

Sergeant Reed was in the act of firing when a Cheyenne bullet struck him in the left thigh. He, too, soon recovered from the wound.

With Wessells incapacitated, Chase took charge of the troops. On his orders, a roaring barrage of gunfire lasting almost half an hour was poured into the pit. Finally, the soldiers ceased firing and squinted into the dense cloud of gun smoke to see the result. They had almost decided the fight was over when three Cheyenne warriors suddenly emerged from the death pit singing war songs.[37] A Fort Robinson correspondent described the final moment:

> Just before the final resistance of the Cheyennes three of them, the last alive, jumped out of the pit and faced the troops undaunted. One had a pistol and two had knives, which they brandished like warriors while rushing at the troops. One sprang to jump down the embankment, but was speedily riddled with balls, as were the other two.[38]

When the acrid clouds of battle had finally drifted away, the soldiers edged forward to peer down into the pit. A witness described the scene:

> Huddled together in piles were the twenty-three bodies of the slain. Among the nine still surviving were two young Indian girls, aged fourteen and fifteen, covered with dust and under the bodies of young bucks who had fallen lifeless upon them and at first concealed them. They were saved by digging in under the side of the hole. One is named Blanche, and used to write her name while imprisoned here with her people. The appearance of the pit was as though it had been filled with sand bags.[39]

Lieutenant Chase sent a detail into the pit to bring out the bodies that were strewn about. Among the dead the soldiers found three women miraculously unhurt, but a man, four women, and a child had been wounded, three of them mortally.[40] One of the surviving women was the handsome daughter of Wild Hog who, although wounded in the arm, fought the soldiers fiercely as they carried her from the pit.[41] Also among the dead was Little Finger Nail, whose singing and artistry had so pleased rancher Bronson. Strapped to his dead body the troops found Little Finger Nail's sketchbook. Pierced by two bullets from a Springfield rifle, it survived as a remnant of battle and is held today by the American Museum of Natural History in New York, providing an artifact of the Northern Cheyenne ordeal.

"Two of the boys," Johnson wrote, "were the two little boys who had been left behind the day before to decoy Major Evans, and found their way across the country and joined these others in the fight. One of the little boys died before he got home."[42]

The wounded warrior's leg had been shredded by the gunfire. Surgeon Pettys, who treated the wounded at Antelope Creek, bandaged the Cheyenne's leg and asked if he could do anything more for him. The warrior said no, that he wanted to be thrown back into the pit where the others had died. He died soon after and was laid out with the others per his wish.[43]

Of the thirty-two people in the pit, twenty-three were killed on January 21—seventeen men, four women, and two children. The following day a man, a woman, and a child died, bringing the total to twenty-six Cheyenne fatalities in the Antelope Creek engagement. Only six of those in the pit survived the ordeal.[44]

Pettys's official list of the twenty-three outbreak survivors itemizes their wounds and reveals the carnage inflicted on the Cheyennes. Six died shortly after arriving at Fort Robinson. They included six-month-old and one-year-old baby girls, both of whom had fractured thighs, and a five-year-old girl who suffered a penetrating wound of the abdomen. Almost all of the survivors had multiple wounds, including Medicine Woman, whose right eye had been shot out.[45]

A Board of Officers inquiry into the breakout provided a list—considered incomplete—of the Cheyennes' weaponry. It included five Springfield carbines, four of which were taken from soldiers killed during the outbreak; seven Springfield breech-loading rifle muskets, all bearing brass tacks that indicated lengthy Cheyenne ownership; three Sharps carbines; one Sharps rifle; one Colts revolver, caliber 36; one Colts revolver, navy old pattern; and one Remington revolver, army old pattern.[46]

"Even at the last moment," a reporter noted, "when fate had set its seal against the Cheyennes, they moved their unloaded rifles frantically about over the edge of the pit to produce, if possible, some alarm."[47]

The troops also found in the hole a number of blankets, a soldier's overcoat, pantaloons, bed covers, and a "good stock of half-dried beef three feet high and two feet wide."[48]

Companies F and E had been deployed in such a position that they were less actively engaged in the action. Lawson, however, led twenty-two of his Company E during the final charge. He was the first to descend into the pit when the fighting was over. There he saw a small, bewildered girl who looked at him with imploring eyes. He took the child by the hand and helped her from the tangle of Cheyenne dead. This was Lame Girl, who had miraculously survived the onslaught. Lawson also assisted a Cheyenne woman from the pit and called on his men to help with the others who were still alive.[49]

Evans had moved down from the bluffs to Hat Creek road with Companies B and D too late to take part in the action. After the battle the remaining troops reported to him there. He had learned that the Cheyenne were gone only when Sgt. William B. Lewis made a risky climb to the top, an act for which he received the only Medal of Honor awarded for the Cheyenne retreat.[50]

When he departed from the scene of the fight to rejoin Evans, Lawson left a detail behind to place the bodies of the Cheyennes in the pit. The next day Evans ordered a wagon and a detachment of men with implements to be sent out to bury the dead.[51] The consolidated command began its march back to Fort Robinson along the Hat Creek road with the dead and wounded. A telegraph line ran along the road, and six miles northeast of Bluff station Evans had a man tap out a message to General Crook reporting the event.[52]

Observers noted that eighteen Cheyenne warriors, some of them mere youths, had held four companies of U.S. Cavalry at bay. In doing so, the warriors had killed several soldiers and wounded others. The Cheyennes had again shown themselves to be superior shots and fearless to the extreme, as Colonel Evans recognized in his report on the battle: "The Cheyennes fought with extraordinary courage and fierceness, and refused all terms but death."[53]

The *Omaha Bee* observed: "Their adventure certainly forms a remarkably interesting and thrilling chapter of Indian history, reflecting great credit upon them as warriors and strategists, while, on the other hand, our military forces are covered with anything but glory."[54]

20
Little Wolf's RETURN

AFTER SEPARATING FROM DULL KNIFE'S PARTY BEYOND THE PLATTE, Little
Wolf's band had continued northwestward into the sandhills along
the Niobrara River in western Nebraska. There they subsisted for a
time on the numerous antelope and deer in the region.[1] During early November 1878 Capt. James F. Simpson, Third Cavalry, sent a courier to Fort
Robinson from the head of Ash Creek to report that his command of four companies of Third and Seventh Cavalry had picked up Little Wolf's trail and were
following it in the direction of the Niobrara.[2] Nothing came of this, however,
and it was the last supposed sighting of Little Wolf by the military for some time.

During early 1879 several incidents of stolen stock and killings were
reported in the region. Rightly or wrongly, Little Wolf's band was blamed.

On January 17 two ranchers arrived at Fort Robinson to report the loss
of fifty head of horses.[3] At the same time, five companies of Fifth Cavalry
under Capt. Robert H. Montgomery were ordered out from Fort Russell
near present Bosler, Wyoming, in search of unknown Indians depredating
ranches in northwestern Nebraska. The raiders were thought to be Little
Wolf's men, but they were able to avoid discovery.[4] In early February a
cowherder galloped fifty miles from the Niobrara to Cheyenne, Wyoming, to
tell of two men killed on January 26 by thirteen Indians and of two others
who had been killed later.[5]

During the bitter cold of mid-February, a battalion of Fifth Cavalry conducted a six-day search for Little Wolf through the sandhills country of western Nebraska. Marching eastward from a camp on the Snake River, the troops crossed the Clifford, Boardman, and Loup Forks of the Snake before returning to their base camp. The command found it impossible to follow any trails because the snow was so deep. The men suffered badly from the thirty-degrees-below-zero temperatures, snow blindness, and the lack of wood or water in the region.[6]

A dispatch from Deadwood, Dakota Territory, on February 24 may have provided a clue to Little Wolf's movement northward from the sandhills. According to the report, two wagon trains carrying freight on the Fort Pierre road forty miles east of Deadwood had been corralled by Indians firing at them from overhanging cliffs. Six people had been reported killed within the past week, and large numbers of citizens from Rapid City and neighboring communities had turned out to provide protection. Two companies of Seventh Cavalry sent out from Fort Meade, Dakota Territory, to rescue the wagon trains, however, found no signs of Indians other than pony tracks. The prevailing opinion was that the depredations were committed by Little Wolf's band of Cheyennes, who were on their way to join Sitting Bull in Canada.[7]

In late February 1879 1st Lt. William P. Clark at Fort Keogh was ordered into the field to intercept the Northern Cheyennes. Clark, an 1868 graduate of West Point, had served as Second Cavalry adjutant but resigned the desk post in favor of field duty. While campaigning with Mackenzie in Wyoming, he had commanded the Lakota and Arapaho scouts during the capture of Dull Knife's village in 1876. Afterward, at Fort Robinson, Clark supervised the Cheyenne scouts under Little Wolf. A strong friendship and mutual respect had developed between the Cheyenne war leader and the cavalry officer, popularly known as "White Hat" among the Cheyennes.[8]

Now stationed at Fort Keogh, Clark knew only that the Cheyennes had left Indian Territory because of some dissatisfaction and that some whites had been killed during their march. He believed that if he contacted Little Wolf, the Cheyenne leader might trust him more than others and surrender peacefully.[9]

Clark's command consisted of Company E, Second Cavalry, under himself; Company I, Second Cavalry, under Lt. Frederick W. Kingsbury; a detachment of twenty men and a three-man artillery squad under Lt. John C.F. Tillson; acting Assistant Surgeon Sabin; and four Lakota scouts. Ten wagons and forty pack mules transported Sibley tents and other supplies and equipment.

With the thermometer hovering consistently around thirty-three degrees below zero, Clark marched northeastward down the Yellowstone to Sheridan Buttes near the mouth of the Powder River. There he left a detail of four men to scout that area. Clark also requested that ranchers and teamsters plying the trails of the region report any sightings of Cheyennes. He then moved east to make camp at the mouth of O'Fallon's Creek.

On March 8 Clark sent two of his scouts to reconnoiter southward down the Powder River to where it was crossed by the Fort Keogh/Black Hills trail. They returned three days later to report that they had sighted Cheyenne hunters on foot fifty miles up the Powder. Clark immediately sent three scouts—Billy Jackson, Red War Bonnet, and Lakota mixed-blood Fleury—to locate the Cheyenne that had been sighted. Directing them to complete the original plan of reconnoiter eastward to the Little Missouri River, Clark marched his troops back to his Powder River camp through bitter cold and a four-inch snowfall to await the scouts' return.

Clark requested Cheyenne scouts from Two Moon's band of forty lodges, who had been permitted to remain at Fort Keogh. Six of the Cheyennes arrived on March 19, but there was no interpreter. Since Two Moon's men might object to fighting against other Cheyennes, Clark felt it was necessary to make his intentions regarding Little Wolf entirely clear. The only available interpreter at Keogh was a half-blood named Jules Seminole, who had been discharged from the army's payroll for misconduct. Clark had to use his own money to hire the man.

Through Seminole, Clark explained to the scouts that he would be able to make Little Wolf no promises except that if he and his people would surrender their ponies and guns, he would try to arrange for them to go to the Northern Arapaho Agency. One leading man dissented at first, saying that to shoot at Little Wolf's band would be like shooting at his own relatives. But Brave Wolf declared that if necessary, he was prepared to fight Little Wolf, who was his brother-in-law. He had been a scout at Keogh for two years, Brave Wolf said, and if Little Wolf did not surrender, he would fight him as ordered. The others said they would do likewise.

The council had just ended when scout Billy Jackson arrived in camp after riding 125 miles in twenty-four hours. He told Clark how he and his two companions had been captured by Little Wolf's band. This had occurred, he said, when the grass around their campfire caught fire and gave away their presence near the mouth of Box Elder Creek in far southwestern North Dakota. The scouts had told the Cheyennes they were out on a hunt from Sitting Bull's camp. By Jackson's account, the Cheyennes had believed them. The trio offered to lead the Northern Cheyennes to a good ford of the

William Philo Clark with Sioux chief Little Hawk. Courtesy, Bureau of American Ethnology.

Yellowstone and Missouri Rivers and take them to Sitting Bull in Canada. Many years later Jackson recited the story of how he and the other two scouts escaped from Little Wolf.

Upon reaching Hole-in-the-Rock Creek in far eastern Montana, the scouts began to see numerous signs of Cheyennes. Despite Jackson's caution against it and his insistence that they eat their meal raw, his two Sioux companions built a campfire. While Jackson was looking about from atop a knoll, the fire caught on the prairie grass and began spreading rapidly. Knowing the smoke could cause them to be spotted, Jackson called for his companions to leave quickly. But they had just topped a nearby ridge when they ran into four Cheyennes who demanded they surrender.

Jackson decided to bluff his way out of the situation. Because his hair was long, he felt he could convince the Cheyennes that he and his companions were Sioux hunters from Sitting Bull's camp. The Cheyennes, however, did not understand the Sioux language. Through sign talk they demanded that the three men accompany them to their camp, which proved to be that of Little Wolf. There was one Sioux woman in Little Wolf's camp.

"I talked mighty nice to that woman," Jackson said, "and she did the interpreting for me into Cheyenne."[10]

Little Wolf was suspicious of Jackson's claim that he was from Sitting Bull's camp, but the scout persisted until he and his companions were finally given lodging in the Cheyenne camp. Jackson stayed in Little Wolf's lodge and the other two in a tepee in the center of the camp. Little Wolf, still suspicious, had ordered that their guns and horses be taken away. During the night, however, Fleury and Red War Bonnet cut a slit in their lodge, secured their horses, and escaped, leaving Jackson behind.

Now Little Wolf was even more convinced that the three men were army scouts. Jackson argued that his friends had fled because they feared for their lives. He was convincing enough that he was given permission to accompany a Cheyenne party on a hunt for fresh meat. Little Wolf allowed him to ride his own horse but let him have only six cartridges.

The party soon came across some antelope. Jackson shot and crippled one and then began trailing it. He shot at it occasionally but was careful to miss. When he felt he was far enough away from the Cheyennes, he headed off at a hard gallop, stopping only after dark to rest and let his horse feed. He rode for two days and two nights, reaching Clark's column ahead of Fleury and Red War Bonnet.

Clark calculated that Little Wolf would likely attempt to cross the Yellowstone at the mouth of Cabin Creek, the best place to cross. Accordingly, he rushed a courier to Gen. Joseph N.G. Whistler, commander at Fort Keogh, to send forces to that point. Whistler dispatched a seventy-five-man detachment under Lt. Alonzo L. O'Brien, Second Cavalry, and Lt. Hobart K. Bailey, Fifth Infantry, from Keogh. He also ordered Capt. Simon Snyder, Fifth Infantry, to march down the Yellowstone River from Glendive in an effort to intercept Little Wolf's party. General Miles sent Company F, Sixth

Infantry, up the river from Fort Buford, Dakota Territory, for the same purpose.[11]

Clark broke camp immediately and, taking his pack mules and wagons, headed in the direction of Little Wolf's camp. He soon came upon Fleury and Red War Bonnet, who were making their escape. A cat and mouse game began, with Clark trying to guess what course Little Wolf might have taken when he learned their location and course of march had been discovered. The officer reasoned that the Cheyennes would either turn back to avoid interception or press quickly on in an attempt to cross the Yellowstone before Clark could catch them. The scouts believed Little Wolf would likely head for a place the Lakotas and Cheyennes used as a natural fortress known as "Hole in the Rock," near the mouth of Box Elder Creek. Clark sent two Lakotas and three Cheyennes to scout out Little Wolf's trail.[12]

Leaving his wagons behind and taking eight days' rations on his pack mules, Clark pushed rapidly toward that location on March 24. After marching thirty-five miles, he met the two Lakotas, who reported that Little Wolf was indeed headed for Hole in the Rock. The Cheyenne scouts continued on in pursuit. The following morning Clark discovered a two-day-old camp of Little Wolf's band. In following the trail that led from it, he was met by his three Cheyenne scouts. With them were three of Little Wolf's band.

The scouts said they had gone into the camp to deliver the terms Clark had dictated, and Little Wolf and his people had agreed to accept them. Fearing the troops would frighten his people if they marched into the village, however, Little Wolf wanted Clark to go into his camp. Little Wolf's people would then come over and join him. Clark refused, although he sent Brave Wolf and Young Two Moon to Little Wolf's camp to reiterate his good intentions and invite the chief to meet him. Brave Wolf delivered Clark's message, saying: "I love the soldiers of Keogh; I go with them to fight all their enemies, and if you will not listen you will force me to fight my own people, for you are my relatives."[13]

Clark marched to the Hole in the Rock redoubt, finding the Cheyennes had reinforced it with stone and dirt breastworks. After positioning his two companies of Second Cavalry around the Cheyennes, Clark sent his scouts to reassure Little Wolf of his good intentions. Then Clark walked unarmed into the camp for a parley. He told Little Wolf and his men that the price of peace was for them to give up their guns and horses. He wanted the Cheyennes' guns immediately, but they could keep their horses until they reached Keogh. There were many soldiers and Cheyenne scouts in the region, Clark said, and they would be wise to surrender.[14]

Handing over their guns was difficult for the Cheyennes. Clark adroitly permitted them to keep the weapons until they reached his wagons back up the trail. When the disarming took place, only thirty weapons were produced from among Little Wolf's thirty-three men. Clark, suspicious that they might be withholding guns, called a council of all the men before entering the post. He reasoned that if they still had arms, they would have them on their persons. When the Cheyennes had seated themselves in a circle on the ground, Clark asked that they all rise and throw off their blankets. They did so, and the scouts examined their packs and bundles. No more weapons were found.[15]

The Second Cavalry band played "Hail to the Chief" as Clark's command and the Cheyennes rode into Fort Keogh on April 1, 1879. General Miles was there to greet them. The last of the Northern Cheyenne exiles who had fled Indian Territory had been recaptured. But the stubborn question remained of whether they would be permitted to remain in the north or be returned to the south. The subject had not arisen during their surrender.

"I made them no promises," Clark stated in an official report; "[and] have not even touched on the subject of their going back. I know, however, that the hope of remaining is so strong with them that it amounts to expectation."[16]

The hopes of Little Wolf and his band that they would remain in their homeland were seriously threatened by the Fort Robinson Board of Officers, who concluded that they were guilty of depredations during their march north. The board's report charged Little Wolf's warriors with scouring the countryside, "killing farmers, ravishing and murdering women and children, robbing and burning houses, committing the most horrible atrocities, and bearing each night to their women and children the spoils of the whites."[17]

Little Wolf claimed that "we killed none who did not fire at us first."[18] He had a staunch friend and ally in Lieutenant Clark, who, despite the findings of the board, issued an impassioned appeal on behalf of the Cheyennes under Little Wolf. Admitting to the "horrible atrocities" committed in Kansas, Clark pointed to the actions of the band after it had crossed the Union Pacific Railroad. In a letter written April 6, 1879, to his department commander, Maj. George Gibson, Clark vigorously defended Little Wolf. He supported Little Wolf further by forwarding a letter from the chief to the post adjutant at Fort Keogh with a request that it be forwarded in turn to the proper authorities. In his letter Little Wolf made an impassioned plea for himself and his people to remain in their northern homeland:

> I am anxious and troubled. I think of some of my people killed at Fort
> Robinson after they had surrendered, and the worse than death for the rest

suffered there in being sent back south, for that means slow death by disease and suffering, of our people still south every lodge burdened with some one who is sick. They will leave as we did. Ask the Great Father to give us all a home somewhere here in the North. Perhaps if we could see him and plead with him for a little ground and for life he would heed our prayers. We are poor, but we are brave and we can die. We ask for pity, hope, and life.[19]

The slender thread by which the Northern Cheyennes held any chance of remaining at Fort Keogh was seriously imperiled, however, by an incident that occurred soon after their return. On April 5, 1879, Sergeant Kennedy of the Signal Service and Private Baader, Company E, Second Cavalry, were on their way from the Powder River telegraph station to Fort Keogh when they were fired upon from ambush by six Cheyennes at Mizpath Creek. Baader was killed immediately. Kennedy was wounded while attempting to reach his horse but managed to hide in the brush.[20]

The Cheyennes left but returned that night to scalp Baader and take the men's horses and Baader's revolver and ammunition. Kennedy was rescued the next day and taken to Fort Keogh by a party of Deadwood men who were passing by. A detachment of Second Cavalry troopers and two Cheyenne scouts immediately took to the field in pursuit. After finding three abandoned camps in which they found remnants of clothing, a pipe, a watch, and horse equipment taken from the two soldiers, the pursuers overtook the warriors. The culprits proved to be three Cheyenne men—Black Wolf, Whetstone, and Hole-in-the-Breast—four women, and one child. The troops forced their surrender, recovering the stolen arms, ammunition, and horses. Little Wolf had no sympathy for the trio, telling the commanding officer at Fort Keogh: "Your laws punish such crimes. Hang them or imprison them for life. I never want to see their faces again. They knew I had made peace with you, and they killed your soldiers."[21]

Thus, with Little Wolf's approval, the military gave in to white settlers' demands that the three Cheyennes be tried in civil court of Montana Territory. During January 1879 two Nez Percé chiefs who had been tried before a civilian jury at Pendleton, Oregon, were executed by hanging.[22] In June of that same year, a Gros Ventre was tried by the First Territorial District Court in Miles City for murdering a rancher. He was quickly found guilty and hanged by a civilian court according to the attitude that prevailed among many whites on the frontier that "the only good Indian is a dead one."[23]

The three Cheyennes sat through their trial impassively and declined to ask any questions when an interpreter repeated the testimony in the Cheyenne tongue. They, too, were quickly convicted and sentenced to be hanged the following July 7. Whetstone and Hole-in-the-Breast, however, defied execution by committing suicide.

> They sought death in a cool and deliberate manner, so unparalleled as to provoke the admiration of even their white foes. Although handcuffed and chained by the ankles to a bull-ring in the floor, they had succeeded in hanging themselves in the aperture of the cell door. The same strap was used by both, one waiting until the other was dead, and then lifting down the corpse, deliberately removing the strap and adjusting it for his own strangling.[24]

A pardon was sought for Black Wolf, who was believed to have been less guilty than the others. Before the request could be acted on, however, the Cheyenne learned of his wife's death, and he, too, hanged himself. When asked what he thought of the affair, an old Cheyenne at Fort Keogh replied, "Big fools—stout hearts!"[25]

Little Wolf and his people had beaten all the odds; they had outmaneuvered and outfought the U.S. Army and made it back to their homeland in the north. A reporter observed that the chief was happier at Keogh than he had been for a long time.

21
Sheridan's PROMISE

THE BANDS OF NORTHERN CHEYENNES WHO HAD SURRENDERED to General Miles at Fort Keogh in 1877 had been far more fortunate than the Dull Knife–Little Wolf group. Permitted to remain in the north, their warriors performed excellent service as scouts and fighters against the Nez Percé and Lakotas. Miles readily admitted he would not have been successful without their help.

Once the other tribes had been quieted, however, the government reactivated its efforts to remove the remaining Northern Cheyennes to Indian Territory. The reluctant chiefs asked for an interview with General Sheridan, then headquartered in Chicago, to determine where their bands were to reside. Miles agreed. It was hoped the Cheyennes would be influenced to accept white ways by the "highest evidences of civilization" the Windy City offered.[1]

Miles arranged a visit to Chicago for the Northern Cheyenne delegation composed of Little Chief, Two Moon, Crazy Mule, High Backbone, Old Wolf, and Black Wolf. Ben Clark, who had been called up from the Darlington Agency to escort and interpret for them when they were removed to Indian Territory, served as their escort. Traveling by way of Bismarck, Dakota Territory, the delegation arrived at Chicago's Commercial Hotel in December 1877. Sheridan was away in Washington, so Chicago officials entertained the Cheyennes with carriage rides about the city, a visit to the Coliseum, and an evening at Haverly's Adelphi, where they could "admire the female minstrelsy."[2]

When Sheridan arrived back in Chicago on December 15, the chiefs, fully bedecked in feathered headdresses and war paint, were escorted through gaping crowds to meet with him at army headquarters in the Union Building. The chiefs expressed their desire to remain with General Miles and continue to assist him in the event of Indian outbreaks the coming spring. Sheridan, however, brusquely gave the chiefs the choice of two options. They could go to Lincoln, Nebraska, until May 1, when it could be decided what to do with them, or they could go directly to Indian Territory. The chiefs opted to go to Lincoln.[3]

Sheridan assured them that considerable game would still be found in Indian Territory. He said the country was large and less likely to be taken away by the white men than the Black Hills had been. Sheridan also made a promise the Cheyennes would not forget: that for their assistance in fighting the Nez Percé and helping to capture Chief Joseph, they would be able to keep their few guns as well as their war ponies.[4]

The Lincoln option was never exercised. When the chiefs returned to their people at Fort Keogh, Little Chief hearkened to Sheridan's assurances of good hunting in Indian Territory and decided to move south on a trial basis. He was likely influenced by another factor. Northern Cheyenne family members were spread among the various bands. He had a wife and son who were with Dull Knife's band. Iron Shirt, Crazy Mule, Ridge Bear, and Black Bear were to go with Little Chief, but Miles was able to retain eighty lodges under Brave Wolf and Two Moon for use as scouts.[5]

During the winter Little Chief and his people moved eastward up the Yellowstone to Fort Abraham Lincoln at Bismarck. They expected to leave there in May 1878 but were delayed. During their wait, they became hopeful they would be returned to Fort Keogh and were sorely disappointed when the order for them to go south finally arrived in July. Sheridan had told Little Chief he and his people could travel by steamboat or railroad from Fort Lincoln, but the Cheyennes begged to be supplied with rations and to pack and ride their own horses in their usual fashion. Sheridan consented. Escorted by Ben Clark and a company of Seventh Cavalry, the Northern Cheyennes marched south to Camp Robinson, their discontent increasing the farther they went.

The Cheyennes arrived at Sidney Barracks on September 16 just as news was breaking of the Dull Knife and Little Wolf outbreak and flight north.[6] Fearing that Little Chief's band might join those fleeing north, the army

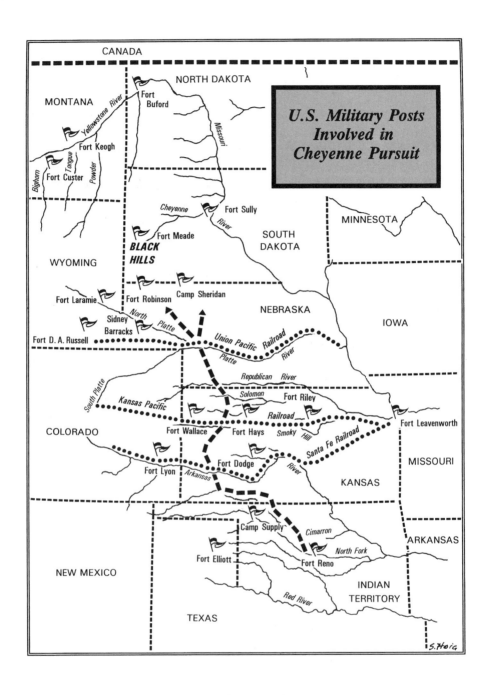

immediately ordered that the Cheyennes be held there temporarily until Dull Knife and Little Wolf were captured. Little Chief's people were taken to a camp a mile outside Sidney to keep them from having contact with other bands from which they might learn that Dull Knife's people had escaped from the southern agency.

Little Chief opined that they were leaving a country that was "heap good, where game is plenty and where our women and children will not starve and going to a country where fever and famine [will] soon kill them all."[7] But when he met with Crook on September 22, he promised Crook that his people would not cause trouble. Authorities were not reassured when one Northern Cheyenne subchief displayed three wounds he had received in Custer's defeat.[8]

Little Chief's men were not tightly controlled, and Sidney residents complained that warriors were occasionally seen lurking around town. They charged that the three Cheyennes who shot and killed a rancher and his two sons on October 19 twenty-six miles north of Sidney may have been members of his band.[9]

As a precaution against their slipping away and joining Dull Knife, General Crook ordered that the Cheyennes' guns be taken from them. The order almost caused a small war to erupt at the Sidney camp. The warriors led by Iron Shirt fiercely resisted giving up the weapons. They had not forgotten the promise Sheridan—whom they called "Three Stars"—had made in Chicago. Eventually, Clark and Little Chief were able to persuade the reluctant warriors to hand over most of the weapons. Before the Cheyennes departed from Sidney Barracks, twenty rifles and a number of pistols were returned to them for hunting.[10]

Mauck and his four companies of Fourth Cavalry arrived at Sidney on October 10, exhausted from their futile pursuit of Dull Knife and Little Wolf. Much to their chagrin, the army saw them as the logical troops to escort Little Chief and his band to Indian Territory. The woman and boy found on Snake Creek plus another woman and boy found on Chalk Creek, all of whom had been left behind during the Dull Knife exodus, were now joined with Little Chief for the return to Darlington.[11]

Leaving Sidney Barracks on October 21, Little Chief's band of 186 people moved south peacefully. As Dull Knife's people had done two years earlier, they traveled by way of Fort Wallace, reaching there on November 3 and Dodge City later that month. They also depended on the hunt for food. With buffalo far less abundant than had been the case two years earlier, riflemen for the entourage killed mostly antelope. When they passed through Dodge City on November 21, a reporter observed that the band looked haggard, sickly, and poorly clothed and equipped. The Cheyennes camped near Fort Dodge, where a large number of sightseers came to see them.[12]

The cavalcade of Cheyennes and cavalry had already left Camp Supply when new orders were sent out from General Pope at Fort Leavenworth. The edict declared that the Cheyennes would have to be disarmed and their horses taken. This change of procedure had resulted when Miles learned that the Cheyennes had been permitted to retain their arms and ponies. The Quaker agent adamantly refused to accept any Cheyenne who was not completely disarmed and dismounted. He had complained strongly to Commissioner Hayt, who in turn contacted the army.[13]

The order was relayed to Captain Mauck, reaching him at night when his party was in camp near present Woodward, Oklahoma.[14] The Cheyennes were camped in a circle and the troops to the outside. Second Lt. Heber Creel, Seventh Cavalry, traveling to Fort Reno with the party to study the Cheyenne language, was camped among the Cheyennes. The following morning Mauck, with great reluctance, read the orders to the Cheyennes. He was not surprised at their reaction. Sheridan had allowed them to keep the guns, Iron Shirt declared angrily, in reward for the service they had rendered to General Miles. In fact, most of the guns were ones they had captured themselves while fighting for the United States against the Sioux and Nez Percé in Montana. For the government to take them away would be an act of deception and injustice. The forty-eight warriors of the band angrily confronted Mauck with rifles, pistols, and knives in hand. Many of the Cheyenne women sat on the ground and began singing their death song.

"You have lied to us long enough," Iron Shirt told Mauck. "We will not surrender. We do not lie; brave men do not lie. Take our guns and ponies if you can!"[15]

He went up and down the line of warriors, saying, "Shiv-e-ta-noth! Shiv-e-ta-noth!" Creel translated this as, "Stand fast! Don't give up! Persevere!"

Creel described the camp as in a wild state of confusion and excitement: "My tent in the midst of the encampment was filled to the utmost capacity with women and children—guns [were] cocked, arrows drawn."[16]

Lieutenant Colonel Dodge, returning to Kansas after temporary service on a court-martial board at Fort Sill, happened to meet the Northern Cheyennes and troops on the trail at the time of the incident. He described the affair in his journal on December 2, 1878:

> When they [the Cheyennes] understood that they were to be disarmed
> they went to their Teepees painted themselves and put on a war aspect.
> Mauck talked, and urged. The Indians pulled out their papers, [and]

insisted that they had the promises of big Chiefs &c, &c, and finally tore
their papers to shreds and stalked back to their tents still keeping their
Arms.[17]

Mauck and Chapman went to the Cheyennes' camp and sat down with
them in council inside a tepee. Chapman attempted to present Mauck's
position, but the Cheyenne warriors angrily rejected any compromise. Finally, Chapman told Mauck they had better leave if they were going to get
away alive. The two men walked slowly away. They had just left when a
knife sliced the tepee where Mauck had been sitting, and a warrior plunged
through the slit crying, "Let me kill [the] thief! Let me kill him!"[18]

Determined to enforce his orders, Mauck brought his four companies of
Fourth Cavalry troops to surround the infuriated Cheyennes. He gave the
order "Advance carbine," and the troopers moved their mounts into line
holding their carbines with their right hands, muzzles pointing upward. The
Cheyennes stood their ground. This potentially explosive face-off continued
for four hours as Mauck attempted to resolve the matter peacefully.

Ben Clark, Amos Chapman, William Rowland, and Heber Creel were
all called forth to persuade the Cheyennes that it would be hopeless for
them to resist. A conference was held with Little Chief, who reminded the
white men of Sheridan's promise. He said he did not think the order came
from Sheridan, as he believed everything the general had told him. Although he did not approve of all that had been done, Little Chief said he
wished to remain a good friend to the soldiers. Through Clark, he was promised that the weapons would be returned once they were on the reservation.
This pacified the warriors enough that the crisis was resolved. Seventeen
firearms were confiscated: thirteen carbines, one new Colts revolver, one
old-style cap-and-ball pistol, one squirrel gun, and a three-band musket cut
down to carbine length. Eleven ponies were taken from the Cheyennes and
sent back to Camp Supply.[19]

Again, not all the weapons were turned in. Some had been issued in
connection with military discharges or ration tickets.

A few of the warriors, fearing the tickets would be telltale documents
for the guns they still possessed, either tore up or chewed and swallowed the
receipts.

On December 9 the entourage reached Fort Reno. The Cheyennes were
first taken to Major Mizner before being turned over to agent Miles. Little
Chief made a speech to Mizner through Clark:

> General Sheridan told us when we go South we should find plenty of
> turkey and deer to hunt while on our way to the Agency. We had just got

to where the turkeys were and found it was so, there were a great many,
but just then we were ordered to give up our guns and ponies. We do not
know why those promises were not kept.[20]

Although Little Chief and his people had willingly come south, Mizner
and Miles would soon learn that the northern band had little intention of
remaining in Indian Territory. Unlike Dull Knife, however, Little Chief
would work persistently to influence the government to live up to its promise that they could return north if they did not like it in the south.

It was the end of a long, difficult, and fruitless episode for the Fort Reno
Fourth Cavalry Troops G and H. Troops I and K had yet to return to their
respective bases at Camp Supply and Fort Elliott. They received little appre-
ciation for their exhausting march of over 1,000 miles after the Northern
Cheyennes. But as the troops settled wearily back into their post routines,
their officers became caught up in bitter rancor over performances during
the ordeal. The man who bore the greatest wrath of officers both above and
below him in rank was Joseph Rendlebrock.[21]

22

The COURT-MARTIALS

IKE MANY OTHERS, RENDLEBROCK HAD SUFFERED CONSIDERABLY during the long, punishing ride from Fort Reno. His age had worked against him, and he was ailing.[1] When the Fourth Cavalry reached Ogalalla on October 4, 1878, he took leave and with his orderly went on ahead of his unit to Sidney. Rendlebrock checked into the Lockwood House before crossing Lodge Pole Creek to Sidney Barracks hospital for a surgeon's examination.[2]

Mauck's command arrived on October 10 and made camp near the military post.[3] Early on October 11 Rendlebrock went to his tent. During the morning he signed a ration return for withdrawing fur caps, boots, and other clothing suitable to the Nebraska locale and season. He also had Feely confine two men who had been quarreling, but he later ordered them released. When asked to sign a forage requisition, however, he said he was no longer in operational command and deferred to Wilder. He told Feely he did not think he could stand the return trip to Fort Reno if the command traveled overland and asked the sergeant's help in applying for a certificate of disability. The post surgeon supported the application, verifying that he had thoroughly examined the officer and found that he suffered from rheumatism and general bad health from his prolonged exposure in the field.[4]

On October 12, the evening before he was to catch a Union Pacific train to Omaha on the first leg of his return to Fort Reno, Rendlebrock invited the other officers to his tent for a post-expedition celebration of sorts. All of the officers—Mauck, Gunther, Hemphill, Wood, Wilder, McDonald, Leeper, Patch, and Martin—dropped by to sit, chat, and drink the beer and whiskey Rendlebrock provided. How robust the celebration was has never been made clear; McDonald referred to the evening as a "little frolic."[5] But whatever camaraderie may have existed that evening, an undercurrent of resentment toward Rendlebrock prevailed, at least with Wilder and Wood—the latter of whom when Rendlebrock left pronounced him "an old fraud."[6] When the two men refused to lend Rendlebrock any assistance in his preparation to leave the next morning, Leeper volunteered to procure his train tickets, saying he thought he could get a special commutation ticket at half fare. Rendlebrock gave him twenty dollars, and Leeper arranged a sleeping car for him at a cost of sixteen dollars.[7]

Although they saw Rendlebrock only from September 10–13, both Wood and Wilder later testified that he was drunk to the point of incapacitation the entire time he was at Sidney. This was contradicted by Leeper, Feely, and several others.[8] That afternoon Rendlebrock paid his bill at the Lockwood House and waited for Leeper and Wilder to arrive with an ambulance to take him to the depot.[9] Before departing, Rendlebrock agreed to take a package back to Fort Reno for Sergeant McGann, who returned a watch the officer had loaned him, and to carry other messages for troopers. Rendlebrock also gave his blankets to his orderly.[10]

Night had fallen when the Union Pacific train pulled out of Sidney with Rendlebrock aboard. When the train reached Omaha the next morning, he was sitting in the corner of a Pullman coach. A correspondent for the *New York Herald* seeking an interview found him there. The journalist described the cavalryman as "so sunburned as to be almost black, wearing a soiled cavalry uniform, with nothing about him to suggest that he was more than a private but a pair of worn shoulder straps bearing the bars of a captain."[11]

Rendlebrock did not want to be interviewed, but he was polite to the reporter. He spoke with a strong German accent the reporter repeated only for one sentence: "Well, I can't tell you nothings you wants to print."[12]

The reporter asked why he was traveling east—was he giving up the chase? Rendlebrock answered with great indignation: "Given up the chase! Do you think I was going to catch the Cheyennes alone? I'm going back to Fort Reno, sick and worn out. I haven't had my clothes off until I went to bed in this car last night since I started from Fort Reno September 10."[13]

Rendlebrock summarized the Cheyenne pursuit. But at one point the veteran officer blundered badly.

"Well, you want to know why the Cheyennes left," he said in frustration. "I will tell you. The principal cause was the perfidy of the interpreter, and they would not have gone but for his misrepresentations. Then Colonel Mizner, of Fort Reno, could have prevented the stampede if he had complied with my wish and sent me two twelve pound Napoleon guns when the Indians were but a short distance from the fort."[14]

This statement was quoted in the reporter's article that appeared not only in the *New York Herald* but also in the *Army and Navy Journal*. It became certain fodder for the filing of court-martial charges by the infuriated Mizner, even though Rendlebrock wrote a public apology to the Fort Reno commander claiming that the reporter had misrepresented his statement regarding the cause of the trouble. What he had meant to convey, he attempted to explain, was his belief that if the two pieces of artillery had been displayed before the Northern Cheyenne village, their dread of the guns might have induced them to come in to the agency as they had been requested to do.[15] This retraction was not enough to save him from Mizner's wrath or from accusations leveled against him by his junior officers who arrived back at Fort Reno on December 9—nearly two months later. The Fourth Cavalry troops returned to their base so sunburned and haggard they were barely recognizable to friends and families. It had been their lot to make the long trip home by horseback in escort to Little Chief's band.

West Pointers Wood and Wilder had been strongly critical of the two foreign-born officers under whom they served. But for a time after their return to Fort Reno, relations among them had remained reasonably harmonious on the surface. The day they returned to the post, Wood accepted Gunther's invitation to have a meal at the captain's quarters. He was a guest on other occasions as well, later explaining this by saying, "Mrs. Gunther is a lady I have great regard for."[16]

The Fort Reno cavalry units were in the field on November 22 when Wood and Wilder responded to General Hatch's request for a report on their recent expedition to the north. In his report Wood was openly critical of Rendlebrock. He made no derogatory mention of Gunther except by omission when he lauded the "courage and energy" of Wilder, McDonald, and, by implication, himself. But his festering dislike of Gunther in particular came to the surface after the holiday season. Ultimately, Wood admitted that for some time he had been mulling over the idea of preferring court-martial charges against Gunther.[17]

On Christmas Eve Wood was among those who paid a Yuletide visit to Gunther's house and afterward to that of Rendlebrock. Wood, whose tongue had evidently been loosened by Yuletide cheer, charged Gunther—who, among other actions, had led troops into the Palo Duro Canyon in 1874— with being a coward.[18] Gunther learned of the remark from Mrs. Rendlebrock, and he in turn told her Wood had called her husband an old fraud. In early January the matter came to a head. Gunther had gone to the guardhouse to relieve Wood as officer of the day. When Wood said he wanted to talk with him, Gunther refused. "You slandered me at Major Rendlebrock's house," he told Wood, "and I will hold you responsible."[19]

Wood denied that such was the case, saying he thought too much of Gunther to do so. The two men went to the base adjutant's office, where Gunther reported to the commanding officer as the new officer of the day. As he was leaving the building, he spied Wood entering Rendlebrock's house. He followed and entered the house to find Wood talking with Rendlebrock. Gunther repeated his accusation that Wood had called him a coward. When Wood denied that he had done so, Mrs. Rendlebrock came into the room.[20]

"Mr. Wood, you did say so, and further than that, you called my husband a fraud!"[21]

"Where?"

"Up at Sidney. If you deny that then you are no gentleman, and you should leave this house and never put foot in it again."[22]

Wood stood up and faced Gunther. "Captain," he said indignantly, "in addition to your other virtues, you are a tale-bearer."[23]

As he was leaving, the junior officer blurted out his feelings in full: "Captain, I want to say to you that you gave the command to charge [during the retreat at Turkey Springs], and I saw you galloping off on your horse."[24]

Gunther denied that he had "galloped" off, and Wood departed. But that was far from the end of it. Wood set about gathering supportive evidence for court-martial charges against both Gunther and Rendlebrock. Wood wrote to Hatch asking that he recommend that Gunther be tried by court-martial. Hatch rejected the action.[25] Mizner, however, was agreeable to bringing Rendlebrock to trial.

It was evidently with his approval that Wood and Wilder called a meeting of all the fort's noncoms to ask if anyone knew of Rendlebrock or Mrs. Rendlebrock selling whiskey to the men of the garrison. Then they asked if anyone knew of them selling eggs or butter to the men. The pair questioned everyone individually and wrote down the answers. Evidently, they found little or no evidence, for no charges were brought on those issues. At the end of the meeting, the officers ordered that none of the enlisted men could visit Rendlebrock without permission.[26]

Rendlebrock was placed under arrest on February 1 and Gunther on February 23. They were escorted by their troops to newly designated Fort Supply where a court-martial board was convened in March to hear their cases. The court-martial board consisted of Col. Jefferson C. Davis, Twenty-third Infantry; Maj. Alexander J. Dallas, Twenty-third Infantry; Capt. John Wilcox, Fourth Cavalry; Capt. G. K. Brady, Twenty-third Infantry; Capt. James Henton, Twenty-third Infantry; Capt. T. E. Rose, Sixteenth Infantry; and Capt. R. I. Eskridge, Twenty-third Infantry. Capt. J. M. Smith, Twenty-third Infantry, served as judge advocate.

Hemphill at Fort (as of December 1878) Supply was likewise arraigned before the board on charges levied against him by Hambright. His case was heard first regarding two counts. One was that he went against Hambright's orders in marching his command to Fort Dodge. The second was that he failed to turn back the Cheyennes when he first engaged them at Sand Creek. Testimony began on March 10, 1879.

The first count—disobedience of orders—centered on whether Hemphill knew Hambright was sending out new rations from Camp Supply on September 13, 1878. Company I, it was shown, was already at Fort Dodge when the information regarding the sending of rations reached Hemphill by courier.

"Captain Hemphill was thrown on his own resources," the court concluded, "to provide for it [an emergency], to the best of his judgment and took the action he did and went to Dodge to provide for it."[27]

The second charge specified: "Neglect of duty to the prejudice of good order and military discipline." Witnesses called in Hemphill's defense included Leeper; J. S. Driscoll (Driskell); Sgt. Samuel A. Trask, Company I; Sgt. Jacob Schaufler, Company I; Sgt. John Dowling, Company I; and Hemphill himself. Leeper testified that he did not think it was possible to have brought the Cheyennes in peaceably at the first Sand Creek engagement.[28] Driscoll felt that going in to Dodge for supplies was proper. Trask and Dowling explained the lack of rations the company experienced. Hemphill defended his action of not sending a courier for more ammunition at Sand Creek, observing, "Had I sent a courier before I could have got reinforcements I would have been out of ammunition."[29] The court concluded:

Whatever his shortcomings in other respects may be, he points with pride to the fact that he did come up with [and] boldly attack with less than forty tired and hungry men of his company engaged for more than two hours and drive back to their stronghold more than a hundred of the bravest and most skilful Indian warriors that ever went on the war path.[30]

The Fort Supply court quickly exonerated Hemphill of the charges. Hambright later issued new charges against him, however. At Fort Riley, Kansas, in October 1879, Hemphill was tried again and found guilty of being so drunk on duty at Camp Supply on September 11 that he could not perform his duties. Accordingly, he was suspended from rank and command for a year, confined to Fort Riley for that period, and required to forfeit half of his pay.[31]

Gunther's trial on March 14, 1879, was more involved, with numerous witnesses called. The charges had been brought by Wood, who insisted he had made up his mind to prefer them long before the incident at Rendlebrock's house.[32] He brought two counts against Gunther. On the first, Wood charged that Gunther galloped away and abandoned his command during the retreat from Turkey Springs. The second accused Gunther of hiding in the grass and behaving in a cowardly manner when a shot was fired and an alarm given in camp during the night of the retreat.[33]

McDonald, Wilder, and Wood were called to testify for the government. McDonald described how he had seen Gunther on the trail and thought he was too sick to set his horse, how he had forced him to continue on, and how later Gunther recuperated enough to form and order a charge against the Cheyennes. He also gave a detailed account of the camp shooting incident. When asked to give his impression of Gunther's manner during the event, he answered that he thought it was the same as his own—a feeling of relief. And when asked: "Relieved from what?" McDonald replied: "From anxiety. None of us wanted to do any more fighting."[34]

Wilder agreed that during the retreat Gunther had looked pale and was so sick that he wanted to get off his horse and lie down and also that his horse was at a walk, not a gallop. Further, Wilder expressed no indication of cowardice in Gunther's behavior during the camp incident, stating only: "He came up to us after we had ascertained what the firing was, holding his piece at about a ready, stooping over, and enquired as to the causes of the shot in a suppressed whisper."[35]

Wood, however, vociferously denounced Gunther. In reference to the retreat, he testified: "His manner as impressed on my mind at the time was that he was deliberately running away and leaving his command because he did not want to get under fire."[36]

In regard to the camp incident, he concurred with Wilder's description of Gunther's presence but came to a far different conclusion than any of the others: "His manner at the time, and knowing what I did of his action in the morning, made me ashamed of him."[37]

A number of noncoms were called to testify in Gunther's behalf, all supporting their longtime officer. On April 4, 1879, the court-martial board rendered its verdict. It found Gunther not guilty on both charges. The interpretation of the board's report by General Pope's headquarters in Fort Leavenworth, however, cast a shadow of suspicion over Gunther's behavior. As reviewing officer, Pope keyed in both on Wilder's statement that he had seen Gunther 300 to 400 yards ahead of the rear guard and on the lack of a satisfactory explanation of the officer's illness. Pope concluded, "While the evidence is insufficient to show shameful cowardice by the accused, it clearly does show that [the] accused left his command and did not show any zeal that day."[38]

Stung by the statement, Gunther rebutted the review by pointing out that according to specifications of the judge advocate general's office, "It is not in the power of the reviewing officer either directly or indirectly or by implication from his language to enlarge the measure of punishment imposed by instance of Court Martial."[39] Gunther held that Wilder's statement had been taken out of context; in fact, he noted, testimony showed that Wilder himself was retreating beside Gunther at the time. Gunther was returned to command of his Fourth Cavalry troops, serving another fifteen years before he retired.[40]

The trial of Joseph Rendlebrock was much more involved than those of Hemphill and Gunther. He was charged on four counts: (1) misbehavior before the enemy, (2) disobedience of the lawful commands of his commanding officer, (3) neglect of duty to the prejudice of good order and military discipline, and (4) drunkenness to the prejudice of good order and military discipline.

Each charge carried several lengthy specifications. Specification One accused Rendlebrock of leading the retreat at Turkey Springs in a careless and unsoldierly manner, of failing to give Wood support at Sand Creek on September 21, of failing to engage the Cheyennes fully on September 22 at Sand Creek, and of failing to join and command his troops at Punished Woman's Fork.

Specification Two claimed he failed to carry out Mizner's orders to pursue the Cheyennes "steadily, perseveringly, persistently, and unrelentingly" (privately issued instructions from Mizner to Rendlebrock as recalled by Wood and Wilder[41]); that he willfully disobeyed orders to "overtake, attack, and force said Indians to return to their agency" at Sand Creek on September 21; and that he failed to do the same on September 22.

Specification Three alleged that under the pretense of procuring supplies, Rendlebrock delayed pursuit of the Cheyennes and permitted them to gain a thirty-six-hour advance; and that he neglected to send a messenger to Fort Dodge to notify Lewis of the Sand Creek engagements, the position of the Cheyennes, and their probable direction of flight.

Specification Four accused him of being too drunk to perform his duties at Sidney Barracks and of conducting himself in such a drunken manner at the Lockwood House as to disgrace the uniform he wore.[42]

Testimony was taken from a large number of witnesses that included Captain Morse and Lt. W. W. Barrett of the Sixteenth Infantry; Gardener and M. Barver of the Nineteenth Infantry; Fourth Cavalry officers Gunther, Hemphill, Wood, Wilder, and McDonald; and ranchmen, scouts, teamsters, and enlisted men. Most notable among the Company G and H men were 1st Sergeants Feely and Gatewood. Once again, Wood was the principal accuser. As had Hemphill and Gunther, Rendlebrock testified in his own behalf.

The court began taking testimony on March 16, 1879, and rendered its decision on March 31. The board found Rendlebrock guilty on charge one, not guilty on charge two, not guilty on charge three, and not guilty on charge four. On the basis of finding him guilty on charge one, the board sentenced Rendlebrock to be dismissed from the service.

At Fort Reno a very distraught Louise Rendlebrock wrote a lengthy letter in German to the secretary of interior, German-born Carl Schurz, on May 20. She pleaded that Schurz use his influence to help her husband obtain justice in the face of the prejudice of West Point officers against others who had risen from the ranks. She cited the observation of two medical officers that he suffered deformity of his great toes on both feet, the condition caused by rheumatic diabetes.

"My husband is utterly unfit for active service," she wrote. "What fear and uncertainty my husband can only know in [Fort] Supply surrounded by a slanderous and malicious set."[43]

In reviewing Rendlebrock's sentence, the judge advocate general observed that in reaching its decision the court-martial board had obviously placed more reliance "in the judgement of Captain Gunther and the other experienced Indian fighters [as witnesses for Rendlebrock], than in the young Lieutenants who denounce their commander; neither of whom had ever been engaged in a fight with Indians till this occasion."[44] He also observed that the disappointment and anger of Rendlebrock's superiors (probably General Pope) were doubtless great because of the lack of military success in stopping the Cheyennes but that there was little to justify such a severe punishment of the accused.

The argument was persuasive to the secretary of war, and General Sheridan joined in recommending executive clemency "on account of his age, his long and creditable service, and the fact that his physical condition has been shown in evidence to have unfitted him for the duties of an active campaign."[45] Accordingly, President Rutherford B. Hayes remitted Rendle-brock's dismissal from the service, and he was placed on the army's retired list as of July 29, 1879.[46]

There is some irony, and a certain injustice, to the fact that Wood was the sole person who won laurels as a result of the Fourth Cavalry pursuit. In February 1880 he was promoted to brevet captain for his "gallant service in action against the Indians at Sand Creek and at Punished Woman's Fork."[47] In the first he had forgotten ammunition for his troops and had gone into action without consulting with or receiving orders from his commanding officer just as he had at Turkey Springs. And at Punished Woman's Fork he himself admitted in his report to General Hatch: "I did not take any particular part in this skirmish. I know nothing of the details."[48]

23

A Search
FOR BLAME

ULL KNIFE, ALONG WITH HIS WIFE, SLOW WOMAN, their one remaining son, and one daughter, had remained alive in their cave by eating their moccasins. After eighteen days of wandering, they reached Pine Ridge Agency, which had been established in Dakota Territory north of Camp Sheridan during fall of 1878 even as Dull Knife and his people were escaping from Indian Territory. As a result, they knew nothing of the site except what they may have been told by the visiting Lakotas. When they finally arrived the night of February 7, 1879, twenty-nine days after escaping from the prison barracks at Fort Robinson, they found refuge in the lodge of Young Man Afraid of His Horses. The Lakota leader duly reported Dull Knife's arrival to agent James Irwin, who wrote to General Crook:

> He [Young Man Afraid of His Horses] stated that the party was in a wretched condition, one or more of them wounded, that the old man from cold, hunger, exposure and anxiety is sick and now prostrated. The Ogalallas were greatly shocked at the Cheyenne affair following the arrival of the Cheyenne women and children at this agency, many of them wounded and altogether a most pitiable sight. Now comes this old man and what is left of his family, and my people [the Sioux] most earnestly insist that the Gov't may show him quarters. I fear it will cause great

trouble if an attempt is made at this time to take the party. His age and great affection and seeking their protection may appeal to their hearts with more force than discretion.[1]

The mass killing of the Cheyennes had so upset the Oglalas that Chief Red Cloud had made an urgent request that the surviving women and children, now widows and orphans, at Fort Robinson be turned over to his people to care for. "My people are sad at heart," the old chief said in a grave tone, "since their brethren were killed here some moons ago. They are very angry with the whites."[2]

With Crook's approval, Irwin telegraphed the commissioner of Indian Affairs imploring that the women and children of Lakota blood be sent to Pine Ridge. The request was passed on to the secretary of war and the secretary of interior. Both departments approved the request, although not on humanitarian grounds. Doing so, they decided, would quiet the Oglalas and make them more attached to the government. Sheridan was ordered to release the Cheyenne women and children survivors of the Fort Robinson holocaust and send them to Pine Ridge Agency.[3]

Twenty-three wounded survivors, along with those not wounded, were loaded into wagons at Fort Robinson on January 31 and driven to the lower camp en route to Pine Ridge.[4] There they were permitted to say tearful goodbyes to Wild Hog and six other surviving Northern Cheyenne men and their families. The wives and children of these seven men were excluded from the group going to Pine Ridge.

Soon after the wagons departed from the lower camp, a disturbance erupted. Wild Hog's wife was seen gesticulating wildly. When the authorities ran to Wild Hog's lodge, they found him bathed in blood and unconscious. Dr. Pettys, who was called forth from where he was testifying before a Board of Officers at Fort Robinson, found the chief had several wounds evidently inflicted with a sharp instrument. Some thought his wife had stabbed him in an effort to save him from being taken to Kansas for trial. Others thought Wild Hog had attempted suicide because he was being sent back to Kansas. No one considered that the cause may have been his deep despair at seeing his people taken away.[5]

A witness described the plight of the widows and orphans as they arrived at Pine Ridge Agency. Among them was another daughter of Dull Knife, the beautiful Cheyenne girl whom the officers at Fort Robinson had known affectionately as "the Princess."

> The survivors were brought into the large council room. The Indians [Sioux] were collecting in great numbers and were loudly bewailing the fate of their allies and kinsmen. A pandemonium prevailed. Some of the

women and children had been wounded. Some had not yet washed the blood from their faces. They presented a horrible sight. The weather was bitterly cold, and there was no fire in the council room. They stood there, shivering with fear and cold.[6]

Public reaction had forced the army to hold an immediate investigation into the bloody affair at Fort Robinson. On January 21, almost as the last shot rang out at Antelope Creek, a Board of Officers was appointed to "examine into and report the facts attending the arrest, confinement, disarmament, escape and recapture of a number of Cheyenne Indians."[7] The board was to assess not only the causes but the blame (military-wise) in the matter. Despite the fact that he had participated in the Cheyenne hunt, Major Evans was named president of the board. He was joined by Capt. John W. Hamilton, Fifth Cavalry, and 1st Lt. Walter S. Schuyler, Fifth Cavalry. The officers assembled at Fort Robinson on January 25 and began taking testimony from officers, soldiers, some of the seventy-nine Northern Cheyenne survivors, and private citizens.[8]

Wild Hog, Old Crow, Blacksmith, and the wounded Big Head were interviewed at length, along with several Cheyenne women and Pumpkin Seed's Son (Big Beaver). Detailed testimony was taken from most of the officers involved in the Fort Robinson breakout as well as interpreter James Rowland. The questioning covered the range of events from the capture of the Northern Cheyennes to the final battle.

Among other matters, the board touched on Wessells's tactics of starvation and withholding fuel for heat to force the Cheyennes to return south. It concluded: "The recourse to measures of starvation bears too strong an analogy to the ancient, but now exploded, practice of torture applied to a prisoner to compel confession, not to startle the supporters of modern leniency."

The board then absolved Wessells, Crook, and the command chain above them by asking, "But what milder course could have been devised?"[9] And finally it concluded:

> The Board has pointed out certain [tactical] errors, it believed to have been committed; but beyond that, attaches no blame to anyone in the Military Service, and in view of all the circumstances of this unfortunate business; of the manifest fact that collision with these Indians and consequent loss of life was unavoidable; of the evidenced desire of everyone concerned to carry out the orders of the Government in the most effective and yet most humane manner; and of the probability that no one else of equal experience and judgment could have done any better, respectfully recommends that no further action be taken.[10]

In truth, blame for the Northern Cheyenne tragedy lay at the feet of many others in addition to the military and Indian Bureau. By no means the least at fault was the nation as a whole for its government's policy that forced relocation of tribes from their native homelands, permitted destruction of their principal food source by white buffalo hunters, and betrayed solemn treaty promises—all causing the Northern Cheyennes and other tribal peoples to suffer sickness, starvation, and decimation.

A *New York Herald* reporter interviewed General Sherman in Washington, D.C., regarding the Fort Robinson outbreak. The old soldier, who had cut his military teeth in the Seminole removal from Florida, was asked if he had read the details of the Cheyenne massacre. Sherman was not sympathetic. "Massacre! Massacre!" he exploded.

> Why do you call it a massacre? A number of insubordinate, cunning, treacherous Indians, who had no more regard for the lives of our officers and soldiers than if they had been dogs, attempted to escape from the custody of troops and used violence to carry out their rebellious act. They were treated just as they deserved to be, and it is folly to attempt to extenuate such a crime by soft sounding words.[11]

The same newspaper sounded a similar theme in an editorial that scoffed at charges that the Cheyennes at Fort Robinson had been half naked. Their outbreak, it told its readers, was a result of their fear of being prosecuted for crimes in Kansas.[12] The *Omaha Daily Herald* answered with anger and indignation, calling the *New York Herald* story a "tissue of lies" and demanding that Congress investigate the affair at Fort Robinson: "Somebody must suffer for this infamous piece of incompetency. If we commence with Crook, the bottom facts can be made to appear sooner than by any other method. If he be guilty, then punish him, but if not, and we are willing to wager heavily that he is not, then let the one who is delinquent be sacrificed."[13]

General Crook was interviewed on the Fort Robinson outbreak by a *Daily Herald* reporter. He justified Wessells's act of cutting off food, water, and fuel from the prisoners on the grounds that "it was impracticable to remove them by physical force, and in their temper could only have resulted in loss of life to the soldiers and the extermination of the Cheyennes. Other measures were therefore resorted to."[14]

Crook, who had tacitly approved Wessells's actions, saw no other option even in retrospect: "I may say regarding that this measure, criticized by the rules for the theoretical management of Indians, seems to have been a severe one, but I ask—what alternative could have been adopted?"[15]

On another occasion Crook revealed what appeared to be a total lack of understanding about the Cheyenne prisoners. "I think they would have gone back two months ago without any trouble," he told the reporter. "They then expected to be taken back."[16]

One of the most damning denunciations of the Cheyenne affair, penned by Episcopal bishop Right Rev. H. B. Whipple, appeared in the *New York Evening Post:*

> I envy no man's head or heart who reads the last fifteen years of Cheyenne history and does not feel the deepest pity for this hunted, outlawed people. ... There is no use of blaming soldiers whom we force into unjust wars, and who are entitled to the sympathy of all good men. It is not the fault of the Department of the Interior. ... The evil lies at the door of Congress, which often fetters the department by its refusal to hear its pleas, and which never has entered upon the work of reform.[17]

In a 1912 interview after he had become a general, Wessells claimed the Cheyennes always had plenty of food and fuel and denied that they were starved for five days.[18]

An officer at Fort Robinson offered another potential, if extreme, solution to a *New York Times* reporter traveling with Secretary Schurz on a visit to Fort Robinson in September 1879. The Cheyennes, he said, should have been shelled out of the barrack. But, he admitted, that would have brought bitter denunciation upon the army: "That is what should have been done, but we were compelled to sacrifice the lives of some soldiers in order to satisfy a mistaken public sentiment."[19]

A basic military blunder had been made, the *Times* reporter suggested, by not separating the Cheyenne women and children from the men. The *Wichita Eagle,* for one, had an entirely different view of the affair. It opined: "If this massacre shall open the eyes of the humane people of this country, and result in putting a stop to our niggardly and dishonest treatment of the Indians, the brave Cheyennes will have accomplished more by their deaths than they could have hoped to accomplish by their lives."[20]

The Fort Robinson outbreak altered the government's plans for returning the Cheyennes to Indian Territory. There was no longer a large body of captive Cheyennes to be returned. But seven Cheyennes of the Dull Knife group, along with their families, were still being held at Fort Robinson. They included Wild Hog, Old Crow, Frizzle Head, Left Hand, Blacksmith, Porcupine, and Noisy Walker.

The fate of these seven survivors of the Fort Robinson outbreak was being debated by the War Department, the Interior Department, and the state of Kansas. Although the army's board of inquiry had strongly indicated that it was likely Little Wolf's band who had committed the depredations, they were still at large. The seven Fort Robinson survivors were the only ones presently available for prosecution.

Kansas governor George T. Anthony telegraphed Mike W. Sutton, county attorney of Ford County at Dodge City, for assistance in finding witnesses to identify the Cheyennes as participants in the killing and raping of Kansas citizens. Earlier, on January 15, Sutton had filed a general complaint against Dull Knife in regard to the deaths of five people in his jurisdiction: "The State of Kansas, Plaintiff, versus Dull Knife and 150 Cheyenne male Indians, commonly known as Warriors, whose names are each unknown and cannot be given."[21]

Anthony wired Sutton: "All that is left of Cheyenne raiders will be at Leavenworth soon—What can be done from your section of the state to aid in identifying them—Answer by mail."[22]

On February 4 the seven Cheyennes and their families, twenty-one in all, departed from Fort Robinson. Escorted by two companies of troops under Captain Vroom, the Cheyennes were taken to Sidney, Nebraska. There they were turned over to Lt. Morris C. Foot and a detachment of ten Ninth Infantry soldiers and entrained on the Union Pacific for a two-day trip to Fort Leavenworth.

At Fort Leavenworth the seven men, heavily restrained with handcuffs and leg irons, were held under close guard in the post guardhouse.[23] In response to Anthony's request, Sutton dispatched Dodge City sheriff W. B. "Bat" Masterson and four others to Topeka. The four were Deputy Sheriff C. E. Bassett, Bat's brother James Masterson, scout Kokomo Sullivan, and Capt. A. J. French, who had encountered the Cheyennes at Meade City. After an interview with the governor, the Dodge men traveled on to Fort Leavenworth.[24]

There they were taken to view and identify the prisoners in their cells at the fort. It was claimed that all of Masterson's party were old plainsmen who had been in the Northern Cheyenne camp a number of times and knew the Cheyennes intimately. Just when these supposed visitations had taken place is not clear, but the seven Cheyennes were turned over to Masterson for transport to Dodge City.[25]

A throng of excitedly curious spectators had gathered at the Leavenworth train station on the morning of February 15, 1879, when the prisoners, minus their families, were brought in wagons from the fort. They were escorted by a squad of Twenty-third Infantry soldiers under Lt. Julius H. Pardee. Pardee formally transferred them to P. S. Noble, adjutant general of Kansas, who in turn released them to the custody of Masterson and his men. The *Leavenworth Daily Times* heralded their appearance at the depot with impassioned headlines:

DUSKY DEMONS
The Cheyenne Robbers and Murderers Fall at Last
Into the Hands of the Civil Authorities
That They Will Never Again Ravish Women
and Kill Children Is a Certainty.[26]

The crowd increased and began pressing forward against the line of soldiers. A path had to be shoved through the crowd to move the prisoners to the depot waiting room. Wild Hog, still in much pain from his self-inflicted wounds, supported himself with a board. Two of the seven suffered from leg wounds and walked with a limp. Big Head, who had been shot in the hand, carried his arm in a sling. Old Crow alone was not in irons, having been vouched for by army officers who cited his loyal military service and the fact that he was a Crow Indian by birth. Two reporters described him as having an intelligent countenance.[27] Before they were put on the train, the Cheyennes were given some clay pipes and tobacco by a Leavenworth law officer who had once furnished the Indians with beef cattle.

At Lawrence a fracas took place when an unruly crowd surged forward and threatened Masterson's control of the prisoners. In the melee the Dodge City lawman struck a man who proved to be the marshal of Lawrence. Hard feelings remained between Masterson and Lawrence officials over the affair, as reflected in a Dodge City newspaper account:

> At every station a mob of hoodlums assembled and made such demonstrations in their eagerness to see the Indians that Sheriff Masterson was compelled to use physical means in preventing his pets from being trampled upon. At Lawrence the mob was almost overpowering, and our officers were involved in a fight which resulted in victory for Dodge City, as usual.[28]

At Topeka the prisoners were taken off the train and lodged in the Shawnee County jailhouse over night. Once again, a large crowd gathered to view some "real live wild Indians."[29] Dodge City citizens were much more blasé about the prisoners, and no one met Masterson and his charges at the station. Upon disembarking at the Dodge depot, the seven prisoners were required to walk some distance to the jail.

"This was the longest walk they had taken since leaving Leavenworth," a Dodge newspaper reported with little sympathy, "and it proved too laborious for the delicate health of one of the wounded chiefs, who, after limping and struggling along for some distance, sank helplessly to the ground, where he remained until a wheelbarrow was procured, upon which, he was placed, and carted to his destination."[30]

Chief Wild Hog (*first row, far left*) and other Cheyennes who survived the Fort Robinson outbreak await trial at Dodge City. Courtesy, Kansas State Historical Society.

The Cheyennes were placed in a basement cell of the jail, their hands and feet still in shackles. "They sat in a row upon the damp floor of the dim dungeon," a reporter observed, "with sorrow and despair deeply etched upon their manly countenances."[31]

Amos Chapman arrived from Fort Supply and held several conferences with the prisoners. Through him they said they understood the charges against them but insisted that other bands did the killing. Dodge City newspapers claimed the prisoners were cared for humanely during their imprisonment there. Their wounds were treated by a physician, and they were amply supplied with beef and tobacco. The main cause of despair among the Cheyennes was their great desire to see their families, who had been left behind in Leavenworth and taken south to Darlington in early March.[32]

Two days after arriving at Dodge, the seven prisoners were taken before a judge for preliminary trial on charges of murder. Sutton handled the prosecution, and Chapman interpreted for the Cheyennes. They requested that a number of officers and soldiers they had served with against the Sioux be called as witnesses. This delayed further proceedings and required that Sutton call for a special term of the court.[33]

The seven Cheyennes remained in the Dodge City jail for almost four months pending trial. Because of the near impossibility of locating prosecution witnesses, they were eventually charged only with the murder of Washington O'Conner at Meade City on September 17, 1868. But even that charge was impossible to sustain, for no evidence indicated that any of the seven Cheyennes had been involved in O'Conner's death. To ensure that the Cheyennes had a fair trial, Miles came up from Darlington and visited with them in their jail cell, finding them in reasonably good spirits. He asked what they were prepared to do if they were returned to Indian Territory. They said that although they much preferred to live in the north, they would be willing to take up farming and send their children to school if given their freedom.[34]

Miles also worked to get Old Crow released on the grounds that he had not been involved in the Kansas atrocities. Miles was successful, and on July 4 the former scout was released and permitted to return to Indian Territory with Chapman.[35]

During April the *Wichita Eagle* ran an interview with Wild Hog. The writer prefaced his article by saying Wild Hog was "doubtless a 'bad Indian' and deserves the fate awaiting him, at the same time he is intelligent and we believed truthful."[36] Wild Hog's interview continued:

> When I went down south I was homesick. A great many of our people died. We did not get enough to eat and were troubled with fleas and vermin. We were not used to it. We had many relatives in the north, and had always been well used there. I was married to a Sioux woman, and my children were born up there and preferred to live with the Sioux. The Sioux always had plenty to eat at the Pine Ridge Agency, and they wanted to come back where they would be used well. We did not think we were doing anything bad.[37]

Capt. J. G. Mohler of Salina volunteered to represent the Cheyennes. His first move was to petition for a change of venue from the Kansas District Court in Dodge, charging that Judge Samuel R. Peters was prejudiced against the Cheyennes. Peters denied the charge but granted the change of venue nonetheless. The trial was moved to the Fourth Judicial District at Lawrence. Once again Bat Masterson was in charge of transporting the prisoners.[38]

The defense lawyers had immediately set about summoning witnesses on behalf of their clients. Among those sought were Col. Nelson A. Miles, General Pope, and Secretary of Interior Schurz, who was asked to bring copies of Cheyenne treaties. Others included Lieutenant Clark from Fort Keogh, Dr. Lawrence A.E. Hodge from Fort Reno, Amos Chapman from Fort Supply, and Dutch Bill Greiffenstein, mayor of Wichita and a longtime friend of the Southern Cheyennes.[39]

The *Dodge City Times* observed that Mike Sutton, "a terror to evil-doers," was just the man to prosecute and win revenge for the deaths of Kansas whites.[40] But his witnesses, he claimed, were scattered all around. One was in Texas, another in Nebraska, another in Arizona, and another in California.[41]

As the prisoners lingered in their Dodge jail cells, the Kansas legislature responded to a request from the governor by passing a resolution to establish a three-man state commission to investigate the crimes committed during the Northern Cheyenne retreat across Kansas. The commissioners held meetings in Dodge City, Hays City, and Norton Center to take testimony regarding depredations and examine claims against the Cheyennes. In early July 1879 the commission issued its report, saying it had examined 116 claims, of which 90 were allowed, at a cost of $202,766.83. The report listed thirty-two people who had been killed by the Cheyennes.[42]

On June 25 the prisoners were transferred to Lawrence. The governor of Kansas sent Masterson railroad passes for the Cheyennes and five guards to entrain to the Douglas County jail.[43] By now the aura of the Cheyennes as dangerous and a threat to the community had lessened considerably, so much so that in late July they were taken to a circus in Lawrence. Still, some women grabbed their children and rushed them out of the circus tent when the Cheyennes arrived. The crowd quieted, however, when the Cheyennes were seated with lawmen at either end, and the show began.

> It was the first thing of the kind they [the Cheyennes] had seen, and they appeared to enjoy it thoroughly. About half-past two o'clock they marched into the menagerie in single file, and were shown one wild animal after another. The herd of elephants puzzled them very much, but they looked quietly and gravely at them, expressing no thought by word or gesture.

The Bengal tigers and the lions, as they jumped and snarled behind the iron bars brought a peculiar gleam to the eyes of the red men. The American lion, the red deer, the brown bear, all drew forth signs from two of the braves, who pointed westward and indicated that they had met these animals before.[44]

The Cheyennes were elated as Frank Melville performed on his horse in the center arena and when Billy Dutton galloped his pony around the ring doing marvelous stunts. But they most enjoyed the clowns. When the thin clown flung the fat clown over the ring and threw a boy on top of him, the Cheyennes shook with glee.

In August 1879 a U.S. senatorial committee composed of Samuel J. Kirkwood of Iowa, H. L. Dawes of Massachusetts, and John T. Morgan of Alabama met with the prisoners in Lawrence. The Cheyennes' legal representative, an attorney from Salina, objected to their being sworn. But with Ben Clark interpreting, the three senators interviewed Wild Hog and Old Crow about the reason they were moved to Indian Territory, their treatment at Darlington, and the causes behind their breakout at Fort Robinson.[45]

"We trust there will be no white-washing in this matter," the *Kansas Daily Tribune* (Lawrence) editorialized, "to shield official incompetence or knavery on the one side, or Indian blood-thirstiness and savagery on the other. Let us have the naked truth, and then let the guilty be punished, without regard to color or previous condition."[46]

From Lawrence the committee traveled to Indian Territory and Fort Reno where military officers and personnel of the Darlington Agency were interviewed at length.[47]

Two days before the trial date of October 13, a delegation from Darlington arrived in Lawrence. It consisted of Old Crow, his wife, son, and daughter, and Wild Hog's wife and two daughters. They were accompanied by interpreter Rowland, Lieutenant McDonald, and Dr. Hodge, post surgeon at Fort Reno.[48]

When the trial date arrived, Mike Sutton failed to appear in court. His absence left no prosecuting attorney. At the last moment attorney A. B. Jetmore appeared bearing authorization from the state attorney general to take the case.[49]

When Jetmore requested a continuance, the defense effectively argued that it would be an unwarranted hardship for witnesses to remain in Lawrence for a week and would constitute no furtherance of justice to keep the Cheyennes in prison any longer unless they were assured a speedy trial. When the prosecution could not promise such, the continuance was denied. Jetmore had no choice but to file a nolle prosequi dismissing the charges. Judge N. T. Stephens then ruled that the six Cheyennes be set free. Agent Miles took them under his charge and escorted them back to the Darlington Agency from which they had fled only thirteen months earlier.[50]

24

The MILITARY SEQUEL

F OR SOME OF THE OFFICERS AND MEN OF THE FOURTH CAVALRY who had
conducted the pursuit to the Platte River and those of the Third
Cavalry who were involved in the Fort Robinson outbreak, the Northern Cheyenne affair was the last significant action of their military careers.
For others, however, more Indian fighting lay ahead. The two regiments
went on to other arenas of conflict in the decade to follow, playing major
roles in the Sioux wars in Montana and the Dakotas, the Ute war in Colorado, and the Apache wars in New Mexico and Arizona.

The scene of Indian fighting in the north quickly shifted from the Northern Cheyennes back to the Sioux. General Miles had pushed Sitting Bull
and his Hunkpapa Sioux into Canada, but General Sherman restrained him
from crossing the border in pursuit. When the hungry Lakotas eventually
returned to northern Montana to hunt, Miles attacked them with seven
companies of Seventh Cavalry, seven of Fifth Infantry, and friendly Indian
scouts. During this action on July 17, 1879, Little Wolf's captor, Lt. William
P. Clark, fought an engagement with a hunting party led by Sitting Bull
himself. The Sioux were driven back into Canada, and pressure was kept on
them until Sitting Bull eventually surrendered at Fort Buford, Montana.[1]

In September 1879 Maj. Thomas Thornburgh led a combined force of
Third Cavalry, Fifth Cavalry, and Fourth Infantry south from Fort Fred Steele,

Wyoming, in an effort to rescue agent N. C. Meeker from his Ute charges in northern Colorado. Shortly after crossing the Milk River, Thornburgh was killed by a Ute sniper.[2]

When they returned to their original bases at Fort Reno, Fort Sill, Fort Supply, and Fort Elliott, the Fourth Cavalry reassumed military oversight of the Indians of the region, which included Little Chief and his band of Northern Cheyennes at Darlington. Their presence imbued stark memories of the Dull Knife–Little Wolf outbreak and cast a threatening shadow over the populace of western Kansas.

Although Little Chief was firmly determined to return to the northern homeland, he promised not to break away as had occurred in 1878. As a result, the military role at Fort Reno shifted from Indian control to that of restraining white settlers, known as Oklahoma Boomers, who in 1879 began invading Indian Territory to occupy lands unassigned to any particular tribe.

After visiting Washington Little Chief was eventually given permission to take his people north to Pine Ridge Agency. On October 6, 1881, Little Chief and his band were issued two months' rations and their annuity goods before departing from Darlington under escort of a company of Fourth Cavalry. By Miles's count the group consisted of 235 people, including a number of small children.[3]

Although they still had 400 miles to travel to reach the Pine Ridge Agency, the Cheyennes were very happy, their faces bearing "a smiling expression, and some of them returned the laughter of the jovial crowd of white men, women, and children."[4]

Little Chief and his band were not the last of the Northern Cheyennes in Indian Territory. By count, 684 remained. In 1883, when Congress approved their being returned north as well, nearly half chose not to go because of family ties to Southern Cheyennes. But on July 18, 1883, rations of flour, sugar, coffee, beef, and other supplies were issued to those who had declared their desire to go north. The following morning, under escort of a company of Ninth Cavalry, 360 Northern Cheyennes headed up the trail to Fort Supply and as far as Sidney. From there Troop H, Fifth Cavalry, from Fort Robinson escorted them to Pine Ridge Agency. In November 1881 Ninth Cavalry troops replaced those of the Fourth Cavalry at Fort Reno who had been ordered west to Colorado.[5]

The Ute disturbance and killing of Thornburgh caused a punitive U.S. strike force to form. Six troops of Fourth Cavalry under Ranald Mackenzie joined a larger force of Third and Ninth Cavalry and infantry units under Gen. Wesley Merritt. The planned expedition against the Utes was curtailed, however, when the conflict was resolved largely through civilian diplomacy.[6]

During 1881 and 1882, when the Apache war erupted, Mackenzie took command of the Department of New Mexico. He brought with him the Third and Fourth Cavalry, the former assigned in Arizona Territory and the latter in New Mexico. Mackenzie headquartered at Santa Fe, and Lt. Col. John Mizner, who had earlier moved from Fort Reno to command at Fort Sill, took charge at Fort Bayard.[7] The two cavalry regiments were soon engaged in the Apache war. In early 1882 an international incident occurred when Lt. David McDonald, acting under orders of field commander Lt. Col. George A. Forsyth, led a force of civilian and Indian scouts into Mexico in search of Apache raiders. McDonald was arrested by Mexican authorities but was soon released. Mackenzie, who had invaded Mexico in 1878, recommended a court-martial for McDonald even as he applauded him as a "brave and energetic officer."[8] McDonald was found guiltless, but the incident eventually caused him to resign from the army.

In April five companies of Fourth Cavalry and a company of scouts marched out of Fort Bayard, New Mexico, and engaged a band of Apaches in Horseshoe Canyon, New Mexico, on April 23. Five men were killed and seven others wounded. During this action Lieutenant Wilder rescued a soldier who was severely wounded and under heavy enemy fire. For this heroic deed Wilder was awarded the Medal of Honor.[9]

The Third Cavalry, which had moved from posts in Wyoming to Arizona, saw extensive action against the Apaches. Officers included Lt. Col. Andrew Evans, Capt. Joseph Lawson, Capt. Henry Wessells, Capt. Peter Vroom, 1st Lt. Francis Hardie, and 1st Lt. George Chase. On July 12 a Fort Apache detachment that included Third Cavalry units under Evans, Chase, and Hardie pursued a band of raiders and overtook them at Chevalons Fork, Arizona. In what was known as the Battle of Big Dry Wash, the Apaches were soundly defeated. For his role in this engagement, Evans was eventually awarded a brevet promotion to brigadier general.[10]

Mackenzie received a long-sought promotion to brigadier general in October 1882 and was replaced in command of the New Mexico district by Gen. George Crook. Ordering a strike by a combined command of Third and Sixth Cavalry into Mexico, Crook forced the surrender of Geronimo.[11] In 1885, however, the Apache leader and 134 of his people broke away and returned to Mexico. A troop of Fourth Cavalry and Indian scouts under Capt. Wirt Davis, who had fought the Northern Cheyennes at Red Fork, Wyoming, in 1876, followed in pursuit. A meeting between Crook and Geronimo resulted in an ill-fated truce that led to continued freedom for the famed Apache and replacement of Crook by Gen. Nelson Miles.[12]

GEN. MILES AND STAFF, Fort Bowie, Arizona, 1886. (1) Dr.Leonard Wood,1st.Lt.Medical Corps;(2) Lieut.R.F.Ames 8th Infantry;(3) Lieut.W.L.Wilder,4th Cavalry;(4) Capt.H.W.Lawton,4th Cavalry;(5) BRIG-GEN. NELSON A. MILES, Department Commander; (6) Capt.W.A.Thompson,4th Cavalry AAAG; (7) Major A.S.Kimball,Q.M.Dept; (8) Lieut.J.A. DaFray, ADC; (9) Lieut. Thomas J. Clay, 10th Infantry.

Wilder (3) and Lawton (4) pose with Miles (5) after their capture of Geronimo in Mexico. Courtesy, Western History Collections, University of Oklahoma.

Miles initiated a new invasion into Mexico led by Lt. Henry W. Lawton, who for seven years following the Cheyenne outbreak commanded Troop B, Fourth Cavalry. During August and September 1886 he led a force of scouts into Mexico's rugged Sierra Madre on a severely punishing march in pursuit of Geronimo. Lawton lost forty pounds during the ordeal but kept the pressure on Geronimo, who was forced to "shoot until he had nothing left to shoot with."[13] Geronimo's surrender came about after Lieutenant Wilder daringly led a small party into the Apache camp and arranged peace talks.[14]

A much briefer military future lay ahead for many of the officers who participated in the Northern Cheyenne affair. After his traumatic court-martial, dismissal from the service, and reinstatement, Joseph Rendlebrock and his wife left Fort Reno on August 2, 1879, for Hoboken, New Jersey, and from there returned to their native Germany. Rendlebrock drew a U.S. military pension until he died from heart disease in Godesberg, Germany, on March 13, 1889.[15]

In March 1879, soon after his return from pursuit of the Northern Cheyennes, Clarence Mauck was transferred to the Ninth Cavalry Regiment and promoted to major. He died on January 25, 1881. Joseph Lawson, who had risen to the rank of captain in the Third Cavalry, died the same month—

January 30, 1881. Following his court-martial, William Hemphill was dismissed from the service in November 1881. He died February 11, 1892. The tumultuous life of Gen. Jefferson C. Davis ended November 30, 1879.[16]

Mizner rose to the rank of lieutenant colonel with the Eighth Cavalry in January 1886 and to colonel of the Tenth Cavalry in April 1890. He commanded that regiment until May 1897, when he was promoted to brigadier general, and soon after retired. He died September 8, 1898.[17]

Gunther remained with the Fourth Cavalry until he retired in November 1884. He received no further promotion. David McDonald saw further service with the Fourth Cavalry in New Mexico and Arizona, and was promoted to first lieutenant in 1881. He resigned in 1888 and returned to Tennessee, where he took up farming and other pursuits unsuccessfully. McDonald died January 8, 1902, at age forty-five, having forever longed for his old life as a U.S. cavalryman.[18]

Two officers—Lt. George F. Chase and Capt. Peter D. Vroom—who had pursued the Northern Cheyennes following their Fort Robinson outbreak went on to successful military careers. Chase continued with the Third Cavalry until May 1892 when he transferred to the Seventh Cavalry, rising to the rank of lieutenant colonel in April 1903.[19] Vroom eventually reached the rank of brigadier general as inspector general of the army before retiring in April 1903.[20]

Caleb H. Carlton became a lieutenant colonel in the Seventh Cavalry in 1889, a colonel in the Eighth Cavalry in 1892, and a brigadier general in 1897. During his career Carlton served at Fort Fetterman, Fort Robinson, and Fort Sill, among other places in the West. He retired in June 1897.[21]

A few of the men who had been involved in the Northern Cheyenne episode served in both the Spanish-American War in 1898 and the Philippine insurrection in 1899. Perhaps the most notable of these was Henry Lawton. As brigadier general of volunteers during the Spanish-American War, he led the Second Division of the Fifth Army corps in the advance on Santiago, Cuba. After the surrender of the city, he was appointed military governor of the province. He was promoted to major general of volunteers before being killed while leading a charge during the battle of San Mateo, Philippine Islands, on December 19, 1899.[22]

Henry W. Wessells also served during the Spanish-American War and was severely wounded during the battle of San Juan Hill. Like Lawton, he saw duty with the Third Cavalry in the Philippines. In 1901 he was promoted to colonel and to brigadier general in 1904 before retiring in Washington, D.C.

In 1927 Wessells was awarded the Silver Star for his action in Cuba. He died November 9, 1929.[23]

Because of the severe wrongs done the Northern Cheyennes, literature concerning their retreat has tended to disparage the troops who pursued them. Certainly, there were brutal misdeeds on the part of the military, particularly during the Fort Robinson outbreak, just as there were on the part of the young Cheyennes in Kansas. The actions of the military while engaged in battle with armed hostiles at Turkey Springs, on Big Sandy, and at Punished Woman's Fork can be viewed on a different moral plain than the random killing of women and children at Fort Robinson. Wessells's action in cutting off the Northern Cheyennes' food, water, and fuel to force them to submit to returning to Indian Territory would hardly be accepted by American society today.

It remains a basic axiom that the military as an instrument of political policy cannot excuse inhumane behavior. But the men U.S. officials placed in the field against a desperate band of maltreated people were much less culpable than those whose orders they were obligated to obey. In the end, the transgressions exercised against the Cheyennes weigh far heavier on the national character than on the soldier who so often laid his life on the line.

NOTES

LIST OF ABBREVIATIONS

AAG—Assistant Adjutant General
AGO—Adjutant General's Office
C/A Agency—Cheyenne/Arapaho Agency
CofIA—Commissioner of Indian Affairs
GCM—Gunther Court-Martial Proceedings
HCM—Hemphill Court-Martial Proceedings
HofR—House of Representatives
LR—Letters Received
NA—National Archives
OIA—Office of Indian Affairs
RCM—Rendlebrock Court-Martial Proceedings
RG—Record Group

CHAPTER 1

1. Grinnell, *Fighting Cheyennes,* 230–231.
2. Hebard and Brinnistool, *Bozeman Trail,* 272–275.
3. Carrington to Great Chief of Cheyennes, July 14, 1866, *Sen. Ex. Doc. 33,* 9.
4. Carrington, *Ab-sa-ra-ka,* 110–111.
5. Woodward, "Experiences with the Cheyennes," *United Service,* 194.
6. "Indian Operations on the Plains," *Sen. Ex. Doc. 33,* 37–39.
7. Ibid., 38–39.

8. Carrington to AAG, Dept./Platte, Jan. 3, 1867; "Indian Operations on the Plains," *Sen. Ex. Doc. 33*, 39–41. Utley in *Frontier Regulars* (109, n. 31) expresses the possibility that an unauthorized charge by his troops may have accidentally drawn Fetterman beyond Lodge Trail crest.
9. Carrington, *Ab-sa-ra-ka*, 202–208, 264–268.
10. "Carrington Report," *Senate Ex. Doc. 33*, 42–43; Hebard and Brinnistool, *Bozeman Trail*, 338–339; Hyde, *Red Cloud's Folks*, 148–149.
11. Kappler, *Indian Treaties*, 1012–15.
12. *Second Annual Report of the Board of Indian Commissioners, 1870*, 59–63.
13. Ibid., 69.
14. Ibid., 15–16.
15. Woodward, "Experiences with the Cheyennes," 191.
16. Ibid., 185.
17. Ibid., 188.
18. Hyde, *Red Cloud's Folks*, 199.
19. *Washington Evening Star*, Nov. 9, 1873.
20. *CofIA Report, 1873*, 2–5; *Washington Evening Star*, Nov. 6, 8, 14, 1873.
21. *Washington Evening Star*, Nov. 14, 1873.
22. Ibid.
23. Whirlwind, *Sen. Rep. 708*, 35. To Old Crow, however, it seemed southern chief Little Robe was hostile to the idea. Whirlwind, *Sen. Rep. 708*, 16.
24. Hyde, *Red Cloud's Folks*, 225.
25. Saville to CofIA, Sept. 7, 28, Nov. 13, 30, 1874, with (unratified) Treaty of Nov. 12, 1874, Red Cloud Agency, LR/OIA, NA.
26. March 23, 1876.
27. En route Crook stopped to visit the Fetterman massacre site at the ruins of Fort Phil Kearny on June 5 and 6. *Leslie's Illustrated Newspaper*, Aug. 12, 1876.
28. Greene, *Slim Buttes*, 6.
29. Smith, *Sagebrush Soldier*, 42–43; Utley, *Frontier Regulars*, 268.

CHAPTER 2

1. *New York Herald*, Dec. 1, 11, 1876.
2. *Army and Navy Journal* 14 (Nov. 18, 1876): 229; Utley, *Frontier Regulars*, 275.
3. *History of the Fourth United States Cavalry*, 6–9.
4. North, *Man of the Plains*, 202–203.
5. Stands in Timber and Liberty, *Cheyenne Memories*, 214–216; *Army and Navy Journal* 14 (Dec. 2, 1876): 270, (Dec. 9, 1876): 286; Grinnell, *Fighting Cheyennes*, 359–364. Wheeler in *Buffalo Days* (125) listed the Cheyennes as Thunder Cloud, Bird, Blown Away, Old Crow, and Hard Robe.
6. *New York Herald*, Dec. 1, 11, 1876.
7. Powell, "High Bull's Victory Roster," 15.
8. Smith, *Sagebrush Soldier*, 72.
9. Kime, *Powder River Journals*, 96.
10. *New York Herald*, Dec. 1, 1876.
11. North, *Man of the Plains*, 212–216.

12. Smith, *Sagebrush Soldier*, 72.
13. Heitman, *Historical Register* 1: 697. Company B was under 1st Lt. W. C. Miller; D, Capt. John Lee; E, 1st Lt. F. L. Shoemaker; F, Capt. Wirt Davis; and I, Capt. W. C. Hemphill. First Lt. Henry W. Lawton, Fourth Cavalry, was regimental quartermaster. Wheeler, *Buffalo Days*, 124–126; *New York Herald*, Dec. 1, 1876.
14. *New York Herald*, Dec. 11, 1876.
15. Smith, *Sagebrush Soldier*, 73, n. 5, citing Col. L. A. LaGarde, "At the Dinner of the Order of the Indian Wars, March 6, 1913," in *Order of the Indian Wars Collection*, L-2.
16. Werner, *Dull Knife Battle*, 54–56.
17. *New York Herald*, Dec. 11, 1876.
18. Bourke, *Mackenzie's Last Fight*, 27.
19. *New York Herald*, Dec. 1, 1876.
20. Bourke Diary 19: Apr. 4, 1877.
21. Werner, *Dull Knife Battle*, 33; Wheeler, *Buffalo Days*, 134.
22. Bourke, *Mackenzie's Last Fight*, 20–28.
23. Fourth Cavalry Returns, Nov. 1876.
24. Smith, *Sagebrush Soldier*, 73.
25. Quoted in Kime, *Powder River Journals*, 85.

CHAPTER 3

1. Miles's Report, Jan. 20, 1877, reprinted in *Army and Navy Journal* (Feb. 10, 1877): 425.
2. Johnson to CofIA, Dec. 11, 1877, M-234, Roll 721, NA.
3. Bourke Diary 19: Mar. 7, Apr. 4, 22, 1877; *New York Herald*, May 11, 1877; *New York Tribune*, Apr. 23, 1877; *Chicago Tribune*, Apr. 23, 1877.
4. Quoted in Bourke Diary 19: Apr. 4–12, 1877.
5. Powell, *People* 2: 1143.
6. *New York Herald*, May 11, 1877.
7. *New York Tribune*, Apr. 23, 1877.
8. Bourke Diary 19: Mar. 7, Apr. 4, 1877; *Dodge City Times*, Apr. 28, 1877.
9. Bourke Diary 19: May 7, 1877.
10. *New York Tribune*, Apr. 23, 1877; *Chicago Tribune*, Apr. 23, 1877.
11. Ibid.
12. Bourke Diary 19: Apr. 22, 1877.
13. *New York Tribune*, Apr. 23, 1877.
14. Ibid.
15. Ibid., Apr. 28, 1877.
16. Hastings to Smith, June 21, 1876, LR, Red Cloud Agency, M-234, Roll 720, NA.
17. *New York Times*, May 18, 1877.
18. Northern Cheyenne Big Head claimed Dull Knife had not been considered a head chief for a long time except by the whites, but he was clearly the Cheyennes' leading spokesman during the surrender at Camp Robinson. Big Head, *Report of Board of Officers*, M-234, Roll 429.
19. Marquis, *Wooden Leg*, 308–309.
20. *New York Times*, May 30, 1877.

21. *Dodge City Times*, July 14, 1877.
22. Powell, *People* 2: 1153, citing Lawton Scrapbook, Everett D. Graff Collection, Newberry Library.
23. Marquis, *Wooden Leg*, 312–313.
24. Powell, *People* 2: 1153.
25. Greene and Wright, "Chasing Dull Knife," 26.
26. *Dodge City Times*, July 14, 1877.
27. Marquis, *Wooden Leg*, 310.
28. Wessells, "Hard Military Service," 605.
29. *Dodge City Times*, July 14, 1877; Big Head, Proceedings, 13.
30. *Dodge City Times*, June 9, Aug. 11, 1877.
31. Ibid., July 28, 1877.
32. Miles to Nicholson, Aug. 8, 1877, C/A Agency, LR/OIA, NA; Report of and Inspection of the Condition of the Cheyenne Indians at the Cheyenne and Arapaho Agency, Sept. 29, 1977, C/A Agency, LR/OIA, NA.

CHAPTER 4

1. *Army and Navy Journal* 16 (Dec. 7, 1878): 297.
2. Heitman, *Historical Register* 1: 483–484, 718, 823.
3. Fourth Cavalry Monthly Returns, Aug.–Sept. 1874.
4. Ibid., Jan.–Nov. 1876.
5. Ibid., Mar. 1875–Sept. 1877.
6. Ibid., May–July 1877.
7. Marquis, *Wooden Leg*, 315.
8. *History of the Fourth United States Cavalry*, 11.
9. Enrollment list of North Cheyennes, Aug. 6, 1877, C/A Agency, LR/OIA, NA.
10. Kappler, *Indian Treaties*, 1012–15.
11. Wild Hog, *Sen. Rep. 708*, 7–8.
12. Wild Hog's wife, ibid., 34.
13. Old Crow, ibid., 19.
14. Stubbs to Miles, July 12, 1877, C/A Agency, LR/OIA, NA; Whirlwind, *Sen. Rep. 708*, 25.
15. Miles to Nicholson, Aug. 8, 1877, C/A Agency, LR/OIA, NA.
16. Miles to Nicholson, Sept. 24, 1877, ibid.
17. Miles, *Sen. Rep. 708*, 58.
18. Hodge to Miles, Oct. 2, 1877, C/A Agency, LR/OIA, NA.
19. Nicholson to CofIA, Sept. 18, 1877, ibid.
20. *Army and Navy Journal* 16 (Oct. 19, 1878): 166.
21. Report of and Inspection of the Condition of the Cheyenne Indians at the Cheyenne and Arapaho Agency, Sept. 29, 1977, C/A Agency, LR/OIA, NA.
22. Wild Hog, *Sen. Rep. 708*, 4.
23. Old Crow, ibid., 15.
24. Rowland, Proceedings, 138.
25. Wild Hog, *Sen. Rep. 708*, 5.

26. *New York Herald,* Oct. 27, 1878.
27. Miles, *Sen. Rep. 708,* 59.

CHAPTER 5

1. Clark to Mizner, Dec. 13, 1878, LR/AGO (main series), NA.
2. Stubbs to Miles, July 12, 1877, C/A Agency, LR/OIA, NA.
3. Miles to Hoyt, Oct. 29, 1877, ibid.
4. Whirlwind, *Sen. Rep. 708,* 36.
5. Miles to Hoyt, Dec. 20, 1877, C/A Agency, LR/OIA, NA.
6. *Dodge City Times,* Dec. 8, 1877.
7. Gunther to AAG, Fort Reno, Dec. 4, 1877, C/A Agency, LR/OIA, NA.
8. Cook, *Border and the Buffalo,* 125, 135, 291.
9. Heitman, *Historical Register* 1: 483–484.
10. *Dodge City Times,* Dec. 8, 1877.
11. Carriker, *Fort Supply,* 115, citing Miles to Nicholson, Aug. 31, 1977, *CofIA Report, 1877,* 82; Hambright to AAG, Dept./Mo., Nov. 27, 1877, LR, Dept./Mo., NA. See *Dodge City Times,* Oct. 27, Nov. 3, Dec. 8, 15, 1877.
12. *Dodge City Times,* Dec. 8, 15, 22, 1878.
13. Covington to Hoyt, Jan. 12, 1878, C/A Agency, LR/OIA, NA.
14. Hatch to C/A Ind. Agent, Dec. 8, 1877, ibid.
15. Miles to Gunther, Dec. 13, 1877, ibid.
16. Hambright to CO, Ft. Reno, Dec. 21, 1877, ibid.
17. Old Crow, *Sen. Rep. 708,* 16–17.
18. Wild Hog, ibid., 4–5, 8.
19. Gunther to Miles, Dec. 26, 1877, C/A Agency, LR/OIA, NA.
20. *Dodge City Times,* Dec. 29, 1877, Jan. 12, 19, 1878.
21. Covington to Miles, July 3, 1878, C/A Agency, LR/OIA, NA.
22. Covington to Hoyt, Jan. 6, 12, 1878, ibid.; *Dodge City Times,* Dec. 22, 1877.
23. Mizner, *Sen. Rep. 708,* 111; Berthrong, *Ordeal,* 34.
24. Berthrong, *Ordeal,* 35.

CHAPTER 6

1. Old Crow, *Sen. Rep. 708,* 20.
2. Berthrong, *Ordeal,* 3–4.
3. Ibid., 12; Miles to Mizner, Aug. 22, 1876, C/A Ltr. Bks., I, 657, El Reno Public Library.
4. Old Crow, *Sen. Rep. 708,* 15; Miles, *Sen. Rep. 708,* 58–61; Covington, "Causes of the Dull Knife Raid," 19, citing *Monthly Report,* 296.
5. Wild Hog, *Sen. Rep. 708,* 5, 8.
6. Miles to Hayt, Dec. 2, 1878, C/A Agency, LR/OIA, NA.
7. Marquis, *Wooden Leg,* 320.
8. Wild Hog's wife, *Sen. Rep. 708,* 33.
9. Wild Hog, ibid., 5.
10. Miles to Hayt, May 31, July 3, 1878, C/A Agency, LR/OIA, NA.
11. Miles to Hayt, July 17, 1878, ibid.

12. Ibid.
13. Miles to Hayt, Aug. 13, 1878, ibid.
14. *Wichita City Eagle*, Apr. 3, 1879.
15. Old Crow, *Sen. Rep. 708*, 26–27.
16. Little Wolf, Folder 326, 222, Grinnell Collection, Southwest Museum.
17. Miles to Hayt, May 31, 1787, C/A Agency, LR/OIA, NA.
18. Miles, *Sen. Rep. 708*, 60–61.
19. Mizner to CO, Camp Supply, Sept. 5, 1878, LR/Fort Supply, Oklahoma Collection, University of Central Oklahoma.
20. Heitman, *Historical Register* 1: 483–484, 662, 823, 1035, 1054.
21. *Army and Navy Journal* 16 (Oct. 13, 1878): 150; Donald, *Sen. Rep. 708*, 136–138.
22. Rendlebrock to Hatch, Dec. 12, 1878, LR, Dept./Mo., NA.
23. Gunther, *Sen. Rep. 708*, 147.
24. Mizner to AAG, Sept. 6, 1878, Dept./Mo., LR/AGO (main series), NA; Mizner to Hambright, Sept. 23, 1878, LR/AGO (main series), NA.
25. Carriker, *Fort Supply*, 120.
26. Gunther, *Sen. Rep. 708*, 148; Clark, *Sen. Rep. 708*, 145.
27. Gunther, ibid., 148.
28. Ibid., 61.
29. Covington, ibid., 105–110.
30. Mizner, ibid., 112.
31. *Sen. Rep. 708*, 119; Rendlebrock to Hatch, Dec. 12, 1878, LR, Dept./Mo., NA. Gunther said that as soon as the cannon arrived, Rendlebrock intended to go to the Cheyennes' camp and form a line of battle, and if the Cheyennes did come out of their entrenchments, he would shell them. Rendlebrock opined that because their families were there, a few shells would bring them out. Gunther to Hatch, Nov. 2, 1878, LR, Dept./Mo., NA. In addition to the two artillery pieces, Fort Reno had two Gatling guns, all of which were assigned to the infantry. *New York Herald*, Oct. 27, 1878.
32. Wilcox report, Sept. 1878, LR, Dept./Mo., NA, accompanied by a sketch of the Cheyennes' fortified position.
33. Miles to Nicholson, Sept. 21, 1878, *The Friend* 52 (Nov. 2, 1878): 90–91.
34. Mizner to Rendlebrock, Sept. 8, 1878, LR, Dept./Mo., NA.
35. Miles, *Sen. Rep. 708*, 62.
36. Mizner to AAG, Dept./Mo., Sept. 18, 1878, *Report of Sec. of War, 1878*, 44–45; *Sen. Rep. 708*, 62.
37. Little Wolf, Folder 328, 226, Grinnell Collection, Southwest Museum.
38. Miles to Hayt, Sept. 10, 1878, C/A Agency, LR/OIA, NA; Miles to Nicholson, Sept. 21, 1878, *The Friend* 52 (Nov. 2, 1878): 90.
39. Miles to Nicholson, Nov. 2, 1878, *The Friend* 52 (Nov. 2, 1878): 90.
40. Ibid.

CHAPTER 7

1. "They had no teepees or travaux. The Enemy walked most of the time and packed her baby on her back." Red Feather/The Enemy, Proceedings, 18.

2. Figures regarding the group vary. Miles's name list of the adult males who left in September gives eighty-seven plus ten boys, ages eleven to thirteen, who were capable of bearing arms. Miles's list, Nov. 15, 1878, LR, C/A Agency, NA.

3. He said also: "Of full grown men, fighting young men, there were not over sixty; including the old, and the boys nearly grown, there may have been ninety." Old Crow, Sen. Rep. 708, 21.

4. Miles to Hoyt, Sept. 10, 1878, LR, C/A Agency, NA; The Friend 52 (Nov. 2, 1878): 90.

5. Big Head, Proceedings, 13.

6. Iron Teeth, a woman who made the journey north, explained that "very old Indians occasionally were abandoned when we were moving, sometimes because they became tired of the travel and asked to be left behind, sometimes because pursuing enemies allowed no other choice." Marquis, "Red Ripe's Squaw," 203.

7. Ibid., 207.

8. The Enemy, Proceedings, 18.

9. Miles's list, Nov. 15, 1878, LR, C/A Agency, NA; Clark to Whipple, Oct. 16, 1878, LR/ AGO (main series), NA.

10. Wilder, Sen. Rep. 708, 133.

11. Leavenworth Daily Times, Sept. 12, 1878.

12. Mizner to AAG, Fort Leavenworth, Nov. 8, 1878, LR, Dept./Mo., NA copy in Mari Sandoz Special Collection, University of Nebraska, Love Library.

13. Wilder, Sen. Rep. 708, 135.

14. Feely, RCM, 172.

15. Donald, Sen. Rep. 708, 138.

16. Pope to AAG, Div./Mo., Oct 10, 1878, "Cheyenne Outbreak," Nebraska State Historical Society.

17. Sheridan to Townsend, Nov. 19, 1878, Sen. Misc. Doc. 64, 45/3, 16–17.

18. Miles, Sen. Rep. 708, 63; Army and Navy Journal 16 (Oct. 12, 1878): 150.

19. Gunther, Sen. Rep. 708, 148.

20. Wilder, ibid., 133, 135; "The Great Cheyenne Chase," Ford County Globe, Jan. 7, 1879.

21. Wood to Hatch, Nov. 22, 1878, LR, Dept./Mo., NA.

22. Rendlebrock to Hatch, Dec. 12, 1878, ibid.

23. Gunther, Sen. Rep. 708, 148.

24. Rendlebrock to CO, Camp Supply, Sept. 10, 1878, C/A Agency, LR/OIA, NA.

25. Rendlebrock to Hatch, Dec. 12, 1878, ibid.

26. Scout Donald referred to Chalk as a Mexican Indian. Donald, Sen. Rep. 708, 137.

27. Alva Pioneer, souvenir edition, Jan. 1, 1904; Rendlebrock to Hatch, Dec. 12, 1878, LR, Dept./Mo., NA.

28. The map, dated January 1875, was compiled under the direction of 1st Lt. E. H. Ruffner, chief engineer of the Department of the Missouri.

29. Gunther, Sen. Rep. 708, 148. Although military participants designated Turkey Springs as the general site of the battle, the command did not know the precise location and never actually reached a spring until during their retreat. They simply saw greenery beyond the Cheyenne line and assumed it was Turkey Springs, the only site noted,

imprecisely, in that locale on an 1875 military map. Officer reports and court-martials testimony, however, clearly indicate that the battle occurred a mile or so west of a range of "red hills." These hills are likely those in TS 28 N, R 17 W of Woods County, Oklahoma, but no solid artifact evidence has been found despite several search efforts to locate the battle site.

30. Ibid.; "The Great Cheyenne Chase," *Ford County Globe*, Jan. 7, 1879.
31. Rendlebrock to Hatch, Dec. 12, 1878, LR, Dept./Mo., NA; Donald, *Sen. Rep. 708*, 137.
32. Fort Reno letter, Sept. 11, 1878, *Leavenworth Daily Times*, Sept. 12, 1878.
33. Pope to AAG, Gen. Hdqs., Sept. 12, 1878, File Relating to Military Operations, Cheyenne Outbreak, RG393, M-1495, NA.
34. Carriker, *Fort Supply*, 122.
35. Pope to Sheridan, Sept. 12, 1878, LR/AGO (main series), NA; *Dodge City Times*, Sept. 29, 1878.

CHAPTER 8

1. Rendlebrock to Hatch, Dec. 12, 1878, LR, Dept./Mo., NA.
2. Fort Reno Special Order 118, Sept. 5, 1878, *Report of Sec. of War, 1878*, 45.
3. Mizner to Rendlebrock, Sept. 8, 1878, ibid., 46.
4. Mizner, *Sen. Rep. 708*, 112.
5. McDonald, RCM, 68.
6. Wood, ibid., 115.
7. Ibid., 113–114.
8. "The Great Cheyenne Chase," *Ford County Globe*, Jan. 7, 1879.
9. Donald, *Sen. Rep. 708*, 137.
10. Little Wolf, Folder 328, 227, Grinnell Collection, Southwest Museum.
11. Wilder, *Sen. Rep. 708*, 128; Rendlebrock to Hatch, Dec. 12, 1878, LR, Dept./Mo., NA.
12. Rendlebrock to Hatch, Nov. 12, 1878, LR, Dept./Mo., NA; Miles to Hayt, Sept. 19, 1878, C/A Agency, LR/OIA, NA. Some accounts say it was Dull Knife who replied to Rendlebrock's demand; others that it was Little Wolf, who recalled: "The troops followed us. I rode out and told the troops we did not want to fight; we only wanted to go north, and if they would let us alone we would kill no one. The only reply we got was a volley." *Sen. Rep. 708*, 249.
13. Gunther, *Sen. Rep. 708*, 148. The records do not say, and it is by no means a given, that Chalk spoke Cheyenne. Precisely how communication between him and the Cheyenne leaders was carried out is not clear. Although most accounts of the battle—both white and Cheyenne—imply direct conversation, Gunther's statement indicates that Chalk used sign language and at a distance. The Cheyenne leaders, therefore, would have replied similarly. There is general agreement between Cheyennes and whites, however, about what Rendlebrock demanded and what the Cheyenne leaders said in reply.
14. *Twenty-Fifth Annual Reunion, 1894*, 86–89; Heitman, *Historical Register* 1: 1054.
15. Wood, GCM, 116; Wood to Hatch, Nov. 22, 1878, LR, Dept./Mo., NA.
16. Wood to Hatch, Nov. 22, 1878, LR, Dept./Mo., NA. See also, "The Great Cheyenne

Chase," *Ford County Globe,* Jan. 7, 1879.

17. After later being charged with cowardice by Wood and Wilder, Rendlebrock could hardly have pressed the point of just who initiated the action.

18. In a letter describing the affair, the unidentified noncom in charge surmised that "all would have been lost" had their position been overrun. *Army and Navy Journal* 16 (Oct. 12, 1878): 150.

19. McDonald to Hatch, Nov. 28, 1878, LR, Dept./Mo., NA; "The Great Cheyenne Chase," *Ford County Globe,* Jan. 7, 1879; Rendlebrock, GCM, 76.

20. Wood to Hatch, Nov. 22, 1878, LR, Dept./Mo., NA.

21. Rendlebrock, GCM, 74–75.

22. Ibid.; Rendlebrock to Hatch, Oct. 1, 1878, LR, Dept./Mo., NA; Wilder, *Sen. Rep. 708,* 128; Gunther, *Sen. Rep. 708,* 148; "The Great Cheyenne Chase," *Ford County Globe,* Jan. 7, 1879.

23. *Army and Navy Journal* 16 (Oct. 19, 1878): 150.

24. "The Great Cheyenne Chase," *Ford County Globe,* Jan. 7, 1879.

25. Wilder to Hatch, Nov. 22, 1878, LR, Dept./Mo., NA; McDonald to Hatch, Nov. 28, 1878, LR, Dept./Mo., NA.

26. Wood reported that "there were many cases of ague and other ills from the bad water we had to use in the Cimarron River country." Wood to Hatch, Nov. 22, 1878, ibid.

27. Gunther, GCM, 116.

28. Fisher, ibid., 92.

29. Gunther to Hatch, Nov. 22, 1878, LR, Dept./Mo., NA. Little Wolf's recollection in 1898 was incorrect when he told Grinnell that after the fight he had gone down to where the soldiers had been and found "a sergeant, a soldier, and an Arapaho dead and unburied." Little Wolf, Folder 328, 228, Grinnell Collection, Southwest Museum.

30. Rendlebrock to Hatch, Dec. 12, 1878, LR, Dept./Mo., NA.

31. *Army and Navy Journal* 16 (Oct. 12, 1878): 150. Long Hair, however, was not the only warrior to have claimed the distinction of having killed Custer. Uncapapa Lakota chief Rain-in-the-Face was once thought to have been responsible, but that was later discounted. Thomas Marquis interviewed a Southern Cheyenne named Brave Bear, said by some to have been the one who killed Custer. But Brave Bear and other Cheyennes laughed at the suggestion. Marquis concluded that none of the Cheyennes really knew who killed Custer. See also Howard, *The Warrior Who Killed Custer.*

32. McDonald, RCM, 77; McDonald to Hatch, Nov. 28, 1878, LR, Dept./Mo., NA.

33. Wilder to Hatch, Nov. 22, 1878, LR, Dept./Mo., NA.

34. Wood, GCM, 47.

35. Rendlebrock, ibid., 74–75.

36. Ibid., 72; Gunther, RCM, 136.

37. Quoted in Gunther, RCM, 137.

38. Wright, GCM, 116.

39. Rendlebrock, RCM, 211.

40. McDonald to Hatch, Nov. 23, 1878, LR, Dept./Mo., NA.

CHAPTER 9

1. Wright, RCM, 191.
2. Ibid., 192; Gatewood, ibid., 201.
3. McDonald, GCM, 71.
4. Wood to Hatch, Nov. 22, 1878, LR, Dept./Mo., NA; McDonald to Hatch, Nov. 28, 1878, LR, Dept./Mo., NA.
5. Wood, GCM, 49.
6. Feely, ibid., 102.
7. Ibid., 100.
8. Wood, ibid., 50.
9. Feely, ibid., 98–99.
10. Fisher, ibid., 95.
11. Wood to Hatch, Nov. 22, 1878, LR, Dept./Mo., NA.
12. Sergeant Fisher said Burton was killed just before they came through the last defile prior to reaching the red hills. Fisher, GCM, 97. Gunther testified that one of his men had seen Burton fall from his horse during the second of the three charges. When asked what action had been taken to ascertain his fate, Gunther replied, "None." Gunther to Hatch, Nov. 22, 1878, LR, Dept./Mo., NA. Wood testified, "There was a man killed in some of the charges as I understood. I did not see it and did not know of it till we got to the water though I was looking for that all the time. I understand that his body fell into the enemy's hands." Wood, GCM, 68.
13. Wood to Hatch, Nov. 22, 1878, LR, Dept./Mo., NA.
14. McDonald to Hatch, Nov. 28, 1878, ibid.
15. Rendlebrock, GCM, 72.
16. Davis, RCM, 194.
17. Wilder to Hatch, Nov. 22, 1878, LR, Dept./Mo., NA.
18. Feely, RCM, 174.
19. Rendlebrock, GCM, 74–75; Wood, GCM, 39; Gunther, RCM, 141.
20. Wilder, GCM, 21.
21. Wilder to Hatch, Nov. 22, 1878, LR, Dept./Mo., NA.
22. Feely, RCM, 174–175.
23. Rendlebrock, GCM, 79.
24. Wilder claimed credit for starting the charge. Wilder's testimony, ibid., 85. Fisher testified that it was Donald, the guide, who said, "Let's charge them boys they won't stand it. Lieut. McDonald then said follow me men, and commenced yelling and we made the rush." Fisher, ibid., 93. Rendlebrock's comment was: "You could not call it a charge, every man took his own direction." Rendlebrock's testimony, ibid., 72.
25. Feely, ibid., 102.
26. McDonald to Hatch, Nov. 28, 1878, LR, Dept./Mo., NA.
27. Fisher, GCM, 92; Feely's testimony, GCM, 92; O'Niell, GCM, 106–107; Gunther, GCM, 123–124. Interestingly, none of the junior officers—Wood, Wilder, or McDonald—mentioned Gunther's action in his report to Hatch.
28. Gunther, ibid., 124.
29. Wood, ibid., 57–58.

30. Gunther, RCM, 142; Wood, RCM, 106; Rendlebrock, GCM, 80; Wilder, GCM, 25.
31. *Army and Navy Journal* 16 (Oct. 12, 1878): 150.
32. Fisher, GCM, 97; Gunther, GCM, 124–125.
33. Wilder, ibid., p. 91.
34. Cook, ibid., 120.
35. Gunther, ibid., 125.
36. McDonald, ibid., 6.
37. Ibid., 7.
38. Cook, ibid., 120.
39. General Court Martial Orders, No. 29, Hdqs., Dept./Mo., ibid.
40. *Army and Navy Journal* 16 (Oct. 12, 1878): 150.
41. Gunther, *Sen. Rep. 708*, 148–149.
42. Chalk's tombstone carries the date "May 13, 1881." Barker, *Burials in the Fort Reno Cemetery*, 7.
43. The Fourth Cavalry Returns twice clearly list Pvt. Frank Struad as one of the battle victims. There are tombstones for Lynch, Struad, and Chalk in the Fort Reno cemetery. Ibid., 5–7.
44. McDonald, GCM, 8.

CHAPTER 10

1. *Leavenworth Daily Times*, Sept. 12, 1878.
2. Donald, *Sen. Rep. 708*, 137.
3. The Cherokee Outlet, also known as the "Cherokee Strip," extended across much of northern Indian Territory.
4. Colcord, *Autobiography of Charles Francis Colcord*, 64–67.
5. Ibid., 69–70.
6. Ibid., 73–74. The gravesite of the two cowboy salt haulers, which is well fenced and marked with a granite stone, lies on the Woods County road north of Freedom, Oklahoma.
7. *Leavenworth Daily Times*, Sept. 21, 1878.
8. Kelly et al., Sept. 18, 1878, *Eighteenth Biennial Report of the Kansas State Historical Society*, 23.
9. *Dodge City Times*, Sept. 21, 1878.
10. Shinn et al. to Anthony, Sept. 18, 1878, *Eighteenth Biennial Report of the Kansas State Historical Society*, 23.
11. Anthony to Kelly, Sept. 19, 1878, ibid., 23.
12. Coutant to Anthony, Sept. 21, 1878, ibid., 24.
13. Powers, "Kansas Indian Claims Commission," 208.
14. Johnson to Anthony, Sept. 25, 1878, *Eighteenth Biennial Report of the Kansas State Historical Society*, 24–25.
15. Ibid., 25.
16. Typescript insert to *Indian Raid of 1878*, Kansas State Historical Society.
17. *Eighteenth Biennial Report of the Kansas State Historical Society*, 31; *Arkansas City Traveler*, Sept. 25, 1878; Harold to Post Adj., Fort Dodge, Oct. 19, 1878, LR, Dept./Mo., NA.

18. Harold to Post Adj., Fort Dodge, Oct. 19, 1878, LR, Dept./Mo., NA.
19. Lt. John Harold, who investigated the matter, gave the boy's name as Warren Richardson. Ibid.
20. Brown, "Narrative Accounts," Cheyenne Indian Collection, Kansas State Historical Society.
21. This account is taken from various sources that include Collins, *The Indians' Last Fight*, 249–251; Brown, "Kansas Indian Wars," 135; and Powers, "The Northern Cheyenne Trek," 14.
22. Harold to Post Adj., Fort Dodge, Oct. 19, 1878, LR, Dept./Mo., NA.
23. *Leavenworth Daily Times*, Nov. 20, 1878. Harold states that Murray's body was found on October 2 on Spring Creek. The men's horses and saddles were missing and presumed taken by the Cheyennes. Harold to Post Adj., Fort Dodge, Oct. 19, 1878, LR, Dept./Mo., NA.
24. Collins, *The Indians' Last Fight*, 248–249.
25. Harold to Post Adj., Fort Dodge, Oct. 19, 1878, LR, Dept./Mo., NA.
26. Gillmore to Anthony, Oct. 3, 1878, *Eighteenth Biennial Report of the Kansas State Historical Society*, 29.

CHAPTER 11

1. Hambright to CO, Fort Reno, Sept. 15, 1878, LR, Dept./Mo., NA.
2. Hemphill was eventually court-martialed for his drunkenness at Camp Supply, suspended from rank for a year, confined to Fort Riley, and forced to forfeit half of his pay for that period. General Court Martial Orders N. 73, Oct. 29, 1879, Dept./Mo., HCM.
3. Special Order 115, Camp Supply, Sept. 12, 1878, ibid.
4. Hemphill, ibid., 56.
5. Matthew Leeper had served as an Indian agent in western Indian Territory before the Civil War. In 1872 he became a guide and interpreter for Mackenzie as a second lieutenant in the Fourth Cavalry. Pierce, *Most Promising Young Officer*, 71, 95, 115.
6. Schaufler, HCM, 53.
7. Lewis to CO, Camp Supply, Sept. 17, 1878, Exhibit 10, RCM.
8. Leeper to Hatch, Dec. 7, 1878, LR, Dept./Mo., NA; Hemphill to Hatch, Nov. (n.d.) 1878, LR, Dept./Mo., NA.
9. Ibid.
10. Berryman, "Early Settlement," 568–569.
11. Ibid.; Hemphill to Hatch, November (n.d.) 1878, LR, Dept./Mo., NA; Carriker, *Fort Supply*, 124. The grave of the Cheyenne warrior is located just west of Highway 183 5½ miles south of Sitka, Kansas.
12. Trask, HCM, 50–51.
13. Leeper to Hatch, Dec. 7, 1878, LR, Dept./Mo., NA.
14. Trask, HCM, 50–51.
15. Hemphill to Hatch, November (n.d.) 1878, LR, Dept./Mo., NA. In Hemphill's court-martial defense his counsel noted that of the ranchmen and cowboys there, only six were armed and twenty were unarmed; these last "certainly must have been an incumbrance instead of an aid." Defense summary, HCM, 15.

16. Little Wolf interview, Folder 326, 227–228, Grinnell Collection, Southwest Museum. The only soldier listed as wounded at Big Sandy in the Fourth Cavalry Returns, Sept. 1878, was Pvt. Adolph Esslinger.
17. *Leavenworth Daily Times,* Sept. 21, 1878.
18. Ibid., Sept. 26, 1878.
19. Hemphill to Hatch, November (n.d.) 1878, LR, Dept./Mo., NA.
20. Morse to Post Adj., Fort Dodge, Sept. 27, 1878, ibid.
21. *Daily Oklahoman,* July 31, 1929.
22. Morse to Post Adj., Fort Dodge, Sept. 27, 1878, LR, Dept./Mo., NA.
23. Ibid.; Hemphill to Hatch, Nov. (n.d.) 1878, ibid.

CHAPTER 12

1. Carriker, *Fort Supply,* 125; Hambright to CO, Fort Elliott, Sept. 18, 1878, Exhibit 11, HCM.
2. Wilder to Hatch, Nov. 22, 1878, LR, Dept./Mo., NA.
3. "The Great Cheyenne Chase," *Ford County Globe,* Jan. 7, 1879.
4. Feely, RCM, 176–177. A report on the fight in the *Sidney Plaindealer,* Oct. 10, 1878, was based on interviews with Rendlebrock and Wood.
5. Wood, RCM, 109.
6. Wood to Hatch, Nov. 22, 1878, LR, Dept./Mo., NA.
7. Rendlebrock, RCM, 212.
8. Wood, ibid., 128.
9. Ibid., 127–128.; Wood to Hatch, Nov. 22, 1878, LR, Dept./Mo., NA.
10. Feely, RCM, 178–179.
11. Rendlebrock, ibid., 214, 217; Morse to Adj., Fort Dodge, Sept. 27, 1878, Campbell Collection, University of Oklahoma, Western History Collection.
12. Gunther believed over half the troops would have been slaughtered if the cavalry had been dismounted and ordered to cross the level ground leading to the Cheyennes' position. Gunther, RCM, 149.
13. Wood to Hatch, Nov. 22, 1878, LR, Dept./Mo., NA.
14. Feely, RCM, 176–178.
15. Driscoll (Driskell), ibid., 40.
16. Little Wolf, Folder 328, 229, Grinnell Collection, Southwest Museum.
17. Gunther, RCM, 146.
18. Hemphill to Hatch, Nov. (n.d.) 1878, LR, Dept./Mo., NA.
19. Rendlebrock to Hatch, Dec. 12, 1787, ibid.; Hemphill to Hatch, Nov. (n.d.) 1878, ibid.
20. Wilder to Hatch, Nov. 22, 1878, ibid.
21. Feely, RCM, 180.
22. Morse to Adj., Ft. Dodge, Sept. 27, 1878, LR, Dept./Mo., NA.
23. McDonald, RCM, 149.
24. Rendlebrock, ibid., 216.
25. Wood, ibid., 111; Rendlebrock, ibid., 215.
26. Ibid.
27. Gunther, GCM, 153.

28. Wilder to Hatch, Nov. 22, 1878, LR, Dept./Mo., NA.
29. Ibid.
30. Rendlebrock, RCM, 215.
31. Wood to Hatch, Nov. 22, 1878, LR, Dept./Mo., NA.
32. Exhibit 12, RCM. Lewis had sent instructions to Rendlebrock on September 18 citing the authority of the department commander. Exhibit 11, RCM.
33. Rendlebrock, ibid., 215, 217.
34. McDonald, ibid., 147.
35. Driscoll (Driskell), ibid., 45. According to Charles Colcord, another cattleman named Nelson vigorously protested Rendlebrock's action and led his men off to their own camp. Colcord, *Autobiography*, 14–15.
36. Morse to Post Adj., Fort Dodge, Sept. 27, 1878, LR, Dept./Mo., NA.
37. Rendlebrock, RCM, 214.
38. Rendlebrock to CO, Ft. Dodge, Exhibit 14, ibid.
39. Wilder, *Sen. Rep.* 708, 129; Gunther, RCM, 149; Hemphill to Hatch, Nov. (n.d.) 1878, LR, Dept./Mo., NA; Rendlebrock to Hatch, Dec. 12, 1878, RCM. Both Wood and Wilder urged Rendlebrock to send a courier to Fort Dodge to apprise Lewis of the direction the Cheyennes had taken. He did so the following day.
40. Morse, RCM, 24; Morse to Post Adj., Fort Dodge, Sept. 27, 1878, LR, Dept./Mo., NA.
41. *Daily Oklahoman*, July 21, 1939. Iliff, who was evidently with Wilder's probe, provides a lurid but factually unsound account of the Sand Creek engagements.
42. Rendlebrock, RCM, 214; Gunther, RCM, 154.
43. Rendlebrock, ibid., 214.
44. Powers, "Kansas Indian Claims Commission," 210, citing Claim, 1878 Raid, Folder 19, Ford and Meade Counties.
45. Ibid.
46. Brown, "Kansas Indian Wars," 134–135.
47. Gunther, RCM, 156–157.
48. Kime, *Indian Territory Journals*, 20.
49. *Dodge City Times*, Sept. (n.d.) 1878, Campbell Collection, University of Oklahoma/ Western History Collection; Clark to Whipple, Oct. 16, 1878, C/A Agency, LR/AGO (main series), NA.
50. Telegram, Pope to AAG, Gen. Hdqs., Sept. 18, 1878, Files Relating to Military Operations, Div./Mo., NA.
51. Pope to Sheridan, Sept. 18, 1878, ibid.
52. Pope to Sheridan, Sept. 20, 1878, ibid.
53. Hambright to CO, Fort Elliott, Sept. 18, 1878, Exhibit 11, HCM, NA.
54. Hambright to CO, Fort Reno, Sept. 20, 1878, LR, Dept./Mo., NA.
55. Mauck to Hatch, Dec. 9, 1878, ibid.; Post Returns, Camp Supply, Sept. 1878, NA.
56. Little Wolf, Folder 328, 230, Grinnell Collection, Southwest Museum.

CHAPTER 13

1. Pope to Sheridan, Sept. 12, 1878, LR/AGO (main series), NA; Heitman, *Historical Register* 1: 631; Cullum, *Biographical Register* 2: 382–383; *Leavenworth Daily Times*,

Oct. 13, 1878; Colton, *Civil War in the Western Territories,* 69, 78.

2. Lewis to AAG, Sept. 15, 1878, LR, Dept./Mo., NA; *Leavenworth Daily Times,* Sept. 26, 1878.
3. Pope to Sheridan, Sept. 25, 1878, File Relating to Military Operations, NA.
4. George Brown gave the names of the scouts as Amos Chapman, Ben Jackson, Bill Combs, Levi Richardson, Hugh Bickerdike, Ed Cooley, himself, and a man the others called Kokomomo (Sullivan). Brown, "Dull Knife's Raid," 400–402.
5. Morse to Post Adj., Fort Dodge, Sept. 27, 1878, LR, Dept./Mo., NA.
6. Bradford to AAG, Nov. 4, 1878, ibid.
7. Wood to Hatch, Nov. 22, 1878, ibid.
8. Leeper, RCM, 96.
9. Creel, *Cheyenne Grammar and Ethnology,* Book A, Gilcrease Institute.
10. Leeper to Hatch, Dec. 4, 1878, LR, Dept./Mo., NA; Martin to Hatch (n.d., Box 77), LR, Dept./Mo., NA.
11. Mauck to Hatch, Dec. 9, 1878, ibid. Mauck stated that the "mount and advance" call had been sounded when the Cheyennes appeared, but from all other accounts this appears incorrect.
12. Brown, "Dull Knife's Raid," 400.
13. Gunther testimony, RCM, 160.
14. *Leavenworth Daily Times,* Oct. 9, 1878.
15. Today this cavern, some of the overhang of which has broken off over the years, is known locally as the "Squaw's Den."
16. Mari Sandoz described the battle as having started when a young agency Cheyenne, a southerner, fired too soon. *Cheyenne Autumn,* 76. A person with Lewis's command described it differently, writing: "The troops, suspecting nothing, entered the [main river] cañon, and but for a glimpse of danger by the scouts would have fallen into the trap. Seeing the failure of their plans, the Indians opened fire upon the head of the column." *Leavenworth Daily Times,* Oct. 9, 1878.
17. McDonald, GCM, 17, RCM, 135.
18. Gunther, RCM, 151–152.
19. Gunther to Hatch, Nov. 22, 1878, LR, Dept./Mo., NA.
20. McDonald, GCM, 17.
21. "The Great Cheyenne Chase," *Ford County Globe,* Jan. 7, 1879; McDonald to Hatch, Nov. 28, 1878, LR, Dept./Mo., NA.
22. Wilder testified that the troops were armed with carbines and six-shooting .45-caliber Schofield and Smith and Wesson revolvers. *Sen. Rep. 708,* 135. In his report, Lieutenant Martin addressed the matter of ammunition supply. Cavalry companies, he noted, were issued 100 rounds of ammunition, 40 of which they carried in their belt and 60 in pasteboard packages in their saddlebags. The paper boxes often fell to pieces during a march, and the cartridges became loose in the saddlebags. At Punished Woman's Fork the troopers had no time to dig them out and no place to carry them on their persons. As a result, when the troops were engaged with the Cheyennes, they quickly ran short of ammunition. Martin was forced to send back for more and to refrain from shooting Cheyenne ponies that were easy targets. Martin to Hatch (n.d., Box 77), LR, Dept./Mo., NA.

23. Patch to Hatch, Nov. 23, 1868, LR, Dept./Mo., NA.

24. Martin to Hatch (n.d., Box 77), ibid.

25. Gardener report, Oct. 10, 1878, ibid.

26. Although no company was composed entirely of its own men, the skirmish line was organized west to east by Companies F, G, I, B, and H. Hemphill to Hatch, Nov. (n.d.) 1878, ibid. Maddux and Maddux, *The Battle of Punished Woman's Fork*, 11, and others, based on findings of casings on the battlefield, say Lewis established a command post on the highest point of land northeast of the wagon circle. None of the officer accounts of the battle, however, mention him doing so. Also, the time element of late afternoon and the hurried advance of the troops, of which Lewis took the lead, place doubt on the formation of such a command post. Neither Mauck nor Lewis's adjutant, Lieutenant Gardener, in particular mentions such a post.

27. Martin to Hatch (n.d., Box 77), LR, Dept./Mo., NA.

28. Mauck to Hatch, Dec. 9, 1878, ibid.

29. McDonald to Hatch, Nov. 28, 1878, ibid.

30. Little Wolf, Folder 328, 35, Grinnell Collection, Southwest Museum.

31. *Leavenworth Daily Times*, Oct. 9, 1878.

32. Gardener to AAG, Oct. 10, 1878, LR, Dept./Mo., NA.

33. Brown, "Dull Knife's Raid," 401, indicated that two soldiers sent to carry Lewis down on a stretcher were shot and wounded.

34. Martin to Hatch (n.d., Box 77), LR, Dept./Mo., NA.

35. Mauck to Hatch, Dec. 9, 1878, ibid.

36. Rendlebrock's account, *New York Herald*, Oct. 21, 1878; *Army and Navy Journal* 16 (Oct. 26, 1878): 185.

37. Patch to Hatch, Nov. 23, 1878, LR, Dept./Mo., NA.

38. Rendlebrock, RCM, 216.

39. Gunther, *Sen. Rep. 708*, 150.

40. Mauck to Hatch, Dec. 9, 1878, LR, Dept./Mo., NA; Patch to Hatch, Nov. 23, 1878, LR, Dept./Mo., NA.

41. *Army and Navy Journal* 16 (Oct. 26, 1878): 185; *Survey of Historic Sites and Structures in Kansas*, 55.

42. Mauck to Hatch, Dec. 9, 1878, LR, Dept./Mo., NA. According to Brown, he and another scout named Jackson discovered the Cheyenne horse herd as the fight was going on September 27. The two men were reconnoitering cautiously along the west bank beyond the troops when they made the discovery. Brown, "Kansas Indian Wars," 136.

43. Brown, "Kansas Indian Wars," 136. In another account, Brown stated there were "all kinds of Indian trinkets, paints and brushes, also a nice pair of buckskin gloves with gauntlets which i took for myself." Brown, "Dull Knife's Raid," 401.

44. The three wounded soldiers were Pvt. Zachariah Loar, Pvt. John R. Sanchez, and Pvt. Daniel Z. Badgeley. Fourth Cavalry Returns, Sept. 1878. Lewis's body was eventually taken to Fort Leavenworth and on to his home at Sandy Hill, New York, where he was buried. *Leavenworth Daily Times*, Oct. 13, 16, 1878.

45. Surgeon's report, Sept. 29, 1878, LR/AGO (main series), NA.

46. *Leavenworth Daily Times*, Oct. 16, 1878. Statements that he was buried in Alabama are incorrect.
47. Brown, "Kansas Indian Wars," 137.
48. Mauck to AAG, Gen. Hdqs., Sept. 29, 1878, Files Relating to Miliary Operations, NA.
49. *Leavenworth Daily Times*, Oct. 9, 1878.
50. Lt. Col. R. I. Dodge heard similar criticism at Bluff Creek Station the following December. One of Mauck's main guides who was there charged the officer not only with incompetence but also with cowardice, saying that whenever he came in sight of the Indians he stopped for lunch or for some other reason. Kime, *Indian Territory Journals*, 102.

CHAPTER 14

1. Kime, *Indian Territory Journals*, 15, n. 2, citing Fort Hays LR.
2. *Leavenworth Daily Times*, Sept. 27, 1878.
3. Van Voast to Dodge, Sept. 22, 1878, LR, Dept./Mo., NA.
4. Van Voast to AAG, ibid.
5. Greene and Wright, "Chasing Dull Knife," 26.
6. "The Indian Raid," *Hays City Sentinel*, Oct. 5, 1878, Cheyenne Outbreak Drawer, Fort Robinson Museum.
7. Davis to AAG, Sept. 29, 1878, File Relating to Military Operations, Div./Mo., NA. The *Leavenworth Daily Times* parroted the statement as its own opinion in its October 1, 1878, issue.
8. Kime, *Indian Territory Journals*, 24.
9. Dodge, Diary of Events (Box 75), LR, Dept./Mo., NA; Kime, *Indian Territory Journals*, 25.
10. *Leavenworth Daily Times*, Oct. 2, 1878.
11. Dodge, Diary of Events (Box 75), LR, Dept./Mo., NA.
12. While in the field Dodge was sent orders to take over Dallas's command but did not feel he could contact the unit. Kime, *Indian Territory Journals*, 44.
13. Pope to AAG, Oct. 1, 1878, Files Relating to Military Operations, Div./Mo., NA.
14. Vance to Broderick, Oct. 9, 1878, LR, Dept./Mo., NA; Greene and Wright, "Chasing Dull Knife," 28.
15. Greene and Wright, "Chasing Dull Knife," 30.
16. Ibid.
17. Dallas to Post Adj., Fort Leavenworth, Oct. 25, 1878, LR, Dept./Mo., NA.
18. Twenty-third Infantry Monthly Returns, Regular Army Commands, September–October 1878, M-665, Roll 237, NA.
19. Dodge, Diary of Events, Oct. 2, 3, 1878, LR, Dept./Mo., NA.
20. Ibid., Oct. 4, 1878.
21. Ibid.
22. Ibid.
23. Kime, *Indian Territory Journals*, 42–43. Dodge wrote: "I have had ample experience of trails in a long service, and have never seen such an Indian trail as this [that of the Northern Cheyennes]. They did not move in a compact body as usual—but singly or abreast—no two ponies went out behind the other. They covered a broad space of

from 3 to 8 miles—and except when they crossed streams or fire guards, there was no trail to be seen. I have never yet seen a white man who could have followed that trail at a rate of more than 5 or 6 miles a day." Kime, *Indian Territory Journals,* 40–41.

24. It was also reported that government wagons at Fort Leavenworth were hauling supplies that included hardtack and tobacco to the freight depot for shipment to the troops on the frontier. *Leavenworth Daily Times,* Oct. 1, 1878.

25. Pope to AAG, Oct. 4, 1878, citing Mauck to Pope telegram, Files Relating to Military Operations, Div./Mo., NA.

26. Cook, *The Border and the Buffalo,* 306–307.

27. Rendlebrock to Hatch, Dec. 12, 1878, LR, Dept./Mo., NA; Hemphill to Hatch, Nov. (n.d.) 1878, LR, Dept./Mo., NA.

28. *Leavenworth Daily Times,* Oct. 2, 1878.

29. Dodge, Diary of Events, Sept. 28, 1878, LR, Dept./Mo., NA.

30. Davis Report, Oct. 17, 1878, ibid.

31. Ibid.

32. Mizner to AAG, Dec. 17, 1878, ibid.

33. Greene and Wright, "Chasing Dull Knife," 30.

34. *Army and Navy Journal* 16 (Oct. 26, 1878): 185.

CHAPTER 15

1. Little Wolf, Folder 328, 231, Grinnell Collection, Southwest Museum.

2. Rendlebrock interview, *New York Herald,* Oct. 21, 1878.

3. Dodge, Diary of Events, Sept. 28, 1878, LR, Dept./Mo., NA.

4. Gunther, *Sen. Rep. 708,* 151–152. Wilder gave a similar account of the incident. *Sen. Rep. 708,* 131.

5. *Leavenworth Daily Times,* Oct. 8, 9, 13, Nov. 12, 1878.

6. *Indian Raid of 1878: Report of (Kansas) Commission,* Kansas State Historical Society, 13–14, plus addendum.

7. Berthrong, *Southern Cheyennes,* 404; West, "Battle of Sappa Creek," 150–178.

8. Cheyenne woman, Proceedings, 2.

9. Old Crow, ibid., 5; *Sen. Rep. 708,* 21.

10. Grinnell, *Fighting Cheyennes,* 413.

11. *Leavenworth Daily Times,* Oct. 5, 1878.

12. Ibid., Oct. 13, 1878; *Indian Raid of 1878: Report of (Kansas) Commission,* Kansas State Historical Society, 13; Powers, "Northern Cheyenne Trek," 19, citing Mr. and Mrs. Henry Anthony, "Early Northwest Kansas Reminiscences," typescript interview collated by Raymond L. Stacey, July 5, 1958, Folklore File, Library, Fort Hays, Kansas State College, Hays, Kansas. The *Leavenworth Daily Times,* October 13, 1878, stated that the Cheyennes held the two girls "captive in a grove nearby and let them go, after outraging their persons in a most brutal, fiendish, and inhuman manner." An even more lurid account in the *Omaha Republican* also tells of the two girls being taken to the Cheyennes' camp on a nearby creek where they were "ravished in the heartless manner of the fiendish devils." Reprinted in the *Leavenworth Daily Times,* Nov. 22, 1878. An account by Mr. and Mrs. Anthony, however, states: "Eva and Lou Van

Cleave returned to their home next day, and found their home was not in the path of the Indians. They soon recovered from the severe shock as they had been injured in no way. Eva taught school that fall and Lou went to school." "Early N.W. Kansas Reminiscences," typescript, Decatur County Museum. That the girls were not mistreated is supported by L. M. Foster, "The Last Indian Raid in Kansas," typescript, Decatur County Museum, 2.

13. *Leavenworth Daily Times,* Oct. 9, 1878. A detailed surgeon's report regarding wounds of the victims appears in the November 12, 1878, *Leavenworth Daily Times,* and accounts of the Decatur County attacks are given in the October 13, 1878, edition.

14. Powers, "Kansas Indian Claims Commission," 209; *Leavenworth Daily Times,* Oct. 13, 1878.

15. Powers, "Northern Cheyenne Trek," 19.

16. Wedemeyer Report, Oct. 26, 1878, Campbell Collection, Box 120, University of Oklahoma/Western History Collection.

17. Gus Cook's story, typescript, Decatur County Museum.

18. Quoted in Powers, "Kansas Indian Claims Commission," 210.

19. Raab, "The Indian Raid," typescript, Decatur County Museum.

20. Colvin, "The Indian Raid of 1878," typescript, Decatur County Museum. See also Colvin account in *National Tribune,* June 19, 1911.

21. Colvin, "The Indian Raid of 1878," typescript, Decatur County Museum.

22. Powers, "Kansas Indian Claims Commission," 209; story of Dora Westphalen, typescript, Decatur County Museum.

23. O'Toole, "Billy O'Toole's Story," Decatur County Museum.

24. Mauck to Hatch, Dec. 7, 1878, LR, Dept./Mo., NA.

25. Keith, "Dull Knife's Cheyenne Raid," 118.

26. Foster, "The Last Indian Raid in Kansas," 147.

27. Powers, "Kansas Indian Claims Commission," 210; *Leavenworth Daily Times,* Oct. 9, 12, 13, 1878. Other victims along the South Fork of the Sappa on September 30 were Marcellus Felt, George F. Walters, Moses Abernathy, John Iroin, a man named Lull who had been hunting with Iroin, and John Wright. Along the Beaver on October 1, Paul Janousheck, Rudolph Springler, and Arnold Kubitz had been killed and their wives raped, as was the wife of Frank Vacasek. Another victim along the river was Anton Stenner (or Stermer). Louise Stenner testified later that after killing her father, the Cheyennes whipped her. She managed to crawl into a creek bed where with ten other children she stayed from Tuesday to Thursday with nothing to eat or drink. Most of the women whose husbands were killed and property was taken were left destitute. Other deaths along the Beaver were those of Henoch Janousheck, Frank Lochore, traveling preacher George Femberg, Fred Hemper, a man named Morrison, and one named Zeidler.

28. "The Widows' Wail," Cheyenne Outbreak Drawer, Fort Robinson Museum.

29. *Eighteenth Biennial Report of the Kansas State Historical Society,* 21–22.

CHAPTER 16

1. Street, "Incidents of the Dull Knife Raid," Decatur County Museum.

2. *Leavenworth Daily Times,* Sept. 19, 1878. A dispatch from Omaha stated that a corps

of railroad bridge men saw 200 mounted Cheyennes cross the South Platte at 11:30 A.M. on October 4. *New York Herald,* Oct. 5, 1878.

3. According to reports in the *Leavenworth Daily Times,* Oct. 5, 1878, and the *New York Times,* Oct. 5, 1878, the men were ten army scouts from Sidney Barracks sent to trail the Cheyennes.

4. Thornburgh to Mauck, Oct. 4, 1878, LR, Dept./Mo., NA; AAG to Thornburgh, Oct. 7, 1878, LR, Dept./Mo., NA; enclosure to Mauck to Hatch, Dec. 9, 1878, LR, Dept./ Mo., NA.

5. Thornburgh to Mauck, Oct. 6, 1878, ibid.; enclosure to Mauck to Hatch, Dec. 9, 1878, ibid.

6. Street, "Incidents of the Dull Knife Raid," 15.

7. Ibid.

8. Carlton report, *New York Times,* Oct. 13, 1878.

9. Bourke to AAG, Oct. 15, 1878, Files Relating to Military Operations, Dept./Platte, NA.

10. Davis to Mauck, Oct. 6, 1878, LR, Dept./Mo., NA; enclosure to Mauck to Hatch, Dec. 9, 1878, LR, Dept./Mo., NA; *Army and Navy Journal* 16 (Oct. 19, 1878): 153.

11. Carlton to AAG, Oct, 16, 1878, LR/AGO (main series), Dept./Platte, M-666, Roll 428, NA; Map of Carlton's scout, M-1495, Roll 6, NA; *New York Herald,* Oct. 16, 1878; Buecker, *Fort Robinson,* 133.

12. *Army and Navy Journal* 16 (Nov. 9, 1878): 217.

13. Mauck to Hatch, Dec. 9, 1878, LR, Dept./Mo., NA.

14. *Report of Secretary of War, 1879,* 50–51. Both Vroom and Wessells were sons of well-known men, Vroom the son of a two-time governor of New Jersey and Wessells the son of Gen. Henry Wessells, who served many years on the Western frontier. Heitman, *Historical Register* 1: 990, 1019; *National Cyclopedia of American Biography,* 290.

15. Wood to AAG, Oct. 27, 1878, LR, C/A Agency, Dept./Dak., NA.

16. *Report of Secretary of War, 1879,* 50–51.

17. Little Wolf, Folder 328, 231, Big Beaver, Folder 350, 31, Grinnell Collection, Southwest Museum.

18. Little Wolf to Grinnell, Folder 328, ibid.; Red Feather/The Enemy, Proceedings, 16.

19. Little Wolf, Folder 328, 232, Grinnell Collection, Southwest Museum.

20. Johnson to AAG, Third Cavalry, Oct. 25, 1878, Campbell Collection, University of Oklahoma/Western History Collection; Johnson, Proceedings, 60; *Army and Navy Journal* 16 (Nov. 2, 1878): 201, (Nov. 9, 1878): 217.

21. *Army and Navy Journal* 16 (Nov. 2, 1878): 201, (Nov. 9, 1878): 217.

22. Johnson to AAG, Third Cavalry, Oct. 25, 1878, Campbell Collection, University of Oklahoma/Western History Collection.

23. Ibid.

24. Carlton to AAG, Oct. 27, 1878, Dept./Platte, ibid.; Johnson, Proceedings, 64.

25. Johnson listed the arms taken as a Winchester rifle, a Sharps carbine, a Spencer carbine, a double-barreled shotgun, nine muzzle-loading rifles, a Smith and Wesson revolver, a Colts revolver, a Remington revolver, a muzzle-loaded Dragoon pistol, and fifteen or twenty sets of bows and arrows. Johnson, Proceedings, 61.

26. Chase, ibid., 27; Johnson, ibid., 64. Chase was commissioned as a second lieutenant in

1871. He joined the Ninth U.S. Infantry, transferring to the Third Cavalry in May 1872. Heitman, *Historical Register* 1: 297.

27. Thompson, Proceedings, 68–69; Johnson, Proceedings, 129.

28. Carlton to AAG, Oct. 29, 1878, LR, Dept./Platte, NA; *Army and Navy Journal* 16 (Nov. 9, 1878): 218.

29. Johnson, Proceedings, 63.

30. Chase, ibid., 29–30; Report of Board, ibid., 188.

31. Wessells's *Reminiscences*, cited in Wessells, "Hard Military Service," 604; Bronson, *Reminiscences*, 165.

32. Chase, Proceedings, 32.

33. Ibid., 31; Marquis, *Cheyennes and Sioux*, 22.

34. Chase, Proceedings, 31.

35. Johnson, ibid., 60.

36. Simpson, ibid., 83; Bigalsky, ibid., 148.

37. Simpson, ibid., 94.

38. Pettys, ibid., 125.

39. Big Beaver, Folder 350, 42, Grinnell Collection, Southwest Museum.

40. Wessells, Proceedings, 85; Wessells's *Reminiscences*, cited in Wessells, "Hard Military Service," 604.

41. Big Beaver, Folder 350, 42, Mrs. Howling Wolf, Folder 355, 22, Grinnell Collection, Southwest Museum.

42. Crook to Sheridan, Nov. 1, 1878, *Sen. Misc. Doc. 64*, 13.

43. *Leavenworth Daily Times*, Nov. 9, 1878.

44. Carlton to AAG, Third Cavalry, Oct. 25, 1878, Campbell Collection, University of Oklahoma/Western History Collection; *Leavenworth Daily Times*, Jan. 15, 1879.

45. *Leavenworth Daily Times*, Nov. 9, 1878.

46. Ibid.

47. Carlton to AAG, Nov. 17, 1878, LR, Dept./Platte, NA.

48. Carlton, Proceedings, 180. Little Wolf verified this incident in an 1898 interview. Little Wolf, Folder 328, 34–35, Grinnell Collection, Southwest Museum.

49. Little Wolf to Grinnell, Folder 328, 35, Grinnell Collection, Southwest Museum.

50. Clark to Whipple, Oct. 16, 1878, LR/AGO (main series), NA; *Dodge City Times*, Nov. 23, 1878.

51. Wessells, Proceedings, 72.

52. Ibid.; Wessells, "Hard Military Service," 604.

CHAPTER 17

1. *St. Louis Post and Dispatch,* Jan. 2, 1879.

2. *New York Times,* Jan. 10, 1879.

3. Ibid., Jan. 20, 1879.

4. Ibid.

5. Ibid., Jan. 11, 1879.

6. Ibid., Jan. 13, 1879.

7. Cummings, Proceedings, 164–165.

8. Chase, ibid., 32; Simpson, ibid., 94; Pettys, ibid., 125.
9. *Sen. Misc. Doc. 64*, 47.
10. Crawford to Morton, Jan. 8, 1879, Cheyenne Outbreak Drawer, Fort Robinson Museum.
11. Ibid.; Report of Board, Proceedings, 191; Mrs. C. A. Johnson to sister, Cheyenne Outbreak Drawer, Fort Robinson Museum.
12. Wild Hog, *Sen. Rep. 708*, 10–11.
13. Wessells to AAG, Dept./Platte, Jan. 5, 1879, *Sen. Misc. Doc. 64*, 20; Wessells to AAG, Dec. 8, 1878, LR, Dept./Platte, NA.
14. Wessells to AAG, Dept./Platte, Jan. 12, 1879, *Sen. Misc. Doc. 64*, 6–8.
15. Wessells, Proceedings, 82.
16. Wild Hog testimony, *Sen. Rep. 708*, 12.
17. Quoted in *The Friend* 52 (Feb. 7, 1879): 200.
18. Old Crow, *Sen. Rep. 708*, 23.
19. Vroom, Proceedings, 91. Even then two Nez Percé were executed by hanging at Pendleton, Oregon. *New York Times*, Jan. 12, 1879.
20. *Leavenworth Daily Times*, Jan. 10, 1879.
21. Wessells to AAG, Dept./Platte, Jan. 12, 1879, *Sen. Misc. Doc. 64*, 6–8. George W. Baxter, a North Carolinian by birth, attended West Point. After resigning from the army in 1881, he became a wealthy cattleman in Wyoming and served in several territorial legislatures. He was appointed territorial governor of Wyoming in 1886. *National Cyclopedia of American Biography*, 176; Heitman, *Historical Register* 1: 200.
22. Wild Hog, *Sen. Rep. 708*, 11.
23. *Sen. Rep. 708*, xviii; *Leavenworth Daily Times*, Jan. 17, 1879.
24. Old Crow, *Sen. Rep. 708*, 22.
25. Tangled Hair, ibid., 13.
26. Old Crow, ibid., 23.
27. Mrs. Howling Wolf, Folder 355, 22–24, Grinnell Collection, Southwest Museum.
28. Red Feather/The Enemy, Proceedings, 17.
29. Simpson, ibid., 91; *Army and Navy Journal* 16 (Jan. 25, 1879): 433.
30. Cummings, Proceedings, 163.
31. *Leavenworth Daily Times*, Jan. 17, 1879.
32. Simpson, Proceedings, 97. There were twenty-one guards on duty. Guard Pvt. O'Hearn testified that six of the guards had gone to the nearby guardhouse to sleep when relieved from their posts at nine o'clock because there was no room in the prison guard room. Emory, Pulver, and O'Hearn, Proceedings, 20–23.
33. Ross, ibid., 169.
34. Tangled Hair, *Sen. Rep. 708*, 13; Simpson, Proceedings, 97; Lannigan, Proceedings, 144; Pumpkin Seed's Son, Proceedings, 12; Red Feather/The Enemy, Proceedings, 17.
35. Wessells, Proceedings, 84; Simpson, ibid., 98; Rowland, ibid., 140.
36. Ross, ibid., 168; Johnson, ibid., 130; Rowland, ibid., 140; Wessells to AAG, Dept./Platte, Jan. 12, 1879, *Sen. Misc. Doc. 64*, 6–8.
37. Report of Board, Proceedings, 190.

38. Old Crow, *Sen. Rep. 708*, 21; Pumpkin Seed's Son, Proceedings, 12; Red Feather/The Enemy, ibid., 17.
39. Red Feather/The Enemy, ibid., 17–18; Pumpkin Seed's Son, ibid., 12.
40. Cheyenne woman, ibid., 15. Wessells said he made the women "work on very bright days policing and unloading grain wagons. This was to give them exercise and on the recommendation of Dr. Mosely, Post Surgeon." Wessells, ibid., 72.
41. Wessells, ibid., 72–73.
42. Old Crow, ibid., 5; Blacksmith, ibid., 9.
43. O'Hearn, ibid., 23.
44. *Leavenworth Daily Times,* Jan. 17, 1879.
45. Iron Teeth stated that the women had kept guns hidden in their clothing. She had one in the breast of her dress: "We hid all of these under a loose board of the floor. My family blanket was spread over this board." Marquis, *Cheyennes and Sioux,* 22.
46. The Cheyenne firearms found after the Fort Robinson outbreak were five Springfield carbines (1873 model), caliber .45, four of which were obtained from dead soldiers and one of which indicated long Cheyenne possession because its stock was studded with brass tacks; seven Springfield rifle muskets, caliber .50, all cut down to carbine length and their stocks ornamented; three Sharps carbines, caliber .50, with brass-studded stocks; one Sharps "Old Reliable" rifle with a round 28-inch barrel, caliber .45; one Colts five-shot revolver, caliber .36; one Colts Navy revolver (old pattern); and one Remington revolver (old pattern, army size). Report of Board, Proceedings, 4.
47. Bronson, *Reminiscences,* 176.
48. Wessells, Proceedings, 73.

CHAPTER 18

1. Pulver, Proceedings, 20; Ross, Proceedings, 168. A report to the *Leavenworth Daily Times* (Jan. 15, 1879) said the guard on the east side of the prison barrack had just called out "ten o'clock, all's well." It appears, however, that the breakout began before ten. Wessells gave the time as "about 10 P.M." Proceedings, 73.
2. Old Crow listed the leaders of the young men as Roman Nose and Little Finger Nail. Proceedings, 6.
3. Mrs. Black Bear stated that Little Shield fired the first shot. Mrs. Black Bear, Folder 348, 57–58, Grinnell Collection, Southwest Museum. Asst. Surg. Edward B. Moseley said that five minutes afterward Schmidt was drawing an occasional breath, but no pulse could be found at his wrist. Grange, "Treating the Wounded," 279. The *Army and Navy Journal* 16 (Jan. 18, 1879), gave the soldier's name as Richard Smith. See also Report of Board, Proceedings; Powell, *People,* 1202.
4. *Army and Navy Journal* 16 (Jan. 18, 1879): 409; Grange, "Treating the Wounded," 279–280.
5. Timmey (Timmany), Proceedings, 21; Grange, "Treating the Wounded," 281–283.
6. Pulver, Proceedings, 20.
7. Ross, ibid., 168. Powell indicates that in leaving the barracks the Cheyennes stopped to grab four carbines the guards had left behind in their flight from the first sergeant's room. *People,* 1201. Private Ross testified that he had left a loaded carbine standing in a corner of the room when he came off guard duty. Proceedings, 169.

8. Grange, "Treating the Wounded," 282–283.
9. Ibid., 281.
10. Young, Proceedings, 19.
11. Janzohn, ibid., 142–143.
12. Mitchell, Proceedings, 150–151; Powell, *People*, 1203.
13. Mitchell, Proceedings, 151.
14. Report of Board, ibid., 194.
15. Simpson, ibid., 98.
16. Big Beaver, Folder 350, 44, Grinnell Collection, Southwest Museum; Lannigan, Proceedings, 144–145.
17. Lannigan, Proceedings, 144–145.
18. Wessells, ibid., 73; Wessells to AAG, Dept./Platte, Jan. 12, 1879, *Sen. Misc. Doc. 64*, 6–8; Wessells's Interview, Ellison Papers, Denver Public Library.
19. Wessells to AAG, Dept./Platte, Jan. 12, 1879, *Sen. Misc. Doc. 64*, 7.
20. *Leavenworth Daily Times*, Jan. 15, 1879.
21. Powell, *People*, 1203, citing James Rowland to Grinnell.
22. *Army and Navy Journal* 16 (Jan. 18, 1879): 409.
23. Simpson, Proceedings, 99; Pettys, ibid., 126; *Leavenworth Daily Times*, Jan. 15, 1879.
24. Marquis, *Cheyennes and Sioux*, 22–23.
25. Marquis, "Red Ripe's Squaw," 208.
26. Grange, "Treating the Wounded," 290; Wessells's Interview, Ellison Papers, Denver Public Library.
27. Chase, Proceedings, 34–35.
28. Bronson, *Reminiscences*, 183–184.
29. Big Beaver to Grinnell, Folder 350, 44, Grinnell Collection, Southwest Museum.
30. Pumpkin Seed's Son, Proceedings, 11.
31. Chase, ibid., 35.
32. Ibid.
33. Johnson, ibid., 132; Cummings, ibid., 165. Petty listed the victim as White Antelope and indicated she had a gunshot wound to the thigh and a stab wound. Petty, ibid., 127.
34. Powell, *People*, 1202, n. 23, stated that this may have been Dull Knife's daughter, Walking Woman. She is identified as the beautiful girl known by officers at the post as "the Princess." Bronson, *Reminiscences*, 184; *Army and Navy Journal* 16 (Jan. 18, 1879): 408–409. The Jordan manuscript, however, which tells of the survivors who arrived at Pine Ridge after the outbreak, gives a personal acquaintance account of a meeting with Dull Knife's daughter "the Princess" at the old Red Cloud Agency. Charles P. Jordan manuscript, Red Cloud Agency ms. No. 71, Cheyenne Outbreak Drawer, Fort Robinson Museum.
35. Bronson, *Reminiscences*, 184; *Army and Navy Journal* 16 (Jan. 18, 1879): 408–409; Charles P. Jordan manuscript, 17, Red Cloud Agency ms. No. 71, Cheyenne Outbreak Drawer, Fort Robinson Museum.
36. Bronson, *Reminiscences*, 181–182; Powell, *People*, 1207.

37. *Army and Navy Journal* 16 (Jan. 18, 1879): 409.
38. Lawson, Proceedings, 109.
39. Mrs. C. A. Johnson to her sister, Jan. 15, 1879, Cheyenne Outbreak Drawer, Fort Robinson Museum.
40. Wessells, Proceedings, 74.
41. Vroom, ibid., 88.
42. Wessells, ibid., 74; Crawford, ibid., 134; Wessells to AAG, Dept./Platte, Jan. 12, 1879, *Sen. Misc. Doc. 64*, 6–8.
43. Chase, Proceedings, 36.
44. Rowland, ibid., 140–141.
45. Cummings, ibid., 158.
46. Clifford, ibid., 152–153.
47. Cummings, ibid., 160.
48. Ibid., 161.
49. Simpson, ibid., 105–106.
50. Ibid., 104.
51. Cummings, ibid., 158; Pettys, ibid., 127–128.
52. Wessells to Sheridan, Jan. 10, 1879, *Sen. Misc. Doc. 64*, 23.
53. Crawford to Morton, Feb. 26, 1879, Cheyenne Outbreak Drawer, Fort Robinson Museum.
54. Big Beaver, Folder 350, 47, Grinnell Collection, Southwest Museum. Powell lists Dull Knife's surviving party as Dull Knife; his wife, Pawnee Woman; Bull Hump; Bull Hump's wife, Red Leaf; their child; and Dull Knife's grandson Calf. Powell, *People*, 1242.
55. Sheridan to Townsend, Jan. 13, 1879, *Sen. Misc. Doc. 64*, 23.

CHAPTER 19

1. Vroom, Proceedings, 88.
2. Grange, "Treating the Wounded," 283.
3. Wessells, Proceedings, 75.
4. Baxter, ibid., 118; Grange, "Treating the Wounded," 283–284. See also *Leavenworth Daily Times*, Jan. 15, 1879; Bronson, *Reminiscences*, 187–192.
5. Cummings, Proceedings, 162–163.
6. This may have been Young Pumpkin Seed (Big Beaver), who said an officer shook hands with him, then hoisted him onto his horse and took him back to the fort. Grinnell, *Fighting Cheyennes*, 423–424; Big Beaver, Folder 350, 46, Grinnell Collection, Southwest Museum.
7. Grange, "Treating the Wounded," 286.
8. Ibid., 285–286; Lawson, Proceedings, 110.
9. Proceedings, 110.
10. Chase, ibid., 38–39; Grange, "Treating the Wounded," 284. Lieutenant Chase said: "Sergeant Bigalsky that night obtained Corporal Ore's body and brought it into Camp Robinson." Proceedings, 39.
11. Chase, Proceedings, 38–41.

12. Baxter, ibid., 119.
13. Wessells, ibid., 76.
14. *Army and Navy Journal* 16 (Jan. 18, 1879): 409; *New York Times,* Jan. 16, 1879.
15. Shangreau interview, Cheyenne Outbreak Drawer, Fort Robinson Museum.
16. Ibid.
17. Ibid.; *Army and Navy Journal* 16 (Jan. 28, 1879): 408–409.
18. Shangreau interview, Cheyenne Outbreak Drawer, Fort Robinson Museum; Wessells, Proceedings, 76; Grange, "Treating the Wounded," 286–287.
19. Shangreau interview, Cheyenne Outbreak Drawer, Fort Robinson Museum; Grange, "Treating the Wounded," 286–287; *Army and Navy Journal* 16 (Jan. 25, 1879): 433; *New York Times,* Jan. 19, 1879.
20. Shangreau interview, Cheyenne Outbreak Drawer, Fort Robinson Museum.
21. Lawson's testimony, Proceedings, 112; Chase, ibid., 46. Evans had commanded one prong of Sheridan's winter campaign into Indian Territory in 1868, routing a Comanche village in Devil's Canyon of the Wichita Mountains on Christmas Day. Hoig, *Tribal Wars,* 264–267.
22. Wilson, "Coliseum Butte."
23. Shangreau interview, Cheyenne Outbreak Drawer, Fort Robinson Museum; *St. Louis Post and Dispatch,* Jan. 23, 1879.
24. Antelope Creek Fight transcript, Cheyenne Outbreak Drawer, Fort Robinson Museum; *Army and Navy Journal* 16 (Jan. 25, 1879): 433.
25. Chase, Proceedings, 46.
26. Ibid., 48.
27. Woman's Dress was erroneously reported as having died during the return to Fort Robinson. *Army and Navy Journal* 16 (Feb. 1, 1879): 453.
28. Ibid.
29. Grange, "Treating the Wounded," 289.
30. *Leavenworth Daily Times,* Jan. 14, 1879.
31. Wessells, Proceedings, 78.
32. Chase, ibid., 50.
33. Grange, "Treating the Wounded," 288.
34. Ibid., 288–289.
35. *Army and Navy Journal* 16 (Feb. 1, 1879): 453.
36. Chase, Proceedings, 50–52.
37. Carter P. Johnson, Antelope Creek Fight transcript, Cheyenne Outbreak Drawer, Fort Robinson Museum, stated that three Cheyennes appeared out of the pit; Chase, Proceedings, 52, said he saw two.
38. *Army and Navy Journal* 16 (Feb. 1, 1879): 453.
39. Ibid., citing the *New York Herald.*
40. Ibid.
41. Powell, *People,* 1227.
42. Antelope Creek Fight transcript, Cheyenne Outbreak Drawer, Fort Robinson Museum.
43. Pettys, Proceedings, 126.
44. Report of Board, ibid., 198; *Army and Navy Journal* 16 (Mar. 15, 1879): 571. Chase,

Proceedings, 51, listed seventeen men and seven women and children dead (total twenty-four), whereas eight women and children survived.

45. Pettys, Proceedings, 127–128; Grange, "Treating the Wounded," 290–291.
46. Buecker and Paul, "Cheyenne Outbreak Firearms," 9, citing Board of Officers Ordnance Report, 326. The Army and Navy Journal 16 (Feb. 1, 1879): 453, reported the arms found in the redoubt after the battle included ten rifles—"the best sporting rifles of calibers fifty and forty-four with short and long cartridges"—and five pistols. Their ready ammunition, however, was said to be virtually exhausted, with very few bullets in their belts. Boxes of reloading caps, 2 pounds of powder, and bullet molds were found, but there was no lead.
47. Army and Navy Journal 16 (Feb. 1, 1879): 453.
48. Ibid.
49. Lawson, Proceedings, 113.
50. Rodenbough, Fighting for Honor, 396; Buecker, Fort Robinson, 147.
51. Lawson, Proceedings, 113.
52. Leavenworth Daily Times, Jan. 24, 1879; Antelope Creek Fight transcript, Cheyenne Outbreak Drawer, Fort Robinson Museum.
53. Evans to Crook, Jan. 23, 1879, Army and Navy Journal 16 (Feb. 1, 1879): 453.
54. Reprinted in the St. Louis Post and Dispatch, Jan. 22, 1879.

CHAPTER 20

1. Little Wolf to Grinnell, Folder 328, 35, Grinnell Collection, Southwest Museum.
2. Leavenworth Daily Times, Nov. 9, 1878.
3. New York Times, Jan. 19, 1879.
4. Grinnell, Fighting Cheyennes, 410; Leavenworth Daily Times, Jan. 19, 1879; Army and Navy Journal 16 (Jan. 25, 1879): 433.
5. New York Times, Feb. 9, 1879.
6. Army and Navy Journal 16 (Feb. 22, 1879): 512.
7. Ibid. (Mar. 1, 1879): 529; Report of Secretary of War, 1878, 52.
8. Clark's adeptness at sign language won him the friendship of the tribes and helped him to organize a 400-scout unit in support of U.S. troops. Leslie's Illustrated Newspaper, June 23, 1879, 276–277; Heitman, Historical Register 1: 306.
9. Report of Lt. Clark, Sen. Rep. 708, 246–250.
10. "Billy Jackson's Capture by the Cheyennes," 102.
11. New York Times, Mar. 31, 1879; Report of Secretary of War, 1878, 52.
12. Report of Lt. Clark, Sen. Rep. 708, 246–250.
13. Ibid.
14. Ibid.
15. Ibid. A brief summary of Little Wolf's capture by Lieutenant Clark appeared in the Army and Navy Journal 16 (Apr. 5, 1879): 617.
16. Clark to AAG, Apr. 6, 1879, LR, Dept./Dakota, NA.
17. Report of Board, Proceedings, 185.
18. Report of Lt. Clark, Sen. Rep. 708, 249.
19. Quoted in Clark to Post Adj., Fort Keogh, May 5, 1879, LR/AGO (main series), NA.

20. *Report of Secretary of War, 1879,* 52–53.
21. Roberts, "Shame of Little Wolf," 42, citing G. N. Whirler to AAG, Apr. 17, 1879, Dept./Dakota, NA (RG 393).
22. *New York Times,* Jan. 12, 1879.
23. Ibid., June 23, 1879.
24. Ibid.; "Billy Jackson's Capture by the Cheyennes," 103.
25. *New York Times,* June 23, 1879.

CHAPTER 21

1. *Chicago Tribune,* Dec. 16, 1877.
2. Ibid., Dec. 14, 16, 1877.
3. Ibid., Dec. 16, 1877.
4. Ben Clark, *Sen. Doc.* 708, vii, 142–143.
5. Clark to Mizner, Sept. 8, 1879, LR, Dept./Mo., NA.
6. Ibid.; Buecker, *Fort Robinson,* 130.
7. *Leavenworth Daily Times,* Sept. 19, 1878.
8. Ibid.; Buecker, *Fort Robinson,* 130.
9. *New York Herald,* Oct. 20, 1878.
10. Ben Clark, *Sen. Doc.* 708, 142–143.
11. *Leavenworth Daily Times,* Oct. 1, 1878; *Dodge City Times,* Nov. 23, 1878.
12. *Dodge City Times,* Nov. 23, 1878; *Leavenworth Daily Times,* Nov. 24, 1878; Greene and Wright, "Chasing Dull Knife," 31.
13. *Leavenworth Daily Times,* Dec. 19, 1878.
14. *Dodge City Times,* Dec. 7, 1878. Col. R. I. Dodge, who met the party on his way to Camp Supply from Fort Reno, said the affair took place four miles above his camp at Cedar Bluffs, said to be 16 to 17 miles from Supply. Kime, *Indian Territory Journals,* 95–96.
15. Creel account, Ricker Interview, March 16, 1913, Cheyenne Outbreak Drawer, Fort Robinson Museum.
16. Kime, *Indian Territory Journals,* 97, n. 58, citing Creel to Major Barbar, June 5, 1879.
17. Ibid., 96–97.
18. (Wilder), "The Experience of Major Mauck," 91.
19. *Leavenworth Daily Times,* Dec. 19, 1878.
20. Clark to Mizner, Dec. 10, 1878, LR, Dept./Mo., NA.
21. Fort Reno dispatch, Dec. 9, 1878, *Leavenworth Daily Times,* Dec. 19, 1878.

CHAPTER 22

1. Gunther, RCM, 163.
2. Wilder, ibid., 84, 90, 93; Rendlebrock, ibid., 218.
3. McDonald, ibid., 69.
4. Rendlebrock to AAG, Oct. 11, 1878, LR, Dept./Platte, NA; certificate of Post Surgeon, Sidney Barracks, Oct. 11, 1878, LR, Dept./Platte, NA; Feely, RCM, 185–186; Rendlebrock, RCM, 218.
5. McDonald, RCM, 76.
6. Wood, GCM, 44.

7. Leeper, RCM, 96; Rendlebrock, RCM, 218.
8. Wilder, ibid., 83; Wood, ibid., 117: McDonald, ibid., 75; Feely, ibid., 185; Crozier, ibid., 185.
9. Rendlebrock, ibid., 218.
10. Ibid., 186–187.
11. *New York Herald,* Oct. 21, 1878. See also *Army and Navy Journal* 15 (Oct. 26, 1878): 185.
12. *New York Herald,* Oct. 21, 1878.
13. Ibid.
14. Ibid.
15. *Army and Navy Journal* 15 (Nov. 9, 1878): 223.
16. Wood, GCM, 51.
17. Ibid., 46.
18. Ibid., 51, 60; Gunther, ibid., 127.
19. Gunther, ibid., 127.
20. Ibid.; Wood, ibid., 44–45.
21. Ibid.
22. Ibid.
23. Ibid., 128.
24. Wood, GCM, 44.
25. Ibid., 65.
26. Feely, RCM, 187.
27. Exhibit 12, HCM, 4.
28. Leeper, ibid., 45.
29. Hemphill, ibid., 63.
30. Exhibit 12, ibid., 8.
31. General Court-Martial Orders No. 28, General Court-Martial Orders No. 79, Fort Leavenworth, Kansas; Heitman, *Historical Register* 1: 521.
32. Wood, GCM, 46.
33. General Court-Martial No. 29, Apr. 4, 1869, Dept./Mo., GCM.
34. McDonald, ibid., 8.
35. Wilder, ibid., 22–23.
36. Wood, ibid., 40.
37. Ibid., 42.
38. Hdqs. Dept./Mo., Apr. 4, 1879, GCM. Pope's statement also appeared in the *Army and Navy Journal* 16 (Apr. 19, 1879): 652.
39. Gunther to AG, Apr. 16, 1879, LR, Dept./Mo., NA.
40. Heitman, *Historical Register* 1: 483–484.
41. Wood, RCM, 115.
42. Ibid., 4–5; General Court-Martial Orders No. 36, June 21, 1872, AGO, Hdqs./Army, ibid.
43. Louise Rendlebrock to Schurz, May 20, 1879, Rendlebrock papers, microfilm, Oklahoma Historical Society, Archives and Manuscript Division.
44. Judge Advocate General W. M. Dunn to Sec. of War, June 6, 1879, RCM.
45. *Army and Navy Journal* 16 (July 12, 1879): 884.
46. Ibid.; Rendlebrock papers, microfilm, Oklahoma Historical Society, Archives and Manuscript Division; Fort Reno Post Returns, August 1879.

47. Heitman, *Historical Register* 1: 1054.
48. Wood to Hatch, Nov. 22, 1878, LR, Dept./Mo., NA.

CHAPTER 23

1. Irwin to Crook, Feb. 10, 1879, LR/AGO (main series), NA.
2. *New York Times*, Jan. 10, 1879.
3. Ibid.; Johnson, "Cheyennes in Court," 8, citing Crook to Irwin, Jan. 18, 1879, File 1224, AGO; Williams to Irwin, Jan. 18, 1879, File 1224, AGO.
4. Pettys, Proceedings, 127–128; Grange, "Treating the Wounded," 290–291.
5. *Army and Navy Journal* 16 (Feb. 8, 1879): 478; Buecker, *Fort Robinson*, 147.
6. Red Cloud manuscript 71, Cheyenne Outbreak Drawer, Fort Robinson Museum.
7. Special Orders No. 8, Jan. 21, 1879, AAG, Dept./Platte, Proceedings, 1.
8. Proceedings, Jan. 25, 1879, LR/AGO (main series), NA.
9. Report of Board, ibid., 201.
10. Ibid.
11. Quoted in *Army and Navy Journal* 16 (Jan. 25, 1879): 433.
12. Quoted in Fast, *The Last Frontier*, 305–306.
13. *Omaha Daily Herald*, Jan. 17, 1879.
14. *Leavenworth Daily Times*, Jan. 15, 1879.
15. *New York Times*, Nov. 6, 1879.
16. *Leavenworth Daily Times*, Jan. 15, 1879.
17. *Army and Navy Journal* 16 (Feb. 22, 1879): 512, citing the *New York Evening Post*.
18. Wessells's interview, Ellison Papers, Denver Public Library.
19. *New York Times*, Sept. 28, 1879.
20. *Wichita Eagle*, Feb. 6, 1879.
21. Epp, "State of Kansas v. Wild Hog et al.," 141.
22. Miller and Snell, "Cowtown Police Officers," 392.
23. St. John to Pope, Feb. 13, 1879, LR/OIA (main series), NA; *Leavenworth Daily Times*, Feb. 6, 12, 1879.
24. Miller and Snell, "Cowtown Police Officers," 392–393.
25. *Leavenworth Daily Times*, Feb. 15, 1879.
26. Ibid., Feb. 16, 1879.
27. Ibid., Feb. 15, 16, 1879; *Dodge City Times*, Feb. 25, 1879.
28. *Ford County Globe*, Feb. 17, 1879.
29. *Topeka Commonwealth*, Feb. 16, 1879.
30. *Ford County Globe*, Feb. 17, 1879.
31. Ibid.
32. *Dodge City Times*, Feb. 22, 1879; *Leavenworth Daily Times*, Feb. 25, 1879.
33. *Ford County Globe*, Feb. 25, 1879.
34. Berthrong, *Ordeal*, 40.
35. Ibid., 40–41.
36. Apr. 13, 1879.
37. Ibid.
38. Powers, "Northern Cheyenne Trek," 23.

39. Epp, "State of Kansas v. Wild Hog et al.," 143.
40. Feb. 22, 1879.
41. *Dodge City Times,* Oct. 18, 1879; Powers, "Northern Cheyenne Trek," 23; Epp, "State of Kansas v. Wild Hog et al.," 143.
42. Powers, "Kansas Indian Claims Commission," 202–203; *Topeka Commonwealth,* July 9, 1879.
43. Miller and Snell, "Cowtown Police Officers," 398.
44. *Western Home Journal,* July 31, 1879.
45. *Leavenworth Daily Times,* Aug. 13, 18, 1879.
46. *Kansas Daily Tribune,* Aug. 13, 1879.
47. *Sen. Rep. 708.*
48. *Lawrence Daily Tribune,* Oct. 11, 1879. A photo of the group with the other prisoners appears in Powers, "Kansas Indian Claims Commission," 202.
49. Epp, "State of Kansas v. Wild Hog et al.," 143.
50. *Dodge City Times,* Oct. 18, 1879; Epp, "State of Kansas v. Wild Hog et al.," 145.

CHAPTER 24

1. Utley, *Frontier Regulars,* 286–288; Heitman, *Historical Register* 1: 306.
2. Utley, *Frontier Regulars,* 335–337.
3. Berthrong, *Ordeal,* 46.
4. *Dodge City Times,* Oct. 27, 1881.
5. *Annual Report of Commissioner of Indian Affairs, 1883,* 30; Buecker, *Fort Robinson,* 152; Hoig, *Fort Reno,* 231.
6. Utley, *Frontier Regulars,* 335–342. Hatch died as a result of a carriage accident at Fort Robinson on April 11, 1889. Buecker, *Fort Robinson,* 171–172.
7. Pierce, *Most Promising Young Officer,* 211; Fourth Cavalry Returns, Apr. 1881.
8. Pierce, *Most Promising Young Officer,* 215–216.
9. Third Cavalry Returns, Apr. 1882; Utley, *Frontier Regulars,* 375; Heitman, *Historical Register* 1: 1035.
10. Heitman, *Historical Register* 1: 409; Utley, *Frontier Regulars,* 376–377.
11. Utley, *Frontier Regulars,* 377–380; Debo, *Geronimo,* 172–192.
12. Schmitt, *General George Crook,* 255; Utley, *Frontier Regulars,* 377–386; Debo, *Geronimo,* 172–192.
13. *Harper's Illustrated Weekly,* Sept. 18, Oct. 2, 1886.
14. Fourth Cavalry Returns, Aug., Sept., Oct., 1886; *Harper's Illustrated Weekly,* Sept. 18, Oct. 2, 1886; Miles, *Serving the Republic,* 225–226; Debo, *Geronimo,* 281–298; Utley, *Frontier Regulars,* 387–393.
15. Rendlebrock papers, microfilm, Oklahoma Historical Society, Archives and Manuscript Division.
16. Heitman, *Historical Register* 1: 358–359, 521, 619, 697.
17. Ibid., 718.
18. *Twenty-Fifth Annual Reunion, 1894,* West Point Archives.
19. Heitman, *Historical Register* 1: 197.
20. *National Cyclopedia of American Biography,* 205.

21. Heitman, *Historical Register* 1: 282–283.
22. *Harper's Illustrated Weekly*, Sept. 18, Oct. 2, 1886; Debo, *Geronimo*, 281–298; Miles, *Personal Recollections*, 513–514; Utley, *Frontier Regulars*, 387–389.
23. Wessells, "Hard Military Service," 601–605.

BIBLIOGRAPHY

ARCHIVES

DECATUR COUNTY MUSEUM, OBERLIN, KANSAS
  Typescript Manuscripts
    Anthony, Mr. and Mrs. Henry. "Early N.W. Kansas Reminiscences."
    Colvin, H. D. "The Indian Raid of 1878."
    Cook, Gus. "Tells Story of Last Indian Raid."
    Foster, L. M. "The Last Indian Raid in Kansas."
    "The Great Cheyenne Chase: A Truthful Account by a Dragoon Who
      Participated in It." From the *Ford County Globe,* Jan 7, 1879.
    "History of William Laing, Sr., and Family."
    "Kansans Recall Terror of the Last Indian Raid."
    Laing family data sheet.
    O'Toole, Billy. "Billy O'Toole's Story of the Raid."
    Raab, Joseph. "The Indian Raid."
    Street, Wm. D. "Incidents of the Dull Knife Raid."
    "Story of Dora Westphalen." From the Decatur County Museum.
    "Story of 'Dull Knife' and the Last Indian Raid in Kansas." From the *Goodland
      News Republic,* May 27, 1926.
  Booklet
    "Authentic Accounts of Massacre of Indians and Cheyenne Raid in Western
      Kansas."

DENVER PUBLIC LIBRARY
  Johnson, Carter P., Interview.
  Wessells's Interview, Robert S. Ellison Papers, 1876–1940.
EL RENO PUBLIC LIBRARY
  Cheyenne/Arapaho Letterbooks.
FORT ROBINSON MUSEUM
  Cheyenne Outbreak Drawer
    Antelope Creek Fight typescript, Ricker Interview of Carter P. Johnson.
    Brown, George W., account. *National Tribune,* July 22, 1920.
    Carlton, Mabel. Caleb H. Carlton typescript.
    Colvin, H. D., account. *National Tribune,* June 19, 1911.
    Crawford, Lt. Emmet, to Lt. Morton. Letters.
    "The Indian Raid." *Hays City Sentinel,* Oct. 5, 1878.
    Johnson, Mrs. C. A. Letter to sister, Jan. 15. 1879.
    Kansas' Last Indian Uprising.
    Lemmon, G. E., account. *Developing the West.*
    Red Cloud manuscript.
    Ricker Interview with Brig. Gen. H. M. Creel, March 16, 1913.
    Shangreau, John, Interview by Judge Ricker, Nov. 6, 1906.
    Trask, Samuel A., account. *National Tribune,* Oct. 19, 1911.
    "The Widows' Wail." *Atchison Champion.* Oct. 17, 1878.
GILCREASE INSTITUTE
  Herber M. Creel. *Cheyenne Grammar and Ethnology,* Book A.
KANSAS STATE HISTORICAL SOCIETY
  Emerson L. Brown. "Narrative Accounts of Indian Raid of 1878," Cheyenne Indian
    Collection (ms. 1227.03).
  *Indian Raid of 1878: The Report of (Kansas) Commission, Appointed in Pursuance of
    the Provisions of Senate Joint Resolution No. 1 Relating to Losses Sustained by
    Citizens of Kansas by the Invasion of Indians during the Year 1878.*
  Second Biennial Report, 1879. Adjutant General, State of Kansas.
NATIONAL ARCHIVES
  File Relating to Military Operations, Cheyenne Outbreak, RG 393, M-1495, Roll 6.
  Fort Reno Special Order 118.
NEBRASKA STATE HISTORICAL SOCIETY
  "Cheyenne Outbreak."
  Excerpt taken from account by Carter P. Johnson.
  Interview with John Shangreau, Nov. 6, 1906.
  Judge Eli S. Ricker papers.
NEWBERRY LIBRARY, EVERETT D. GRAFF COLLECTION
  Henry W. Lawton Scrapbook.
OKLAHOMA HISTORICAL SOCIETY, ARCHIVES AND MANUSCRIPT DIVISION
  M. L. Ervin Boyle Rendlebrock papers (microfilm).
SOUTHWEST MUSEUM
  Grinnell Collection.

UNITED STATES ARMY MILITARY HISTORY INSTITUTE
Order of the Indian Wars Collection.
UNITED STATES MILITARY ACADEMY
Bourke Diaries.
UNIVERSITY OF CENTRAL OKLAHOMA, OKLAHOMA COLLECTION
Letters Received, Fort Supply.
UNIVERSITY OF NEBRASKA, UNIVERSITY ARCHIVES, LOVE LIBRARY
Mari Sandoz Special Collection.
UNIVERSITY OF OKLAHOMA, WESTERN HISTORY COLLECTION
Campbell Collection, Boxes 99, 120, 121.
Fourth Cavalry Monthly Returns.
Military Map of Indian Territory, Dept. of the Missouri, 1875, Comp. by First Lt. E. H. Ruffner.
WEST POINT ARCHIVES AND SPECIAL COLLECTIONS
Fiftieth Annual Report of the Association of Graduates, U.S. Military Academy, 1919. Saginaw, Mich.: Seeman and Peters, 1919.
Twenty-Fifth Annual Reunion of the Association of the Graduates of the U.S. Military Academy, 1894. Saginaw, Mich.: Seeman and Peters, 1894.

ARTICLES/THESIS

Berryman, J. W. "Early Settlement of Southwest Kansas." Kansas State Historical Collections 17 (1926–1928): 561–570.
"Billy Jackson's Capture by the Cheyennes." Forest and Stream 49 (Aug. 7, 1897): 102–103.
Brill, Charles A. "Cheyenne Defiance." Daily Oklahoman, Mar. 29, 1936.
Brown, George W. "Dull Knife's Raid." Early History of Scott County, Kansas. Scott City, Kan., Scott County Historical Association, 1977, 400–402.
———. "Kansas Indian Wars." Collections of Kansas Historical Society 17 (1926–1928): 134–139.
Buecker, Thomas R., and R. Eli Paul. "Cheyenne Outbreak Firearms." Museum of the Fur Trade Quarterly 29 (summer 1993): 1–13.
Colcord, Charles F. "Reminiscences of Charles F. Colcord." Chronicles of Oklahoma 12 (March 1934): 5–18.
Covington, James Warren. "Causes of the Dull Knife Raid." Chronicles of Oklahoma 26 (spring 1948): 13–22.
"Dull Knife's Cheyenne Raid of 1878." Nebraska History 7 (October–December 1924): 116–119.
Dusenberry, Verne. "The Northern Cheyenne." Montana Magazine of History 5 (winter 1955): 23–25.
Epp, Todd D. "The State of Kansas v. Wild Hog et al." Kansas History 5 (summer 1982): 139–146.
Foster, L. M. "The Last Indian Raid in Kansas." Westerners' Brand Book, Denver Posse, 1963, 140–150.
Grange, Roger R., Jr. "Treating the Wounded at Fort Robinson." Nebraska History 45 (Sept. 1964): 273–294.

Greene, Jerome A., and Peter M. Wright, eds. "Chasing Dull Knife: A Journal of the Cheyenne Campaign of 1878 by Lieutenant George H. Palmer." *Heritage of Kansas, a Journal of the Great Plains* 12 (winter 1979): 25–36.

Johnson, Barry C. "Cheyennes in Court." *English Westerners' Brand Book* 4 (July 1962): 6–12; 5 (Oct. 1962): 2–6.

Keith, A. N. "Dull Knife's Cheyenne Raid of 1878." *Nebraska History* 7 (October–December 1924): 116–119.

"Lieutenant W. P. Clark, U.S.A., and Little Wolf." *Leslie's Illustrated Newspaper*, June 23, 1879, 276–277.

Marquis, Thomas B. "Red Ripe's Squaw." *Century Magazine* 118 (June 1929): 201–209.

Miller, Nyle H., and Joseph W. Snell, comps. "Some Notes on Kansas Cowtown Police Officers and Gun Fighters." *Kansas Historical Quarterly* 27 (autumn 1961): 391–399.

Pickering, I. O. "The Administration of John P. St. John." *Kansas State Historical Collections* 9 (1905–1906): 378–394.

Powell, Peter J. "High Bull's Victory Roster." *Montana Magazine* 25 (winter 1975): 14–21.

Powers, Ramon S. "The Kansas Indian Claims Commission of 1879." *Kansas History* 7 (fall 1984): 199–211.

———. "The Northern Cheyenne Trek." *Trail Guide* (Westerners Kansas City Posse) 17 (September–December 1972): 2–33.

Roberts, Gary L. "The Shame of Little Wolf." *Montana Magazine* 28 (summer 1978): 37–47.

Wessells, Henry W., IV. "Hard Military Service: Two Officers in the 19th-Century West." *Cite AB* (Oct. 5, 1998): 601–605.

West, C. Derek. "The Battle of Sappa Creek." *Kansas Historical Quarterly* 34 (summer 1968): 150–178.

"Wilber Elliott Wilder." *Medal of Honors Records* (April 1952), USMA. 43

(Wilder, Wilber). "The Experience of Major Mauck in Disarming a Band of Cheyennes on the North Fork of the Canadian River in 1878." *Papers of the Order of Indian Wars,* U.S. Army Military History Institute, 89–92.

Wilson, Luella. "Coliseum Butte." *Harrison Sun-News,* April 19, 1962.

Woodward, George A. "Some Experiences with the Cheyennes." *United Service* 1 (April 1878): 184–195.

Wright, Peter M. "The Pursuit of Dull Knife from Fort Reno in 1878–1879." *Chronicles of Oklahoma* 46 (summer 1968): 141–154.

———."Fort Reno, Indian Territory. 1874–1885." Master's Thesis, University of Oklahoma, 1965.

BOOKS

Appleton's Annual Cyclopedia. New York: Appleton, 1862–1903.

Baldwin, Alice Blackwood. *Memoirs of the Late Frank D. Baldwin, Major General, U.S.A.* Los Angeles: Wetzel, 1929.

Barker, Carolyn. *Burials in the Fort Reno Cemetery, 1874–1948.* El Reno, Okla.: Carolyn Barker, 1996.

Berthrong, Donald J. *The Cheyenne and Arapaho Ordeal.* Norman: University of Oklahoma Press, 1976.

———. *The Southern Cheyennes.* Norman: University of Oklahoma Press, 1963.

Bode, E. A. *A Dose of Frontier Soldiering: The Memoirs of Corporal E. A. Bode,* ed. Thomas T. Smith. Lincoln: University of Nebraska Press, 1994.

Bourke, John G. *Mackenzie's Last Fight with the Cheyennes: A Winter Campaigning in Wyoming and Montana.* Governor's Island, N.Y.: Military Service Institution, 1890.

————. *On the Border with Crook.* New York: Charles Scribner's Sons, 1891.

Bronson, Edgar Beecher. *Reminiscences of a Ranchman.* New York: McClure, 1908.

Buecker, Thomas R. *Fort Robinson and the American West, 1874–1899.* Lincoln: Nebraska State Historical Society, 1999.

Carriker, Robert C. *Fort Supply and the Indian Territory: Frontier Outpost on the Plains.* Norman: University of Oklahoma Press, 1970.

Carrington, Frances C. *My Army Life and the Fort Phil Kearney Massacre.* Philadelphia: J. B. Lippincott, 1910.

Carrington, Margaret I. *Ab-sa-ra-ka, Land of Massacre.* Philadelphia: J. P. Lippincott, 1879.

Carroll, John M., intro. by. *The Papers of the Order of Indian Wars.* Fort Collins, Colo.: Old Army, 1975.

Chalfant, William Y. *Cheyennes and Horse Soldiers: The 1857 Expedition and the Battle of Solomon's Fork.* Norman: University of Oklahoma Press, 1989.

————. *Cheyennes at Dark Water Creek: The Last Fight of the Red River War.* Norman: University of Oklahoma Press, 1997.

Colcord, Charles Francis. *The Autobiography of Charles Francis Colcord, 1859–1934.* Privately printed, 1970.

Collins, Dennis. *The Indians' Last Fight or the Dull Knife Raid.* Girard, Kan.: Press of the Appeal to Reason, 1914.

Colton, Ray C. *The Civil War in the Western Territories.* Norman: University of Oklahoma Press, 1959.

Cook, John R. *The Border and the Buffalo: An Untold Story of the Southwest Plains.* Topeka: Crane, 1907.

Cullum, George W. *Biographical Register of the Officers and Graduates of the U.S. Military Academy at West Point.* 2 vols. Boston: Houghton Mifflin, 1891.

Debo, Angie. *Geronimo: The Man, His Time, His Place.* Norman: University of Oklahoma Press, 1976.

Dodge, Richard I. *Our Wild Indians: Thirty-three Years among the Red Men of the Great West.* Hartford, Conn.: A. D. Worthington, 1882.

Eighteenth Biennial Report of the Board of Directors of the Kansas State Historical Society, 1910–1912. Topeka: State Printing Office, 1913.

Fast, Howard. *The Last Frontier.* Cleveland: World, 1941.

Finerty, John F. *War-Path and Bivouac, or the Conquest of the Sioux.* Norman: University of Oklahoma Press, 1961.

Greene, Jerome A. *Slim Buttes, 1876: An Episode of the Great Sioux War.* Norman: University of Oklahoma Press, 1982.

Grinnell, George Bird. *The Cheyenne Indians.* 2 vols. New Haven: Yale University Press, 1923.

————. *The Fighting Cheyennes.* Original printing by Charles Scribner's Sons, 1915. Norman: University of Oklahoma Press, 1958.

Hebard, Grace Raymond, and E. A. Brinnistool. *The Bozeman Trail.* Cleveland: Arthur H. Clark, 1922.

Heitman, Francis B. *Historical Register and Dictionary of the United States Army.* 2 vols. Washington, D.C.: Government Printing Office, 1903.

Hoig, Stan. *Fort Reno and the Indian Territory Frontier.* Fayetteville: University of Arkansas Press, 2000.

————. *Tribal Wars of the Southern Plains.* Norman: University of Oklahoma Press, 1993.

Howard, James H., trans. and ed. *The Warrior Who Killed Custer: The Personal Narrative of Chief Joseph White Bull.* Lincoln: University of Nebraska Press, 1976.

Hyde, George E. *Life of George Bent, Written from His Letters,* ed. Savoie Lottinville. Norman: University of Oklahoma Press, 1968.

————. *Red Cloud's Folks: A History of the Oglala Sioux.* Norman: University of Oklahoma Press, 1937.

————. *Spotted Tail's Folks: A History of the Brulé Sioux.* Norman: University of Oklahoma Press, 1974 [1961].

Johnson, Virginia Weisel. *The Unregimented General: A Biography of Nelson A. Miles.* Boston: Houghton Mifflin, 1962.

Kappler, Charles J., comp. and ed. *Indian Treaties.* New York: Interland, 1972.

Kime, Wayne R., ed. *The Indian Territory Journals of Colonel Richard I. Dodge.* Norman: University of Oklahoma Press, 2000.

————. *The Powder River Expedition Journals of Colonel Richard Irving Dodge.* Norman: University of Oklahoma Press, 1997.

Leckie, William H. *The Buffalo Soldiers: A Narrative of the Negro Cavalry in the West.* Norman: University of Oklahoma Press, 1967.

Maddux, Albert G., and Vernon R. Maddux. *The Battle of Punished Woman's Fork.* N.p., n.d.

Marquis, Thomas B. *Cheyennes and Sioux: The Reminiscences of Four Indians and a White Soldier.* Stockton, Calif.: University of the Pacific, 1973.

————. *Wooden Leg: A Warrior Who Fought Custer.* Original printing, Midwest, 1931. Lincoln: University of Nebraska Press, 1962.

Miles, Nelson A. *Personal Recollections and Observations of General Nelson A. Miles.* Chicago: Weiner, 1897.

————. *Serving the Republic.* New York: Harper and Brothers, 1911.

Monnett, John H. *Tell Them We Are Going Home.* Norman: University of Oklahoma Press, 2001.

National Cyclopedia of American Biography. New York: James T. White, 1900. Reprint by University Microfilms, Ann Arbor, Mich., 1967.

North, Luther. *Man of the Plains: Recollections of Luther North,* ed. Donald E. Danker, foreword by George Bird Grinnell. Lincoln: University of Nebraska Press, 1981.

Nye, W. S. *Carbine and Lance: The Story of Old Fort Sill.* Norman: University of Oklahoma Press, 1969.

Pierce, Michael D. *The Most Promising Young Officer: A Life of Ranald Slidell Mackenzie.* Norman: University of Oklahoma Press, 1993.

Porter, Joseph C. *Paper Medicine Man: John Gregory Bourke and His American West.* Norman: University of Oklahoma Press, 1986.

Powell, Father Peter John. *The Killing of Morning Star's People.* Chadron, Nebr.: Mari Sandoz Society, 1994.

————. *People of the Sacred Mountains.* 2 vols. San Francisco: Harper and Row, 1979.

Robinson, Charles M. *Bad Hand: A Biography of General Ranald Mackenzie.* Austin: State House Press, 1993.

Rodenbough, Theodore F., ed. *Fighting for Honor.* New York: G. W. Dillingham, 1893.

Russell, Don. *The Lives and Legends of Buffalo Bill.* Norman: University of Oklahoma Press, 1960.

Sandoz, Mari. *Cheyenne Autumn.* New York: McGraw-Hill, 1951.

Schmitt, Martin F. *General George Crook, His Autobiography.* Norman: University of Oklahoma Press, 1946.

Shrewder, Dorothy Berryman, and Melville Campbell Harper, eds. *Notes on Early Clark County, Kansas.* Clark County Chapter of Kansas State Historical Society, Ashland, Kansas, n.d.

Smith, Sherry L. *Sagebrush Soldier: Private William Earl Smith's View of the Sioux War of 1876.* Norman: University of Oklahoma Press, 1989.

Stands in Timber, John, and Margot Liberty, with assistance of Robert M. Utley. *Cheyenne Memories.* New Haven: Yale University Press, 1967.

Starita, Joe. *The Dull Knifes of Pine Ridge: A Lakota Odyssey.* New York: G. P. Putnam's Sons, 1995.

A Survey of Historic Sites and Structures in Kansas. Topeka: Kansas State Historical Society, 1957.

Svingen, Orlan J. *The Northern Cheyenne Reservation, 1877–1900.* Niwot: University Press of Colorado, 1993.

Terrell, J. B., ed. *David Thompson's Narrative of His Explorations in Western America.* Toronto: Champlain Society, 1916.

Thoburn, Joseph. *A Standard History of Oklahoma.* Chicago: American Historical Society, 1916.

Utley, Robert M. *Frontier Regulars: The United States Army and the Indians, 1866–1891.* New York: Macmillan, 1973.

Werner, Fred H. *The Dull Knife Battle.* Greeley, Colo.: Werner, 1981.

Wheeler, Col. Homer W. *Buffalo Days: Forty Years in the Old West.* New York: A. L. Burt, 1923.

GOVERNMENT DOCUMENTS, PUBLISHED

Annual Report of Commissioner of Indian Affairs, 1867–1883. Washington, D.C.: GPO.

Annual Report of Secretary of War, 1878, 1879. Washington, D.C.: GPO.

"Escape of Indians from Fort Robinson." *Sen. Misc. Doc. 64,* 45th Cong., 3d sess. 1879.

General Court-Martial Orders, Nos. 28, 29, 36, 79. Office of Judge Advocate, Dept./Mo., NA.

The History of the Fourth United States Cavalry. Gov. Doc. D 101.21C 31/2.

"Indian Operations on the Plains." *Sen. Ex. Doc. 33,* 50th Cong., 1st sess., 1887–1888.

"Northern Cheyenne Indians." *H.R. Doc. 17,* 49th Cong., 1st sess., 1886.

Record of Engagements with Hostile Indians within the Military Division of the Missouri from 1868 to 1882. Chicago: Headquarters, Military Division of the Missouri, 1882.

"Removal of the Northern Cheyenne Indians." *Sen. Report 708,* 46th Cong., 2d sess, 1880.

Second Annual Report of the Board of Indian Commissioners, 1870. Sen. Ex. Doc. 39, 41st Cong., 3d sess., 1870–1871.

"Shooting of Black Wolf." *Sen. Ex. Doc. 176,* 48th Cong., 1st sess., 1884.

The War of the Rebellion: A Compilation of the Official Records of the Union and Confederate Armies. Washington, D.C.: Government Printing Office, 1891–1898.

GOVERNMENT DOCUMENTS, UNPUBLISHED

Camp Supply Post Returns, Returns from U.S. Military Posts, 1874–1884 (M-617), NA.

Correspondence Relating to Disturbances Caused by Indians of the Cheyenne and Arapaho Agency, Indian Territory, June 1885, September 6, 1886, and Lt. Gen. Philip Sheridan Report, July 24, 1885 (M-689, Rolls 362–363), NA.

Correspondence Relating to the Planned Reduction of Beef Rations for the Arapaho and Cheyenne, Comanche, and Kiowa Agencies: The Fears of Army Officers. LR/AGO (main series) (M-689, Roll 88), NA.

Files relating to Military Operations: Cheyenne Outbreak, Sept. 1878 (RG 393, M-1495, Roll 6, 10), NA.

Fort Reno Post Returns, Returns from U.S. Military Posts, 1874–1884 (M-617, Roll 998), NA.

Fourth Cavalry Monthly Returns, Regular Army Commands, 1877–1883 (M-744, Roll 43, NA).

Gunther Court-Martial Proceedings, Office of Judge Advocate, Dept./Mo., NA.

Hemphill Court-Martial Proceedings, Office of Judge Advocate, Dept./Mo., NA.

Letters Received, AGO (main series) 1871–1880 (M-666, Roll 422), NA.

Letters Received, Dept. of Missouri, RG 393, NA.

Letters Received, OIA, Cheyenne/Arapaho Agency (M-234, Rolls 122–124), NA.

Letters Received, Red Cloud Agency (M-234, Rolls 720–721), NA.

Letters Sent, Fort Supply, Vol. 29, RG 98, NA.

"Military Operations against the Northern Cheyennes, 1878–79." LR/AGO (main series), 1871–1880 (M-666, Roll 428), NA.

Proceedings of a Board of Officers, LR/OIA (M-666, Roll 429), NA.

Rendlebrock Court-Martial Proceedings, Office of Judge Advocate, Dept./Mo., NA.

Twenty-third Infantry Monthly Returns, Regular Army Commands, 1874–1884 (M-665, Roll 237), NA.

PERIODICALS

Arkansas City Traveler

Army and Navy Journal

Chicago Tribune

Daily Oklahoman

Dodge City Times

Emporia News

Ford County Globe

Leavenworth Daily Times

Leslie's Illustrated Newspaper

Medal of Honor Records

National Tribune

New York Evening Post

New York Herald

New York Times

New York Tribune

Omaha Daily Herald

The Friend

Harper's Illustrated Weekly

Harper's Monthly Magazine

Hays City Sentinel

Kansas Daily Tribune

Lawrence Daily Tribune

Lawrence Standard

Omaha Republican

Sidney Plaindealer

St. Louis Post and Dispatch

Topeka Commonwealth

Washington Evening Post

Washington Evening Star

Western Home Journal

Wichita Eagle

Winfield Courier

INDEX

Page numbers in italics indicate illustrations.

Canyon, 30; Punished Woman's Fork, 110–129, 131, 133–135, 137; Red Fork, 10–13, 16, 18, 109, 174, 233; San Mateo, 235; Turkey Springs, 59, 63–72, 81, 84, 93, 108, 129, 133, 135, 243; Warbonnet Creek, 9

Baxter, 2nd Lt. George W., 165, 175, 182, 184, 188, 190, 258

Bayless, F., 139, 141

Bear Butte, Dakota Territory, 150

Bear Creek, 58, 93, 99, 149–150

Bear Who Pushes Back His Hair (Cheyenne), 6

Beaver Creek, 41–42, 130–134, 137–138, 140, 144, 255

Beecher, Henry Ward, 169

Belle Fourche, Dakota Territory, 18, 47

Bent, George, 42

Berrymen, J. W., 94

Bickerdike, Hugh, 251

Biddle and Spencer cattle camp, 91

Big Antelope (Cheyenne), 176–177

Big Antelope's wife (Cheyenne), 176

Big Back (Cheyenne), drawing by, 14

Big Beaver (Cheyenne), 157, 173, 176, 180, 222. See also Young Pumpkin Seed

Big Head (Cheyenne), 25, 222, 226, 239

Big Piney Creek, 1

Big Sandy Creek, 90–91, 149, 236, 249. See also Sand Creek

Big Springs, Nebraska, 146

Big White Clay Creek, 149

Big Wolf, 8, 25

Bigalsky, Sgt. Gottlob, 183–184, 188, 261

Bighorn Mountains, 1, 9, 47, 150

Bighorn River, 150–151

Bird (Cheyenne), 238

Bismarck, North Dakota, 205

Bissonnette, Joseph, 6

Black Bear (Cheyenne), 205

Black Bear, Mrs. (Cheyenne), 259

Black Coal (Arapaho), 3

Black Hawk (Cheyenne), 6

Black Hills, 8, 22, 150, 187, 205

Black Horse (Cheyenne), 2

Black Kettle (Cheyenne), 41

Black Wolf (Cheyenne), 202–204

Blacksmith (Cheyenne), 168, 222, 224

Blanche (Cheyenne), 192

Blown Away (Cheyenne), 238

Bluff Creek, 89–91, 93, 95

Bluff Creek station, Nebraska, 186–187, 194, 253

Board of Officers, 169, 201, 221; inquiry of, 193; members, 222

Boardman Fork of Snake River, 196

Bohemian Colony, 138

Bolenti, Pvt., 76

Bosler, Wyoming, 195

Bourke, Lt. John, 15–17, 19–21, 148

Box Elder Creek, 197, 200

Bozeman Trail, 2

Bradford, Capt. James H., 111, 119, 123

Brady, Capt. G. K., 215

Brave Bear (Cheyenne), 245

Brave Wolf (Cheyenne), 197, 200, 205

Bridle, Robert, 143

Bristow, Reuben, 85

Bronson, Edgar Beecher, 169, 176–177, 192

Brown, Emerson, 89

Brown, George W., 90, 107, 131, 191, 251–252; discovers horses, 123; scouts for Lewis, 112

Brulé Lakota Indians, 149. See also Sioux Indians

Brunot, Felix, 8

Buffalo, 8, 46; slaughter of, 39

Buffalo Creek, 81

Buffalo Days, 16

Buffalo, Oklahoma, 27

Buffalo station, Kansas, 91, 108, 139–141,

Bull Elk (Cheyenne), 138

Bull Hump (Cheyenne), 14, 157–158, 261

Bull Hump's wife (Cheyenne), 261

Burrows, Pvt., 69

Burton, Pvt. Francis E., 76, 246

Cabin Creek, 199

Calf (Cheyenne), 261

Ryan, Cpl. Patrick F., 17
Ryder, Nathan, 144

Sabin, Asst. Surg., 196
Sac and Fox Indians, 44
Salina, Kansas, 230
Saline River, 130
Salt Fork of Arkansas, 60, 84–85, 91
Salt Fork of Cimarron, 88
Salt haulers, grave of, 86, 247
Sanchez, Pvt. John R., 252
Sand Creek, 94, 97–99, 102, 105–107, 109,
    215, 217, 219; action at, 100–101, 250.
    See also Big Sandy, Little Sandy
Sandoz, Mari, 84, 251
Sandy Hill, New York, 110, 124, 252
Sans Arc Lakota Indians, 150
Santa Fe, New Mexico, 233
Santa Fe Railroad, 39, 87, 97, 149
Sappa Creek, 137, 139–141, 143–145, 255;
    1875 attack on, 138; South Fork of,
    131–132, 134, 140–141, 255, 131
Saville, J. J., 8
Schaufler, Sgt. Jacob, 93, 215
Schmidt, Pvt. Frank, 170, 259
Schurtz, Secretary of Interior Carl, 218,
    224, 229; agrees with Sheridan on
    return of Cheyennes, 162; defends
    department, 160
Schuyler, 1st Lt. Walter S., 222
Scott County, Kansas, 108
Second Cavalry, 151, 196, 199–202
Secretary of War, 221
Sedgwick, Maj. John, 39
Selma, Alabama, 39
Seminole Indians, 223
Seminole, Jules, 197
Seminole wars, 110
Senate, investigating committee of, 36
Seventh Cavalry, 11, 16, 41, 63, 112, 150,
    154, 195–196, 205, 208, 231, 235; Little
    Bighorn battle, 9
Shangreau, John, 185–188
Shawnee County, Kansas, 226
Sheedy (rancher), 89, 97

Sheridan, Kansas, 11, 22
Sheridan Butte, 197
Sheridan County, Kansas, 133–134, 138,
    140
Sheridan, Gen. Phil, 62, 108, 111, 149–
    150, 161–162, 180, 204–205, 218, 221,
    262; attacks Indian Bureau, 160;
    Montana invasion by, 8, notes difficulty
    of overtaking Indians, 57; promise of,
    207, 209; staff of, 20
Sheridan station, 124, 132, 136, 139;
    incident at, 129
Sherman, Gen. William T., 3, 8, 223, 231
Shinn, Lloyd, 25
Shoemaker, 1st Lt. F. L., 239
Shoshone Indians, 11; Red Fork action of,
    15; scouts, 13
Sidney, 30, 211–212, 214, 232
Sidney and Black Hills Stage Line, 179
Sidney Barracks, Nebraska, 23, 25, 56,
    134, 146, 149, 159, 205, 207, 211, 218,
    225, 256. *See also* Fort Sidney
Sidney, Nebraska, 30, 132, 134–135, 146,
    162, 207, 211–212, 214, 232
Sidney Plaindealer, 249
Sidney Road, 147, 181
Sierra Madre Mountains, 234
Simmonds, George, 90
Simpson, Capt. James F., 166, 173, 179,
    183–184, 195
Sioux, The (Cheyenne), 152
Sioux Indians, 1, 4–6, 8, 11, 13, 149–150,
    159, 165, 179, 198, 208, 220–221, 228;
    attack fort, 3; attack wagon trains, 2;
    fight with Crook, 9; forced to surrender,
    11; language of, 199; at Little Bighorn,
    9
Sioux wars, 231
Sitka, Kansas, 248
Sitting Bull (Lakota Sioux), 196–199, 231
Sixteenth Infantry, 25, 29, 97, 131, 140,
    215, 218
Sixth Cavalry, 233
Sixth Infantry, 151, 199–200
Sleeping Bear Creek, 81